The Politics of Becoming

The open access publication of this book has been made possible through the generous support of (in alphabetical order):

The Austrian Political Science Association

The Centre for Deliberative Democracy and Global Governance at the University of Canberra

The Faculty of Business, Government, and Law at the University of Canberra

The Participatory and Deliberative Democracy specialist group of the Political Studies Association

Participedia

The Politics of Becoming

Anonymity and Democracy in the Digital Age

HANS ASENBAUM

OXFORD
UNIVERSITY PRESS

Great Clarendon Street, Oxford, OX2 6DP,
United Kingdom

Oxford University Press is a department of the University of Oxford.
It furthers the University's objective of excellence in research, scholarship,
and education by publishing worldwide. Oxford is a registered trade mark of
Oxford University Press in the UK and in certain other countries

Published in the United States of America by Oxford University Press
198 Madison Avenue, New York, NY 10016, United States of America

British Library Cataloguing in Publication Data

Data available

Library of Congress Control Number: 2022951437

ISBN 978–0–19–285887–0

DOI: 10.1093/oso/9780192858870.001.0001

Printed and bound by
CPI Group (UK) Ltd, Croydon, CR0 4YY

Acknowledgements

During my research for this book, I have been privileged to encounter many brilliant people and engage in inspiring conversations which helped shape my thinking. Their support, advice, and inspirations are reflected on these pages. First among them is Graham Smith, who as my PhD supervisor has provided invaluable guidance to completing the research this book is based on. His work on democratic innovations and his openness to pluralism in democratic theory have been an important source of inspiration. I deeply appreciate Anne Phillips' and Anastasia Kavada's engagement with my work in examining my thesis. Anne Phillips' concept of the politics of presence has been a fundamental source of inspiration and orientation for this book. I am deeply grateful to Selen Ercan, whose generosity, encouragement, and relentless support have accompanied this book from its inception to its completion. My thanks also go to John Dryzek, Nicole Curato, and Simon Niemeyer, who have supported this project from the beginning and offered conceptual ideas and invaluable advice.

I am indebted to Matthew Fluck, Amanda Machin, Rahel Süß, Rod Dacombe, Sonia Bussu, Paulina Tambakaki, David Chandler, and Christian Fuchs for providing insightful comments on draft chapters.

I am particularly grateful to Chantal Mouffe and Carole Pateman for engaging with my project. Their work had a strong impact on my thinking. Chantal Mouffe highlighted the importance of rearticulating identities after their deconstruction and Carole Pateman stressed the importance of the socio-economic context of participation. Special thanks go to Jane Mansbridge for sharing insights on identity and self-transformation and to Donatella della Porta and John Parkinson for sharing their expertise on participation in public spaces. This book also benefitted from thought-provoking conversations with Ricardo Fabrino Mendonça, Lucy Parry, Marta Wojciechowska, Kimmo Grönlund, Maija Setälä, Lauri Rapeli, Marina Lindell, Henrik Serup Christensen, Kim Strandberg, Kaisa Herne, Brigitte Geissel, Rikki Dean, Petra Guasti, Jonathan Rinne, Jan-Peter Voß, Jean-Paul Gagnon, Andrea Felicetti, Marco Deseriis, Taina Meriluoto, Paolo Spada, Alice el-Wakil, Dimitri Courant, Dannica Fleuß, and Alfred Moore.

I would also like to thank the editorial team at Oxford University Press and in particular Dominic Byatt, the commissioning editor, who believed in and supported this project.

Finally, I would like to acknowledge that parts of this book build on previously-published journal articles. I am grateful to Cambridge University Press and Oxford University Press for the permission to reprint excerpts from:

Asenbaum, Hans. 2018. 'Anonymity and Democracy: Absence as Presence in the Public Sphere'. *American Political Science Review* 112 (3): 459–72. https://doi.org/https://doi.org/10.1017/S0003055418000163.

Asenbaum, Hans. 2020. 'Making a Difference: Toward a Feminist Democratic Theory in the Digital Age'. *Politics & Gender* 16 (1): 230–57. https://doi.org/10.1017/S1743923X18001010.

Asenbaum, Hans. 2021. 'Rethinking Digital Democracy: From the Disembodied Discursive Self to New Materialist Corporealities'. *Communication Theory* 31 (3): 360–79. https://doi.org/10.1093/ct/qtz033.

Asenbaum, Hans. 2021. 'The Politics of Becoming: Disidentification as Radical Democratic Practice'. *European Journal of Social Theory* 24 (1): 86–104. https://doi.org/10.1177/1368431020935781.

Contents

Contents

1

Becoming Subject to Change

An Introduction

We live in a time of disruption. Populist leaders divide us. The gig economy replaces stable class affiliations. Robots become both our professional competitors and personal companions. Social media curate our public image. Gender fluidity confuses the heterosexual matrix. Pandemics redefine our living spaces. Deep economic, societal, and cultural ruptures destabilize our sense of self. This disorder of the things that define us causes fear of a loss of control over identity, but at the same time this disorder also creates new opportunities to challenge and break down entrenched structures of domination.

Such identity reconfigurations are a distinct feature of the current digital age. New communicative channels provide novel means to articulate who we are. The #MeToo movement, for example, illustrates how active identity expressions online can disrupt established power asymmetries. By narrating the self in personal stories of sexual harassment and rape, and by linking these stories to personal social media profiles, public identity performances can challenge domination. Social media provide a space of appearance—a stage on which democratic subjects actualize themselves through political action (Arendt 1958; Butler 2015).

The expression of the self online often takes the form of a subversion of identity. Anonymity today becomes the core radical democratic practice of many protest movements. Groups such as Anonymous, Pussy Riot, and the Zapatistas all utilize masks as a way to conceal identities and signal collectivity. After the uprisings in parts of the Arab world in 2011, *Time* magazine declared the anonymous protester the person of the year. The white, impishly grinning Guy Fawkes masks worn by many in the Occupy movement has become an emblem of political contestation along with the black balaclava of black bloc formations and the hoods of Black Lives Matter. But governments push back. A series of laws introduced around the world prohibits publicly concealing one's face. This move meant to limit and control political resistance coalesces with the controversy around the public wearing of veils by Muslim women who are 'using the deliberately assumed invisibility of the burka as a form of protest' (Zakaria 2017: 59). These contestations result in a complex discursive clash around privacy rights, freedom of expression, and identity. Hence, 'the political struggle over anonymity when one acts is among the defining struggles of our time' (Isin and Ruppert 2015: 67).

The Politics of Becoming. Hans Asenbaum, Oxford University Press. © Hans Asenbaum (2023).
DOI: 10.1093/oso/9780192858870.003.0001

In this book, I explore the democratic affordances of anonymity in both online and offline modes of participatory engagement. I propose a politics of becoming as a political strategy realized through radical democratic acts of disidentification. Disidentification means distancing ourselves from the persona we perform in our everyday interactions and exploring our inner multiplicity. This temporary rearrangement of the self disturbs the order of things and opens spaces for systemic transformation. Democratic spaces, from public assemblies to social movement gatherings both online and offline, can employ anonymity to advance the freedom to live the multiple self. I conceptualize the subject itself as *subject to change.*

The struggle over anonymity unfolds in parallel with a broad movement for a radicalization of democracy. Radical democratic aspirations manifest in various democratic spaces which fulfil the function of breaking up established modes of governmentality: 'participatory approaches explicitly seek to disrupt the order of hierarchical institutions, creating new and different spaces in which different rules of the game offer otherwise silenced actors a chance to speak and be heard' (Cornwall 2002: 7). Democratic spaces take three basic forms: firstly, state-sponsored democratic innovations such as citizens' assemblies or participatory budgets (Smith 2009); secondly, social movements' participatory assemblies including public gatherings and internal group meetings (della Porta and Rucht 2013); and thirdly, representative state institutions such as parliaments and local councils (Bächtiger et al. 2005). Shielding their participants from external social inequalities, these democratic spaces strive to facilitate freedom and equality through their structural settings. In that manner, they form particular spaces of appearance. They aim to interrupt external hierarchy with internal democracy.

But things are not that simple. Judith Butler (2015) highlights how deeply structural inequalities affect the configuration of the space of appearance. It restricts who can appear and who is rendered invisible. For those who are granted access, the spatial arrangement regulates appreciation and credibility along identity markers of gender, sexuality, race, class, bodily ability, and age. This observation is at the heart of a feminist debate in democratic theory known as 'difference democracy'. Difference democrats argue that in societies dominated by social hierarchies, democratic participation is affected by the identities inscribed in the subjects' bodies. They advance a *politics of presence* that draws attention to inequalities and particular standpoints of subordinate groups through their visibility in the space of appearance (Phillips 1995). Difference democracy advocates institutional quota regulations and social movements' identity politics to reclaim marginalized identities (Mansbridge 1999b). The politics of presence is a promising approach to advancing equality. However, this strategy also undermines freedom. It curtails the freedom of the democratic subject to explore its multiple self. It tends to essentialize the subject and restricts it to its embodied identity. This is what difference democrats call 'the dilemma of difference' (Young 1989: 268).

The Politics of Becoming proposes a solution to this dilemma. This solution cannot and should not simply seek to overcome identity. Phillips (2015: 36) is right to argue: 'We should not have to pretend away key aspects of ourselves, ask for forbearance in the face of our particularities, or appeal to people to see who and what we are "beyond" our gender, skin colour, sexuality, or disability.' Identities fulfil important functions in democratic politics, not only in differentiating individuals and recognizing their group affiliations, but also in advancing claims for inclusion of marginalized groups. Rather than overcoming identity, the solution I propose entails creating conditions to afford the experience of inner multiplicity, experimenting with the plasticity of identity, and exploring the transformative potential of the self. I follow the core ideal articulated by Young (1990) and Fraser (1990) of a society that celebrates the differences of equals. The core argument I advance is that such a diversity among equals cannot always be achieved through a traditional politics of presence facilitated by the visibility of the physically embodied and officially identified persona. Instead, presence needs to be reinterpreted as being constituted by mutable and transformative performances of the multiple self through diverse media in various democratic spaces.

To make this argument, I enrich established radical democratic thinking with queer theory, and in particular intersectional, trans, and Black queer theory, that understands the democratic subject as constituted by a series of performative acts (Muñoz 1999; Lloyd 2005; Bey 2022). From this angle, I observe that anonymity in pamphleteering, graffiti, and online participation does not simply conceal identity. It simultaneously creates new and multiple identities through text, images, or online avatars. The politics of becoming frees inner multiplicity. Rather than presenting a naïve celebration of anonymity, I engage with and build on the feminist critique of anonymity. I elaborate a concept of anonymity as inherently contradictory, allowing for hate speech and deception but simultaneously facilitating meritocracy, democratic contestation, and honesty. This contradictory character of anonymity cannot be overcome. Nevertheless, anonymity opens up new perspectives by allowing for a temporary interruption of established identities and a process of disidentification. Reassembling identities online and offline allows the subject freedom to explore its multiple self while simultaneously affording the visibility of marginalized groups in order to advance equality.

The politics of becoming, then, does not stand in opposition to, but rather augments, the feminist politics of presence. Presence is reconfigured through disidentification and anonymity in both analogue and digital spaces. This does not entail a negation of identity and the body, but a rearrangement of embodied identity articulations. The politics of becoming combines the potential for expressing marginalized identity with the freedom for the subject to change.

Democratic Spaces as Interruption

New spaces for democratic engagement aim to reinvigorate and transform democracy. Such democratic spaces include both formalized institutions such as citizens' assemblies and social movements formations (Cornwall 2004a). Democratic spaces are not confined to Western imaginations but include democratic experiences worldwide (e.g. Roque and Shankland 2007; Aiyar 2010) from participatory budgeting and participatory health councils in Brazil (Avritzer 2009) to the Indian Gram Sabha village assemblies (Parthasarathy, Rao, and Palaniswamy 2019).

Radical democrats agree that 'we need to invent new social and political forms that introduce radical dislocation in the present forms of domination' (Wenman 2013: 17). However, there is a rift running through radical democratic thinking between those promoting a mere augmentation of existing democracy in a reformist sense on the one side and those advocating systemic transformation on the other. With Aletta Norval, I argue in favour of looking beyond this divide and understanding both democratic augmentation and systemic transformation as steps in a continuous effort of radical democratization (Norval 2007: 185; see also Cornwall 2004b: 85). While it is crucial to always question the power relations in which democratic spaces are embedded and the intentions with which they are created (Lee 2014; Hammond 2021), they all signify a democratic potential (Cornwall and Schattan Coelho 2007). By bringing people together who would otherwise not meet, by rearranging the constellation of bodies that potentially constitute democratic space, new modes of participation can work to challenge the established order of things. In Butler's words: 'In wresting that power, a new space is created, a new "between" of bodies, as it were, that lays claim to existing space' (Butler 2015: 85).

In this book, I will argue that the intentional rearrangement of bodies to form democratic space constitutes an *interruption*. It temporarily brings the established order of things into disarray and provides the ground for the emergence of new democratic subjectivities. Democratic spaces, whether in the form of governmental democratic innovations or of social movement formations, always function as an intervention that allows those who are usually unheard a chance to express themselves. By giving voice to the governed, democratic innovations 'can challenge the existing institutional order' (Smith 2009: 3). Against the neoliberal credo suggesting that there is no alternative, they demonstrate that things can be otherwise.

The term 'interruption' is of particular value in comprehending democratic innovation. Interruption features differently in radical democratic thinking. In *Antigone, Interrupted*, Bonnie Honig (2013) discusses interruption as a conversational intervention that can have either democratic or dominant effects: 'interruption postulates both equality, as when two people interrupt each other to knit together a conversation in tandem, and inequality, as when one party must yield the floor as it were, to the other' (13). Nancy Fraser focuses solely on the negative workings of interruption as it thwarts mutual understanding and hinders justice (Fraser 1997). Nicole Curato, on the contrary, evaluating the role of interruptive protest in the deliberative system, defines interruption 'as political practices that break the continuity of dominant patterns' (Curato 2021: 393). This positive reading of interruption is also reflected in the work of Jacques Rancière, who conceptualizes interruption as inherently democratic: 'Politics occurs because, or when, the natural order of the shepherd kings, the warlords, or property owners is interrupted by a freedom that crops up and makes real the ultimate equality on which any social order rests' (Rancière 1999: 16). It is the Rancièrian notion of interruption facilitating experiences of freedom and equality that democratic spaces potentially harness.

What makes interruption such a curious concept is that it does not articulate a permanent break. Rather, it establishes a recess—a pause—within continuity. The prefix *inter*—the Latin 'between'—indicates that after this *inter*lude, things go back to normal. Just like the two interventions marked by dashes in the previous two sentences, the *inbetweenness* of interruption makes us pause. It provides a space to think—a space to experience alterity and explore alternatives. 'To conceive rupture as a systemic or total upheaval would be futile. Rather, rupture is a moment where the future breaks through into the present. It is that moment where it becomes possible to do something different in or by saying something different' (Isin and Ruppert 2015: 57). It is in this sense that I believe a separation between reformists and revolutionaries in progressive debates is often counterproductive. What is needed are interruptions of modes of domination as part of a continuous process of radical democratization. By defining the boundaries of a before and an after, interruptions provide openings in which things can be different. Such openings can also be conceived of as spaces, in which different thinking is possible. Innovation and interruption thus go hand in hand.

While it might appear that after the interruption things go back to normal and return to their designated places, this is not the case. After the interruption, things are never entirely as they were before. Ostensibly, after citizens' assemblies and university occupations end, participants go home. Their bodies shift back to their assigned place in society. But the experiences of equality, of speaking freely, of being taken seriously do not go away. While the hierarchies of capitalist societies might remain unaffected, traces of the democratic experience persist. They change how political issues are perceived, they challenge established attitudes, and induce critical reflection. By affecting perception, democratic spaces alter the order of things.

To comprehend in which way democratic spaces interrupt the established order of things, we need to understand that these spaces themselves consist of a certain arrangement of things. The spaces that facilitate new forms of participation consist of material objects such as walls, pavements, and chairs that both afford and limit interaction. These material infrastructures are populated by sentient bodies of human and nonhuman animals that relate to each other in contingent constellations of social relations, power structures, and emotional ties. These sentient bodies articulate performative expressions such as words, gestures, sounds, silences, and images. The disruptive nature of democratic spaces is constituted by the temporary rearrangement of the constellation of these things.

But what makes these spaces radically democratic? In this book, I respond to this question by drawing on participatory, deliberative, agonistic, difference, and transformative approaches in democratic thought, all of which, in my view, contribute to radicalizing democracy. If radical democracy is taken to mean what its etymology implies—the roots, original meaning, or essence of the rule of the people (Holman et al. 2015)—then all of these perspectives are part of the radical democratic project (Saward 2003: 150; Dahlberg and Siapera 2007: 7; Norval 2007: 13, 38; Little and Lloyd 2009: 2). In this sense, Aletta Norval (2001: 26) writes: 'Radical democracy may be characterised as an ethos of radicalisation. This ethos is constitutive of agonistic, antagonistic and discursive, as well as deliberative models of democracy, all of which form part of contemporary radical democratic theory.' What might appear as an ecumenical approach does not, however, entail eroding the boundaries between different perspectives in democratic theory. Rather, I contend that there is value in perspectival pluralism (Dean, Gagnon, and Asenbaum 2019; Asenbaum 2021a). I follow Smith (2019: 581) who argues that '[t]he theoretical enterprises of deliberative, participatory, agonistic and other approaches to democracy differ in significant ways. It is precisely where these different theoretical lenses offer alternative perspectives on the same object of study that we can gain novel insights.'

The Democratic Subject as Assemblage

Democratic subjects, those who participate in democratic spaces, are situated in capitalist societies that are characterized by deeply entrenched inequalities along the lines of identity categories. These inequalities concern financial resources just as much as respect, recognition, and political power. In fact, all of them are inherently linked. This is pointed out by feminist difference democrats who promote an understanding of difference as a resource for democratic engagement (Young 1997b) and promote a politics of presence (Phillips 1995), giving marginalized groups visibility in the space of appearance. The identified body functions as a claim for equality (Phillips 2015). Examples of the politics of presence include parliamentary gender quotas (Mansbridge 2005) and social movements' identity politics. In SlutWalks, as an illustrative example, women expose their bodies to protest rape culture and advance women's rights to express their sexuality (O'Keefe 2014). Here the body is conceived as an affective thing. Without the need to speak, it articulates a political claim (see Mansbridge 2005: 62).

The politics of presence comes at a price, however. While it effectively advances equality, it works to limit the freedom for democratic subjects to explore multiple sides of their selves, to experience that which is marginalized *within* themselves. This book is interested in how equality can be advanced through active identity articulation while simultaneously affording the freedom of the subject to change. This endeavour calls for a different conception of the democratic subject, one that acknowledges the subject's inner multiplicity. From this vantage point, any act of stabilizing identity constructions is an act of domination. The coherent public persona that we perform every day is the result of masquerade (Butler 1990: 50). Here I borrow Sheldon Wolin's attribute of fugitivity, which he applies to democracy (Wolin 1994), and understand the *subject* as being on the run. The *fugitive self* constantly tries to escape the reification of identity. It behaves like eye floaters— the spots in our eyes we never can get a hold of. As we try to focus on them, they move away.

Identity and the self can be explained as an agentic assemblage of things—just like democratic space, as argued above. Jane Bennett explores how food enters the body, nourishes it, is converted into energy, and leaves it. She proposes 'a conception of the self ... as itself an impure, human-nonhuman assemblage' (Bennett 2010: xvii). The body appears as an assemblage of blood vessels, veins, fat, bones, cartilage, brain cells, eyeballs, guts, skin, and hair. The assemblage of the body interacts with discursive concepts of gender, sexuality, race, class, age, etc. and with political affiliations, personal experiences, motives, and desires. The identity assemblage also includes social protocols, gender and racially-coded body language, and culturally-coded objects such as makeup and clothing (see Young 1994). The democratic subject appears as a network of things that affect and are affected by each other.

The understanding of the self as assemblage resonates with Jon Elster's (1986) concept of the multiple self. According to this notion, we are constituted by different, competing parts such as desires, emotions, reasons, and passions. The Freudian theory of the id, ego, and superego is one approach to the multiple self, the notion of a *homo sociologicus* pursuing the common good and a *homo economicus* pursuing self-interest is another, and the successive self, changing over time, is yet another. People feel and act differently according to their current body chemistry, blood sugar levels, hormones, etc. The multiple self is composed as an assemblage of affective things which together develop a decentred kind of agency akin to swarm intelligence (Bennett 2010: 21). Rather than a rational and coherent actor, the self as assemblage is torn in many directions and set in motion by multiple forces.

Conceptualizing the subject as assemblage has far-reaching consequences for our understanding of democratic spaces. First, spatial arrangements bring out different sides of the multiple self. The constellation of material objects, sentient bodies, and performative expressions at a given moment in a given place affects some aspects of the self and not others. Second, the democratic subject's identity is constitutive of space. As the bodies of those present engender space, alteration in their identities—how they express themselves and are perceived by others—alters the entire space.

The proposed assemblage thinking clashes with some core assumptions of radical democratic theory. If we think in terms of distributed agency and affective networks, what role do we still assign to human intentionality and political responsibility? I see humans as fulfilling a double role. On the one hand, they are indeed just part of spatial assemblages. As sentient bodies, humans affect others through their physical presence—just like other things that constitute space. In this regard, it also makes sense to think about how human bodies should be arranged—along with other things—to facilitate equality and freedom. At the same time, humans fulfil the role of subjects who reflect on their actions and consciously engage in politics. This conscious engagement is, however, to be understood in terms of distributive agency. Humans as subjects do not simply act rationally; rather, their actions result from a conscious and unconscious navigation of various sides of the multiple self.

Anonymity and Disidentification

Anonymity is literally about the 'unnamedness' of people or their unknowability more broadly. That sounds simple enough. But consider the following examples. What makes participants in Alcoholics Anonymous anonymous insofar as people identified by their first names sit in a circle and have face-to-face conversations about intimate aspects of their lives? How is a person anonymous who wanders about an unknown city filled with people? How does a sexual act—possibly the most intimate thing imaginable—between two people who have met very recently and have no intention of seeing each other again qualify as anonymous? Is it the face, body, name, content, occupation, family status, social security number, or IP address of a person that needs to be hidden in order to facilitate anonymity?

The assemblage thinking developed above proves helpful for making sense of anonymity. If we understand the identity of a subject as an assemblage of many things, anonymity interrupts these assemblages. Often anonymity temporarily injects identity assemblages with foreign objects. Masks, for example, can interrupt everyday identity performances. Walls often work to interrupt identity. Think, for instance, of voting booths for casting a ballot, confession booths to whisper words through a grid, and public toilet booths whose walls serve the scribbling of graffiti. Other examples include public walls that display street art, a piece of paper filled with words of political instigation, or a computer screen filled with racial slurs. Online nicknames, pseudonyms, avatars, and digital images can also serve as things that interrupt identity. They are improper names that disturb the established order (Rancière 1999; Deseriis 2015).

Yet, these things do not simply negate and do away with identity. Rather, the things that interrupt identity assemblages are always interfaces; they are the means for new identity articulations. The objects that efface the democratic subject at the same time serve as the surface for new, temporary faces. They not only interrupt but simultaneously mediate identity. The gap that constitutes the temporary interruption is not empty; it is full of newness. The interruption is a moment of innovation of the self. And in the context of democratic spaces, it is potentially a democratic innovation. It is this moment of innovation as democratic self-transformation that this book sets out to explore.

Anonymity is a practical means of realizing radical democratic disidentification. Disidentification is the process by which a subject rejects the names assigned to it by society. The fugitive self tries to expand its freedom to explore its multiplicity by eluding the reification of its identity. This sounds quite abstract. Think of the debate about gender pronouns as a concrete example. People who identify as non-binary, trans, or gender fluid often prefer they/them as gender pronouns. It has become a trend to add the personally preferred pronouns to social media profiles or email signatures. This example does not only emphasize the democratic principles of diversity and personal agency of self-definition, it also illustrates potential disidentification. They/them functions as a signifier—an interruptive object entering the identity assemblage—that rejects the gender identity assigned at birth. Research on the use of alternative pronouns aptly observes how they/them enables trans youth 'to destabilise and disrupt gendered categories and embody non-normative, fluid and transgressive gender and sexual identities' (McGlashan and Fitzpatrick 2018: 240).

In the case of Anonymous it is the Guy Fawkes mask, for Pussy Riot it is the colourful Balaclava, for the Guerrilla Girls it is the gorilla mask, for some Muslim feminists it is the veil, and for the Ku Klux Klan it is the white hood that interrupts and constitutes identity at the same time. While we have undoubtedly witnessed a rise in the use of the mask in social movements, the idea of anonymity is nothing new. The hood that conceals identity in the Black Lives Matter movement to protest racially motivated police brutality is mirrored in the tale of Robin Hood stealing from the rich and giving to the poor. The ubiquitous use of avatars in virtual online roleplay environments, which plays an increasingly significant role in staging online protest, strangely relates to the tale of the long-nosed Cyrano de Bergerac who employed a handsome human avatar to convey his beautiful words to the lovely Roxane. From the uncertain origin of many texts attributed to William Shakespeare to the revolutionary writings now attributed to Thomas Paine and

Karl Marx and Friedrich Engels, anonymity has historically played a crucial role in Western societies.

As the diversity of these examples demonstrates, anonymity does not always have democratic effects. While this book is interested in the employment of anonymity for radical democratic acts of disidentification, anonymity plays a highly ambiguous role in democracy. In her investigation of the history of the hood as an object of political relevance, Allison Kinney (2016: 71) states: 'For as long as powerful forces have weaponized hoods ... wearing them to conceal their own violence, other people have relied on hoods' anonymity and everyday ubiquity in order to fight back, escape, and protest.' I will argue that the objects that afford anonymity always have liberating effects. They free the subject to act. This newly acquired freedom, however, might have detrimental effects for democracy. Anonymous subjects can use their freedom to exclude, submit, and deceive, thereby exacerbating power asymmetries. In the context of democratic politics, the lack of accountability that anonymity entails is particularly problematic. How can legitimacy be secured if actors remain unidentified? However, anonymity can also work to include the marginalized, to subvert concentrations of power, and to vent honest sentiments.

Whether anonymity's effects advance or undermine democracy, they often bring to the fore elements of the multiple self that were previously hidden. Anonymity provides a channel from the private sphere into the public space of appearance. The rearrangement of the identity assemblage is intertwined with the rearrangement of democratic space: 'Anonymity ... redefine[s] the contours of the democratic sphere, that is, the way we conceive it and the relations we are able to establish within it' (de Lagasnerie 2017: 58).

Behold the Rise of the Cyborg

Smartphones have become a central feature of our everyday lives. They wake us up in the morning. They remind us of the tasks of the day ahead. They allow us to communicate with our friends and meet new sexual and romantic partners. They count our steps and monitor our fitness. At night they remind us to go to bed. They lull us to sleep and monitor our sleep patterns to report it back to us in the morning, when their alarms ring and the cycle begins anew.

The everyday use of smart devices signals a profound shift in who we are. In *Seeing Ourselves Through Technology*, Jill Walker Rettberg (2014) discusses how the quantification of the self through smartphone apps alters how we perceive ourselves and others. Such reconfigurations of the self are well captured by Donna Haraway's metaphor of the cyborg (Haraway 1991 [1985]). The science fiction notion of the cyborg as the hybridization of organic human body parts and technological prosthesis is currently realized through the increasing use of cardiac pacemakers and robotic limbs. Everyday cyborgization goes much further, how-ever, and has deep implication for politics (Asenbaum 2018). Just as robotic limbs extend the physical abilities of humans, so too do hearing aids, eyeglasses, and contact lenses. Smart devices follow the same logic. They can make us hear and see things that are far away (Gergen 2000: xviii). Looking through the eyes of a cyborg, we see things differently. The new generation growing up today is social-ized through computer screens. It looks at the world through digital devices. It is raised by YouTube and Instagram—for better or worse.

The cyborgian transformation of the self through online engagement involves the design and curation of alternative self-representations and the potential expression of previously hidden elements of the multiple self. The term 'cybor-gization' then signifies a process of reconfiguring the assemblage of the self. By including smart devices, computer screens, apps, and digital self-representations into the assemblage of the organic body, culturally-coded objects, discursive iden-tity ascriptions, and social conventions, the definition of the self changes. Today we are constituted amid a web of cloud computing, big data, wireless connectivity, and the Internet of Things that connects us to our refrigerators, thermostats, and light bulbs in our homes.

The connection between our bodies and our smart devices is growing ever closer as mouse clicks are replaced by touches, swipes, and taps, which make the use of smart devices feel more intuitive, natural, and organic. The haptic engage-ment with smart devices also further develops an intimate, personal connection with them. The link between the human subject and the communication tool, which no longer simply constitutes an object of use but instead becomes a part of the cyborgian assemblage, is further strengthened by fingerprint and face recogni-tion technology. For authentication the early generation of smartphones required personal passwords—pin codes consisting of four-digit numbers. These passwords granted access to whoever knew it so that multiple users could use the same device. The introduction first of fingerprint and then face recognition to access smart-phones signals a major shift. The smart device is now exclusively accessible by one individual person via the organic body. This is of particular relevance in respect of governmental surveillance and commercial tracking. While for the early gener-ation GPS could tell where a smart device was located, for the current generation GPS can tell where the actual person is located (Eve 2016: 59).

Cyborgian self-constitution heavily relies on social media as a mirror. Every image of the self shared online functions as a digital thing in the cyborgian assem-blage. The audience of such communications is not exclusively and maybe not even primarily the other, but always also the self: 'When we share photos of our children or a new home or a night out with friends our target audience is not just our friends, but also ourselves' (Walker Rettberg 2014: 12). Social media create spaces that give the subject a certain degree of control over the arrangement of digital things that assemble the networked self (Papacharissi 2011; Cohen 2012).

This creative process is possible through the interruption of identity. Even if users create performances of the self that continue identity expressions from offline to online, the interruption of communication by an interface always calls for the active (re)creation of the self, which can never be true to the original (Adorno 1973 [1966]). There is a moment of anonymity and a potential for disidentification built into the very logic of digital communication. This provides the potential for democratic openings.

From the Democratic Microverse towards Systemic Transformations

We life in a time of systemic challenges, in which ravaging neoliberalism, environmental devastation, and a looming age of pandemics erodes the material foundations of our existence. How can a politics of becoming concerned with identity transformation respond to these challenges? Self-exploration through online communication is, moreover, severely limited by digital divides and digital inequalities. If the politics of becoming is not embedded in a more ambitious emancipatory project, self-transformation becomes a fanciful endeavour only for those with the required resources.

Here Nancy Fraser's work on overcoming the division between a politics of identity recognition and a politics of redistribution of economic resources is helpful. Fraser (1997) criticizes the 'increasingly bitter split between "the social left" and "the cultural left" ... critical theorists should rebut the claim that we must make an either/or choice between the politics of redistribution and the politics of recognition. We should aim instead to identify the emancipatory dimension of both problematics and to integrate them into a single, comprehensive framework' (4). Along with Carole Pateman I assert that in thinking about democratic spaces it is crucial to always keep the bigger picture in mind and account for structural inequalities and systemic configurations (Pateman 2012; Pateman and Smith 2019).

This book offers conceptual work that aims at going beyond the recognition vs. redistribution divide. The marginalization of and disrespect towards certain identity groups is deeply intertwined with the unequal distribution of economic resources. To think recognition and redistribution together, I understand the politics of becoming as part of an emancipatory democratic project, which conceptualizes the democratization of self-constitution and the transformation of society towards social equality, a just distribution of resources, and ecological sustainability as inherently linked. Democratic transformations of the self and society go hand in hand.

The concepts of assemblage and interruption applied to identity and self throughout this book, also allow for thinking about systemic transformation. They shed new light on the systems debate in democratic theory (Dean, Rinne, and Geissel 2019). Deliberative systems are mostly thought of in structured and hierarchical ways in terms of bottom up and top down transmission (Dryzek 2009). Assemblage thinking introduces a flat ontology that treats humans, nonhumans, inanimate objects, and natural forces equally. Democracy, then, includes human bodies (Machin 2022), verbal and non-verbal performances (Ercan, Asenbaum, and Mendonça 2023), nonhuman animals (Meijer 2019), material objects (Honig 2017), natural events (Romero and Dryzek 2021), digital technology (Asenbaum 2021b), future generations (Smith 2021), and planetary boundaries (Dryzek and Pickering 2019). Instead of thinking in terms of clear structures and hierarchical relations, assemblage thinking invites us to think about emergence, complexity, informality, spontaneity, and unforeseen change.

To deepen this line of thought, I propose the concept of a democratic microverse. I conceptualize democratic spaces as miniature constellations that prefigure possible democratic futures (Asenbaum and Hanusch 2021). These prefigurative instances interrupt the dominant order of governance. They demonstrate that for a limited time, things can be otherwise. Just as anonymity interrupts established identity assemblages, so do democratic spaces interrupt assemblages of governance and political power. These openings in democratic practice signal systemic ruptures that enable democratic transformations. Reassembling, in this context, does not only refer to a redistribution of recognition but also of economic resources. A democratic microverse functions as a prefigurative real utopia (Wright 2013) that signifies a democratic potential for systemic transformation. It starts from the inner identity constellation of participants, from their hopes and aspirations, and connects them to the societal and potentially the planetary level by projecting possible democratic futures.

Overview of the Book

In summary, the politics of becoming reconfigures presence in the space of appearance. It promotes active articulations of marginalized identities and simultaneously allows for the expression of inner multiplicity. By interrupting everyday modes of performing the self through anonymity which allows for disidentification, identity is reassembled. This reconfiguration of the self is linked to systemic transformations towards democratic futures. To advance this argument, the book proceeds as follows.

Chapter 2 develops a democratic theory of space and in doing so lays the theoretical groundwork of this book. It builds on debates that describe modes of participatory engagement as invited, claimed, and closed spaces and raises the question of why these participatory formats are described in spatial terms. Drawing on Hannah Arendt (1958) and Judith Butler's (2015) work on the space of appearance and taking inspiration from new materialist assemblage theory, I introduce a concept of democratic space as agentic assemblage consisting of material objects, sentient bodies, and performative expressions. The interaction between them affords and limits possible action. The identities of democratic subjects are themselves constituted as assemblages which interact and partly overlap with spatial assemblages. Democratic subjects are simultaneously *products* and *producers* of democratic spaces. Spaces and subjects relate to one another in a dialectical manner so that alterations of identity trigger alterations of space and vice versa.

Having developed a concept of democratic space, Chapter 3 asks how equality can be advanced within such spaces. It revisits feminist difference democracy that draws attention to modes of devaluation and discrimination along the lines of identity markers of gender, race, class, and sexuality (Mansbridge, 1999). The difference democratic argument for a politics of presence (Phillips 1995) advances inclusion by giving marginalized subjects visibility within the space of appearance. Yet, the politics of presence is overshadowed by the dilemma of difference (Young 1989: 268). As difference democrats elaborate, equalizing mechanisms such as quotas and identity politics afford presence, but also entail essentializing tendencies confining the democratic subject to its identified body. While the politics of presence may successfully advance equality, the freedom to explore different sides of the multiple self is compromised.

Chapter 4 seeks a way out of the dilemma of difference and asks how equality in democratic spaces can be accompanied by freedom for the subject to change. The chapter first consults participatory, deliberative, and agonistic perspectives in the search for modes of self-transformation. As these three perspectives render limited results, the chapter introduces a recently evolving perspective that so far has received little attention in the mainstream of democratic theory—transformative democracy. This account calls for a deep transformation of society towards freedom and equality (Hardt and Negri 2004; Newman 2016). The chapter draws on the transformative perspective to develop the concept of a politics of becoming. At the heart of the politics of becoming is the notion of disidentification—the rejection of hegemonic identity interpellations through social movements. This results in the emergence of new collective subjects with improper names that create pseudonymous identities such as the '99 percent' or 'Anonymous' (Rancière 1999; Deseriis 2015). What remains unexplained by the transformative perspective, however, is how disidentification can be experienced on a personal rather than a collective level. To answer this question, the chapter infuses transformative democratic thought with queer theory and in particular intersectional, trans, and Black queer theory (Muñoz 1999; Lloyd 2005; Bey 2022). Understanding identity performances as masquerade (Butler 1990) allows for thinking about how the everyday masks subjects are wearing can be deconstructed or resignified

(Muñoz 1999; Butler 2004). In accordance with the transformative perspective, abolition goes further than resignification and describes identity transformation as intimately linked to societal transformation (Bey 2022).

Chapter 5 asks how such radical democratic acts of disidentification can be practically exercised. It explores anonymity in various modes of democratic participation including voting, campaign funding, masked protests, pamphleteering, graffiti, and online debate. The chapter generates the first concept of anonymity rooted in democratic theory. It shows how anonymity rearranges space by interrupting the established order of things through interfaces such as masks or computer screens. This spatial rearrangement generates a channel from private into public space. The concept of anonymity advanced in this chapter allows for a reconceptualization of the politics of presence. I argue that instead of interpreting anonymity as mere absence of identity, anonymity facilitates a different mode of presence. This new mode of presence is made possible through the interruption of continuous identity performances, which allows for hidden aspects of the multiple self to appear. In doing so, anonymity affords three sets of contradictory freedoms: inclusion and exclusion, subversion and submission, honesty and deception. Anonymity is always liberating—freeing the subject to express its multiple self. This freedom is, however, used in both constructive and destructive ways. Anonymity appears as inherently contradictory.

Chapter 6 explores how modes of disidentification come into play in online engagement. It revisits the poststructuralist-inspired debate on cyberdemocracy that explains the digital self as existing only through the words it utters (Rheingold 1993; Turkle 1995; Poster 1997). This debate imagines an increase in personal freedom by 'leaving the body behind' and conceptualizes cyberspace as a separate realm that follows its own logics. Current debates, in contrast, insist on collapsing digital and physical space (Isin and Ruppert 2015). The chapter develops a new theory of digital space beyond these two positions. It explains digital space as an assemblage of material objects, sentient bodies, and performative expressions, in which the material dimension is reconfigured. Physical space is mediated and interrupted by interfaces. This theory of digital space allows for rethinking of the politics of presence in the digital age. Employing cyberfeminist thought to explain the subject as a cyborgian assemblage of organic bodies and technological devices (Haraway 1991 [1985]), the chapter develops the concept of a *digital* politics of presence. Several practical examples demonstrate that a digital politics of presence articulates marginalized identities in digital spaces but at the same time renders identity transformative by expanding the agency of the subject to reassemble the self both online and offline.

The concluding chapter situates the politics of becoming in a larger progressive project of radical democratic transformations. It goes beyond pitting recognition of identity against the redistribution of economic goods. Re-reading the democratic (deliberative) systems debate through assemblage theory, the chapter introduces the concept of a democratic microverse—a miniature participatory configuration that prefigures a potential future constellation. It extends from the individual democratic subject to democratic spaces and finally to a societal and potentially planetary level. A democratic microverse interrupts the dominant logics of the present by rearranging assemblages of human and nonhuman bodies and in doing so opens spaces for democratic transformation. Not only the subject itself, but the political and societal system is subject to change.

2

Becoming Assemblage

Democratic Spaces

> If democracy were a building, the 'under construction' sign would
> never be removed.
>
> Michael Saward 2003: i

Current debates in the scholarship on democracy readily make use of spatial
terminologies to theorize political participation. Theorists of deliberative democracy trace the transmission between *public space* and *empowered space* in the
deliberative system (Dryzek 2009), which is defined as 'a communicative activity that occurs in multiple, diverse yet partly overlapping spaces' (Elstub, Ercan,
and Mendonça 2016: 139). Scholars working in the agonistic tradition observe
that '[o]ur societies are confronted with the proliferation of political spaces
which are radically new and different' (Mouffe 1993: 20). The study of democratic innovations describes new modes of citizen engagement as *participatory
spaces*, differentiating between *invited spaces* such as citizens' assemblies, *claimed
spaces* such as social movement meetings, and *closed spaces* such as parliamentary committees (Brock, Cornwall, and Gaventa 2001; Cornwall and Schattan
Coelho 2007).

 Given the central role of spatiality in democratic thought, it is surprising that, to
date, no clear understanding of 'space' has been provided. Indeed, the use of spatial terminology remains unsubstantiated. Rather than explaining what is *spatial*
about these democratic spaces, authors often limit their definitions to the attributes
of the spaces under discussion. John Gaventa (2006: 25), for example, writes: 'In
this article ... "spaces" are seen as opportunities, moments and channels where citizens can act to potentially affect policies.' Elsewhere the spatiality of participatory
processes is explained through social relations: 'Thinking about participation as
spatial practice highlights the relations of power ... that permeate any site for public engagement' (Cornwall 2004a: 1). Beyond these gestures towards a metaphoric
understanding, the spatiality of democratic space remains unclear. These authors
fail to demonstrate a direct connection between such metaphoric spatiality and
physical space (Brown 1997: 14; Parkinson 2012: 6). Jennifer Forestal argues:
'the role of the physical environment in structuring democratic action is often

The Politics of Becoming. Hans Asenbaum, Oxford University Press. © Hans Asenbaum (2023).
DOI: 10.1093/oso/9780192858870.003.0002

referenced obliquely in much of the literature in democratic theory ... We need a theory of democratic *space*' (Forestal 2017: 151). This chapter aims at answering this call.

The question of what defines space more generally is usually answered by referring to its material qualities—space is explained as the relationality between physical objects. We experience space through movement. Our movement is limited by physical things and the experience of limitation of movements results in our ability to predict limitation without actively experiencing it. Hence the mere sight of an object results in our understanding of distance—the prediction of the movement it *would* take to reach the object. Rather than understanding space in passive terms, however, I define space in terms of what it *does*. Space is a bounded, relational construct that *affords and limits action*. The central claim I am advancing in this chapter is that a thorough understanding of space as part of democratic action cannot be limited to physical things. It is not only physical objects that enable and bind our movements. In participatory processes such as voting, protesting, or deliberating, our democratic agency is afforded and limited by the relations of all sentient bodies present including human and nonhuman participants and by their articulations. Democratic space forms assemblages consisting of material objects, sentient bodies, and performative expressions.

This chapter is crucial for the overall goal of this book. It lays the theoretical groundwork and clarifies the core concepts. By generating a foundational understanding of democracy and self, it demonstrates that democratic space and democratic subjects, whose reconfigurations the book explores, function by the same principles. Democratic space is woven into and partly inseparable from the constitution of the self. To explore how spaces constitute subjects, I draw on Hannah Arendt's concept of the space of appearance. Arendt argues that 'without a space of appearance and without trusting in action and speech as a mode of being together, neither the reality of one's self, of one's own identity, nor the reality of the surrounding world can be established beyond doubt' (Arendt 1958: 208). But space does not simply constitute us in a unidirectional way; rather, spaces are at the same time the product of our making. In her recent work, Judith Butler further develops Arendt's space of appearance by studying the public assemblies that emerged in 2011 across the world, most notably in the Occupy movement (USA, UK), the Indignant movement (Spain, Greece), and the Arab Spring (North Africa, Middle East):

> So though these movements have depended on the prior existence of pavement, street, and square, and have often enough gathered in the square such as Tahrir, whose political history is potent, it is equally true that the collective actions collect the space itself, gather the pavement, and animate and organize the architecture. As much as we must insist on there being material conditions for public assembly,

and public speech, we have also to ask how it is that assembly and speech reconfigure the materiality of public space and produce, or reproduce, the public character
of the material environment.

(Butler 2015: 71)

I will pick up these lines of thought from Arendt and Butler and enrich them
with inspirations from new materialist assemblage theory. By conceptualizing the
democratic subject itself as an assemblage comprising multiple affective things,
I will further explore the interrelation of space and self understood as interwoven, and at times inseparable assemblages. These assemblages of space and the
self create different affordances for the subject to change.

This chapter will first engage with the literature on participatory spaces that
discusses participation in invited, claimed, and closed spaces. The next section
will develop a theory of democratic space as assemblage that includes materiality,
sentience, and performativity. The final step will then consider the role that such
spaces of appearance play in constructing identity and constituting democratic
subjectivity.

Spaces of Democratic Engagement

The term 'participatory spaces' describes various forms of democratic engagement.
This concept originated in feminist development studies and describes 'new architectures of democratic practice' (Cornwall 2002: 1). One of its main achievements
consists in drawing attention to commonalities between three areas of democratic
participation: new formats of public engagement often called 'democratic innovations'; social movements' activism; and representative governmental institutions
(Gaventa 2006; Cornwall and Schattan Coelho 2007; Cornwall and Shankland
2013).

Invited spaces are participatory formats of public engagement including citizens' assemblies, participatory budgets, and townhall meetings (Fung and Wright
2001; Smith 2009). Invited spaces are created by resource-rich actors, such as state
agencies or NGOs, for the participation of citizens. Studies on invited spaces have
analysed different participatory formats around the world such as the Gram Sabha
village assemblies in India (Aiyar 2010; Parthasarathy, Rao, and Palaniswamy
2019) and local forums for citizens' engagement in South Africa (McEwan 2005)
and Angola (Roque and Shankland 2007). The structural settings of invited spaces
aim to foster inclusion and equality among participants (Karpowitz, Mendelberg, and Shaker 2012). However, invited spaces are prone to cooption (Cornwall 2002) and cherry picking among results by those who set those spaces
up (Font et al. 2017). Moreover, their democratic values are compromised by

an increasingly commercialized sphere of public engagement professionals (C. Lee 2014). Despite these dangers, invited spaces always provide some, even if only limited, opportunity for those who are usually unheard to speak. Thus, invited spaces always foster the potential to challenge established power arrangements and facilitate innovative thinking and change (Cornwall and Shankland 2013: 316).

Claimed spaces emerge through citizens' self-organized participation in social movements and citizens' initiatives (Polletta 2002; della Porta 2009; della Porta and Rucht 2013). The dynamics of invited and claimed spaces are fundamentally different, since invited spaces are created by one set of actors for use by another. Claimed spaces, in contrast, are created and used by the same people (Cornwall 2002b: 17). The process of designing these spaces thus raises a different set of questions for designers. Rather than asking *how do I want others to participate?*, the question is *how do I want to engage with others?* Social movement spaces have been subject to a wide range of studies, including analyses of the global justice movement emerging in Seattle (Shukaitis 2005), the squatter movement in Athens (Poulimenakos and Dalakoglou 2017), the Indignant movement in Greece (Kaika and Karaliotas 2016), public assemblies of the Arab Spring (Lopes de Souza and Lipietz 2011), and anti-AIDS activism in Canada (Brown 1997).

Finally, *closed spaces* are participatory institutions to which access is highly restricted (Cornwall 2004a: 5; Gaventa 2006: 26). Participation is possible through channels of public legitimization such as elections, delegation, or appointment. This exclusivity, in my view, justifies the term 'closed spaces'. It is noteworthy, however, that access to such spaces is not entirely closed. Taking a different perspective, Dryzek (2009) calls the same institutions 'empowered space'. The study of closed spaces focuses on the physical architecture of parliamentary buildings (Goodsell 1988; Dovey 1999; Puwar 2010; McCarthy-Cotter et al. 2018) and deliberation in legislative assemblies (Bächtiger et al. 2005).

The concept of participatory spaces builds on the question of who creates participatory designs and for whom. By focusing on the role of creators and participants, it puts power at its core and asks about the intentions behind participatory design (Cornwall 2002b: 8). Besides the central question of power, invited, claimed, and closed spaces also differ in their durability and degree of institutionalization. Closed spaces are highly formalized institutions, following clear protocols and often adhering to traditional procedures over the course of centuries. Invited spaces, in contrast, have a more experimental, semi-institutionalized character and are of shorter duration. Claimed spaces are often short-lived and exhibit merely emergent traces of institutionalization as activists develop common decision-making rules (Cornwall 2002b).

Assembling Democratic Space

The strength of the debate about new participatory spaces lies in generating a broad picture that captures a variety of participatory engagements in democracy. The spatial terminology points to power relations between participants within such spaces and the contexts in which the spaces themselves are situated. However, this spatial terminology remains, for the most part, unsubstantiated. A deeper understanding of what is *spatial* about participatory spaces is missing.[1] In what follows, I will propose a concept of democratic space as assemblage that brings materiality, sentience, and performativity together.

One of the major omissions in existing conceptualizations of participatory spaces is an apparent shying away from the notion of boundaries. This neglect may be explained by a democratic ethos of inclusion or a constructivist aversion to the positivist Newtonian notion of space as a stable measurable phenomenon. In my view, it is precisely such boundedness that defines democratic space, which raises the crucial question of inclusion and exclusion (Gaventa 2006: 26). Democratic space is defined by the relation between things that demarcate an inside and an outside. Here I take inspiration from Laclau and Mouffe's (1985) concept of the constitutive outside. In their radical democratic discourse theory, discursive concepts always rely on the definition of the other—that which is not included. The relationship between outside and inside, however, is not defined by pure exclusivity; rather, it concerns how the outside is reflected within the inside, and vice versa (also see Butler 2015: 4). Applying the notion of the constitutive outside to the concept of democratic spaces makes it clear that such spaces are not simply defined by boundaries; indeed, the reality outside a bounded space is also reflected within that space. Power asymmetries outside democratic spaces, for example, are partially mirrored within those spaces contra their intended design (Cornwall 2004b: 80).

Such an understanding of democratic space does not reduce space to a stable and measurable category. Rather, spaces of democratic engagement are volatile constructs since their boundaries and internal relations are constituted by affective things (Connolly 2013). At this point, it is crucial to demystify some assumptions about the affectivity of things. What does it mean that even inanimate things are affective or even lively? I understand things as affective insofar as through their interpretation by humans and nonhumans, they create affordances and limitations. The affectivity of things—whether organic or not—derives from the relational character of our perception. Affectivity is deeply rooted in the body.

---

[1] Cornwall (2002b) goes the furthest towards explaining the spatiality of participatory spaces by drawing on Foucault (1979).

It is a visceral response to sensory perception that is then emotionally reflected, cognitively processed, and mentally rationalized (Clough 2010). What constitutes space is the cognitive task of relating things to each other. As participants in space, we engage in 'synthesis', the cognitive act of ordering and relating things (Löw 2008). Synthesis is a constant activity of boundary-drawing through sensory perception and cognitive reflection. This process of assembling things produces spatial relationality. Democratic space, then, is ephemeral because it is continuously reinterpreted by democratic subjects, including participants and the publics that observe participation.

So, how does concrete material space relate to abstract metaphoric space? My main argument is that the cognitive act of synthesis does not just relate physical objects to one another, as common definitions of space suggest (see Voß, Schritt, and Sayman 2021). Taking into account the affective nature of all things, a better understanding of what defines space can be developed by asking what space *does*. I understand spaces of democratic engagement as relational, bounded constructs that *enable and limit action*. Hence, to develop a thorough understanding of democratic space, all things that demarcate boundaries—and thereby afford and limit action—need to be considered as part of space. Spatialization through cognition does not stop at the perception of material things; it also includes the relations between sentient bodies and their performative expressions. Democratic space, then, consists of the relationality of material objects, sentient bodies, and performative articulations. Through the cognitive act of synthesis, participants and the publics that observe participation relate these diverse things to each other. I use the term *democratic* space when the relational bounds of material objects, sentient bodies, and performative expressions afford participatory processes that seek to realize freedom and equality as the core values of democracy (Mouffe 2005).

Sentient bodies and their performances participate in assemblages through the same act of synthesis that also produces material space. The things that democratic subjects feel and express follow the same logic of cognitive ordering. Importantly, the order of sentient relations and performative acts produce affordances and limitations. This order itself, however, is the product of human perception. Hence, when human minds assemble objects, bodies, and performances in participatory processes, they produce and bind democratic agency.

Materiality, sentience, and performativity are not to be understood as sealed off and mutually exclusive. Parkinson (2012: 77) is right to ask: 'can we separate the influence of physical form from its social, cultural, and political context?' It is often hard to tell where sentience ends and performativity begins. What is often overlooked is that this is also true for materiality. Material things can only be comprehended through the senses and the discursive terms assigned to them (Butler 1990). They can never be perceived outside sentient and performative space. Materiality, sentience, and performativity are mutually productive. Materiality lays the foundation for the interaction of sentient bodies and their performative expressions; sentient bodies produce material objects and performative expressions, and performance creates the meaning of material objects and sentient bodies. While it becomes apparent just how porous the boundaries between materiality, sentience, and performativity are, an analytical distinction is necessary to generate a clear understanding.

The Materiality of Democratic Space

Given the bounded nature of physical space, we need to understand which material objects demarcate space. Spaces of democratic engagement are shaped by the constellation of buildings around a public square where protesters assemble, the arrangement of chairs and tables in a classroom of a local school that hosts a participatory budgeting process, and the walls that demarcate the lobbies, meeting rooms, and assembly halls of parliamentary buildings. Indeed, to understand how material space affords and limits democratic agency, studying parliamentary buildings is instructive. These closed spaces are characterized by the inscription of democratic practices into physical spatial arrangements. Nirmal Puwar (2010: 298) claims that 'parliament consists of living scripts' that prescribe and regulate democratic performances. It is important to note, however, that such physically inscribed protocols do not determine human behaviour:

> While the physical setting does not by any means deterministically control the attitudes and behavior of people, it does condition their thoughts and actions in preliminary, subtle and interactive ways. Buildings may be seen as a form of non-verbal communication in which messages are encoded by builders and then decoded by occupants, with probabilistic but potentially powerful cueing effects as a result.
>
> (Goodsell 1988: 288)

Ample scholarly work illustrates how social relations and discursive expression are influenced by the physical settings of parliamentary closed spaces. The confrontational culture of the UK Parliament, for example, is reflected in the walls, furniture, and room layout of Westminster Palace. The chamber of the House of Commons is one of the smallest parliamentary assembly halls in the world. It is a quarter of the size of the German Bundestag. The House of Commons only provides seats for 427 of its 650 members. Debates, therefore, literally become heated as the room temperature rises when the chamber is filled with human bodies. Members of Parliament (MPs) sit close together due to the limited space and because the seating consists of benches, unlike the US Senate, for example, which has individual chairs. MPs arriving late have to sit on the stairs in the aisles between the benches, further contributing to a caged and, at times, aggressive atmosphere with jeering and cheering interrupting the speakers. While in the German Bundestag the size of the assembly hall maintains a distance between MPs and the sole microphone at the speaker's lectern minimizes disruption, the small size of the House of Commons and the distribution of microphones throughout the chamber contributes to the adversarial character of the debates (Goodsell 1988: 298; Dovey 1999: 88; McCarthy-Cotter et al. 2018: 54).

Placing MPs in close proximity to each other not only raises the temperature, but also expresses political alliance. The metaphor of standing shoulder to shoulder as an expression of unity becomes physically manifest. Political opposition as a metaphoric term drawing on spatial imagination is materialized in the two opposed seating blocks. In this confrontation, the physical territory of MPs from the government and opposition, respectively, is demarcated by a line on the carpet, which places speakers at a sword's length from each other, so that if they were to engage in a physical sword fight, blades could cross but not reach the body (Dovey 1999).

The adversarial setting of the UK Parliament differs from most other parliamentary assembly halls where MPs are seated in a semi-circle or horseshoe shape, suggesting a more consensual orientation. These three types can be contrasted with the Chinese National People's Congress, which arranges seating in a single block facing a stage. Speakers are elevated and look down on listeners, rather than the other way around as in the European Parliament. In the common semi-circular parliamentary seating arrangements, the different factions are seated in blocks and separated by aisles. In the US Congress, the expression 'working across the aisle' is widely used to address inter-party cooperation (Goodsell 1988: 299). This fan-like seating arrangement emerged in the French Revolution, and it is from this that the terminology of left-wing and right-wing—yet another spatial metaphor—is derived. The parliamentary setting also materializes the relation between the legislative and the executive branches of government. While in the UK Parliament, members of the cabinet, including the Prime Minister, sit together with other MPs of their party, in many continental European parliaments cabinet members sit opposite their own party MPs, who sit together with the opposition. In the US, with its strong division of power between governmental branches, cabinet members are entirely absent from Congressional debates (Goodsell 1988: 294).

Such practices of physical spatialization are not only observable in closed spaces. Those who design invited spaces devote much of their attention to the effects of the physical arrangement on participation. As we have seen, seating arrangements can influence social interaction. If the bifurcated space of the two oppositional blocks in the UK Parliament contributes to confrontation and the semi-circle in many other parliaments encourages a more consensual orientation (McCarthy-Cotter et al. 2018: 56), then the full circle in invited spaces takes this logic further still. Citizens' assemblies and open forums often seat participants in full circles to facilitate egalitarian and consensual communication: 'Not only does a circular arrangement permit eye contact among all participants, it also removes any head of the table, so everyone is equal in status' (Creighton 2005: 174). When there are so many participants that one circle does not suffice, invited spaces split participants into several smaller circles, often around tables, so that everyone has an equal position. An experiment with an invited space that changed a small group discussion setting from opposite rows to circular seating, observed how 'the tone shifted from the accusatory tone of the previous contestation to an inquisitive one [in] a friendly and more respectful atmosphere' (Paxton 2020: 127, 129).

This circular shape is also characteristic of activist meetings in claimed spaces, which often arrange participants in concentric circles. They thus combine the principle of rows characteristic of parliamentary closed spaces with the circular shape characteristic of invited spaces. The egalitarian intention is combined with the reality of large numbers of participants. An activist reports from a meeting of the Indignados movement with its slogan 'toma la plaza!' ('take the square!'):

> Some of the older or less-able participants were given chairs to sit on while others stood around the outside and the more physically flexible sat on the ground so that the meeting was structured in concentric circles going outwards from those sitting on the ground, to those in chairs, to those standing. This concentric circle formation is also an important political statement ... People faced each other, listened to one another and did not privilege the role of facilitator or speaker above the role of participant.
>
> (Maeckelbergh 2012: 220)

What parliamentary and other governmental buildings are for closed spaces, public squares are for claimed spaces. William Mitchell notes that what the various protest movements of 2011 have in common—despite their different causes and diverse cultural contexts from the Arab Spring to Occupy and the Indignants—is the public square. While other movements are represented in media discourses by the faces of their leaders, the square functions as the public face of leaderless movements: 'This is why the iconic moments, the images that promise to become monuments, of the global revolution of 2011 are not those of *face* but of *space*; not figures, but the negative space or ground against which a figure appears' (Mitchell 2012: 9). This leads Paolo Gerbaudo (2017) to term these diverse movements the 'movement of the squares'. Public squares are the result of architectural intent in city planning. Such physical openings in urban landscapes can afford democratic openings for change (Mitchell 2012: 18; also see Lopes de Souza and Lipietz 2011; Parkinson 2012: 73).

The Sentience of Democratic Space

Beyond the relationality between material objects, it is the relationships between participants themselves that constitute democratic space. Such corporeal space is generated through the connections between all sentient beings including human and nonhuman animals. Although humans might not be good at understanding them, nonhuman animals communicate among each other (Meijer 2019). Bees, for example, are known for their decision making procedures which carry consensual and democratic features (Seeley 2010). Plants, melting ice caps, and natural events such as volcano eruptions become participants in democratic interaction (Javier and Dryzek 2020). As the COVID-19 pandemic has demonstrated, even viruses can play a crucial role in democratic governance (Parry, Asenbaum, and Ercan 2021). Democratic space conceived as an assemblage of diverse living bodies is in constant flux. As relations between living bodies change, so too does sentient space. A new person entering the room, changing the constellation of people, can lead to different topics being discussed or certain discussions being shut down altogether. A conflict between two people can result in one of them leaving the room, feeling that there is not 'enough space' for both of them. Löw elaborates:

> The ordering of two people in relation to each other is also space constitutive, depending on their social relationship. People who are socially more intimate leave less space between them than people who are social strangers. The boundaries of this space become highly visible if overstepped by one of the interlocutors.
>
> (Löw 2008: 34)

Taking the example of how difficult it can feel to walk between two people who are talking to each other, it becomes apparent that the sentience of space fulfils the same function as materiality. Sentient relations establish boundaries that afford and restrict democratic agency. As such, sentient space is more of an event than a static arrangement. It not so much *exists* as *occurs* (Daskalaki 2018).

We can begin to grasp how the affectivity of emotional relations constitutes spaces by considering Judith Butler's work on the movement of the squares:

> Over and against an increasingly individualized sense of anxiety and failure, public assembly embodies the insight that this is a social condition both shared and unjust, and that assembly enacts a provisional and plural form of coexistence that constitutes a distinct ethical and social alternative to 'responsibilization'. As I hope to suggest, these forms of assembly can be understood as nascent and provisional versions of popular sovereignty. They can also be regarded as indispensable reminders of how legitimation functions in democratic theory and practice.
>
> (Butler 2015: 15)

Here the coming together of subjects—who, in assembling their bodies, form another collective body—constitutes space. On the grounds of a material space, such as a public square deliberately built as an opening between densely positioned buildings, a social space emerges. The emotivity of these social relations is a central aspect of sentient space. Butler (2015: 15, 26) notes the shared anxiety and anger of assembled bodies. This emotivity directed at the public outside the assembly, and the solidarity felt between participants within the assembly, produces space. The outside constitutes the inside, and vice versa, through the demarcation of boundaries (Laclau and Mouffe 1985).

Butler's performative theory of assembly builds on Hannah Arendt's concept of the space of appearance. For Arendt, the space of appearance is independent of physical locality. Since it consists of the relationships *between* democratic subjects, it depends on human sentience. Addressing the Ancient Greek polis as the ideal form of democratic space, Arendt claims:

> The polis, properly speaking, is not the city-state in its physical location; it is the organization of the people as it arises out of acting and speaking together, and its true space lies between people living together for this purpose, no matter where they happen to be.
>
> (Arendt 1958: 198)

Arendt further elucidates the mobility of space:

> The space of appearance comes into being wherever men [sic][2] are together in the manner of speech and action ... Its peculiarity is that, unlike the spaces which are the work of our hands, it does not survive the actuality of the movement which brought it into being, but disappears not only with the dispersal of men ... but with the disappearance or arrest of the activities themselves.
>
> (Arendt 1958: 199)

Looking at the history of parliamentary democracy in the UK, the dependency of democratic spaces on the presence of particular bodies, rather than a particular location, is evident. The closed spaces of the Great Council that functioned as a royal advisory assembly and constituted an incipient form of parliamentarianism did not repeatedly meet in the same location. These assemblies were called by the king or queen in different places according to their convenience. Only in the mid-thirteenth century did they begin to convene more regularly in Westminster Palace

---

[2] The use of the English term 'men' is misleading here. In Arendt's own German translation of the English original *The Human Condition*, Arendt uses the word 'Menschen' (Arendt 1981 [1960]: 194) which translates to the English 'humans'. Often equated with 'humans' at the time of Arendt's writing, 'men' would today be more accurately translated as 'humans'.

(Maddicott 2010: 163). It was thus the presence of assembled bodies rather than the physical location that constituted the space.

The presence of living bodies is a defining element of sentient space, but it is their lived experience, their sensory perceptions that brings sentient space into being. This corporeal experientiality as part of democratic exchange is the foundational element of sensory democracy (Ryan and Flinders 2018). Until recently, conceptions of democracy have been dominated by notions of rational and enlightened subjects, whose bodies, emotions, and affects were ignored (Young 1990; Machin 2022). The sentience experience of bodies was connected to their weakness and mortality and to hard labour, which was seen in opposition to intellect. Sensory democracy reverses this move and situates seeing, hearing, smelling, tasting, and feeling bodies at the centre of democratic exchange (Curato 2019; Mendonça, Ercan, and Asenbaum 2020). Corporeal sensations trigger visceral reactions which translate into emotions (Clough 2010). Emotions can then be conveyed through affectivity. One person's sadness, for example, can cause another person's sadness through empathy or it can cause the other person's satisfaction, depending on their pre-existing relations. Importantly, affect does not actually travel from one person to another. Rather, the expression of one person's affect causes the other person to experience affect. Each affect is their own. Nevertheless, this constitutes a network of sentient relationality between people. Within a participatory process, this network constitutes a vital part of democratic space. Like their material counterparts, sentience creates affordances and limitations for human interaction.

Material space is a precondition for sentient experience. It is important to note, however, that this relationship works in two ways. Material and sentient space depend upon and produce one another. Many of the material spaces that facilitate democratic interaction are built by sentient bodies: '*Public space is a human construct, an artifact,* the result of the attempt by human beings to shape the place' (Hénaff and Strong 2001: 5). This echoes Winston Churchill's famous saying: 'We shape our buildings and afterwards our buildings shape us' (Commons debates 28 October 1943: col. 403), thereby understanding material and sentient space-making as a dialectical process. Löw (2008) calls this the 'duality of space'.

Nirmal Puwar records a telling example of the production of physical spaces by human bodies. As noted earlier, in contrast to the relative stability of material space, sentient space is ever changing. Yet, according to Puwar (2010: 299), material space is never fixed. It remains a site of contestation and hence is constantly altered by sentient bodies: 'Inhabitation of space enables bodies to move in planned and coordinated ways but also in unpredictable ways. Boundaries etched in architectures of stone and iron grids do not go unchallenged'. Such contestation changes the structural configuration of material space and may produce alterations in democratic affordances. For instance, when the UK Parliament was rebuilt in 1834, it included the first women's gallery in the House of Commons chamber from which women, who were formerly banned from attending parliamentary debates, could listen. Metal grilles were installed in the gallery to 'keep women in their place'. On several occasions, suffragettes challenged this sociomaterial arrangement. In coordinated actions, they threw leaflets promoting votes for women through the grilles into the chamber, transcending the physical boundary. Two activists padlocked their bodies to the grilles, drawing attention to the physical restraint that the grilles posed to their political freedom and to demonstrate their unmovable political convictions. Suffragettes also used the garrets and shafts of the parliamentary building to secretly gain access to and disrupt parliamentary debates, and they inscribed their messages on stone walls and statues. Such contestations and partial alteration of material space were not just aimed at removing physical restrictions, such as the grilles that separated silent women from vocal men; they also sought to reconfigure the arrangement of sentient space, which ultimately led to female bodies joining the exclusive, male assemblage (Puwar 2010).

The Performativity of Democratic Space

To explore how performative expressions constitute democratic space, it is instructive to consider the etymology of the word 'thing'. Medieval *things* were public assemblies, which constituted the common governing bodies throughout Scandinavia and parts of what is now UK territory. They can be seen as successors to the Ancient Greek polis and predecessors of current parliaments. Things took place in public places and fulfilled their legislative and judicial functions with the participation of all free men. Assembly types were differentiated as *althings*, which discussed various matters, compared to *lawthings*, which focused on legislative matters (Sanmark 2013). This terminology can still be found today in the Danish Parliament, the *Folketing* (the people's thing), and the Parliament of Norway, the *Storting* (the great thing). Importantly, the meaning of the term 'thing' shifted from denoting these public assemblies themselves to the topics they discussed. Assemblies were thus called to discuss public things (see Honig 2017). It was not until the thirteenth century that the meaning of 'thing' shifted once again from discursive subject to material object (Olwig 2013; Kullmann 2018).

I want to revive this early meaning of 'things' as subjects of debate so as to explore the performative dimension of democratic space. Performative space consists of continuously changing constellations of the many things expressed in democratic spaces. Referring to these things as *subjects* of debate, rather than as objects, also draws attention to their affective nature. The things humans and non-humans express through words, silences, gestures, mimicry, sounds, noises, songs, dances, images, artefacts, or presence matter (Curato 2019; Mendonça, Ercan, and Asenbaum 2020). The things that are said, are there. Think of a court room, in which the defence objects to the groundless imputations of the prosecutor. No matter how the judge rules, the damage is done. A thing has been created, and it is in the room. The new performative expressions entering the room, such as the judge's ruling 'sustained!', alter the constellation of things, but they cannot erase them. These performative acts—the things that are said and done as part of democratic exchange—point to the theatrical character of democracy. Democratic exchange involves stages, performers, and audiences (Hénaff and Strong 2001). Space is created through experiential perceptions of material objects, sentient bodies, and performative expressions.

So how can we make sense of space as an assemblage of performative acts? Understanding space as 'a sensible manifestation of things', Mustafa Dikeç (2015: 2) conceptualizes the act of spatialization as a cognitive process. Perceiving material space means establishing relationships between physical things through visual, haptic, and/or olfactory perception. Such a process of material spatialization can be equated to the discursive production and perception of meaning: understanding or articulating spoken or written content means ordering concepts—discursive things—and establishing the relationships between them that make them intelligible:

> Political thinking brings together a disposition to be moved by and a capacity to relate and order what we perceive. Spatial imagination—seeing connections that cannot always be deduced rationally from the givens, establishing new relations and gathering, envisaging new forms and configurations—is thus an important part of political thinking.
>
> (Dikeç 2015: 4)

Following this argument, any performative act entails spatialization. Thinking, speaking, and writing all produce space by generating linguistic structures of orientation. Crucially, then, performative space exists not only in the interaction between participants, but extends into their thinking patterns. Such spatialization always entails establishing terms of inclusion and exclusion that demarcate discursive boundaries. Discourses on a particular topic, such as migration, demarcate a performative space. Discursive boundaries limit what is expressible and thinkable in a particular context (Cornwall 2004b: 75; Butler 2015: 4). Drawing on Foucault's (1979) symbolic discourse boundaries, Cornwall (2002b: 8) notes that the availability of words is a prerequisite for expression. This does not only go for words, but any means of expression. Such availability can be limited by the existence of expressions, the limits of the meaning of expressions, the knowledge or recollection of expression, and, crucially, the social norms and protocols governing expressions in particular contexts. This kind of boundary-drawing occurs not just when subjects articulate things, but also when they perceive performative expression. Spatialization occurs in the mind of the listener who, by interpreting articulation, orders, draws boundaries, and synthesizes.

What does the understanding of performative expression as an act of space-making mean for participatory processes? First, it is not only material and sentient space that affect participation. The protocols that govern performative expression and the bounds of the available vocabulary also afford and limit democratic agency. In short, what participants can think, say, and do depends on performative space. In political debate, participants navigate through a web of discursive meanings that are—for the most part—already established. Democratic subjects can only attempt to stretch or alter the meaning of existing concepts or invent new ones (Lloyd 2007). Second, the performativity of democratic space reveals that the architecture of such spaces consists of a set of protocols. Rules of a claimed space that determine a consensus principle, rules of an invited space that determine the random selection of participants, rules of a parliamentary closed space that allow the Speaker to interrupt MPs who swear, all represent a discursive architecture that guides participation.

The Self as Assemblage

With the conception of democratic space as an assemblage bringing together material objects, sentient bodies, and performative expressions, we have laid the groundwork for understanding democratic participation. To make sense of how identities of democratic subjects form and potentially change in these spaces, we need an understanding of what identities actually are and how they relate to space. Hannah Arendt's concept of the space of appearance is a good starting point. She argues that democratic space and the identity of the democratic subject are directly linked. The public visibility of the speaking and acting body constitutes democratic subjectivity: 'It is the space of appearance in the widest sense of the word, namely, the space where I appear to others as others appear to me, where men [sic][3] exist not merely like other living or inanimate things but make their appearance explicitly' (Arendt 1958: 198–9). Butler deepens Arendt's work on the space of appearance by drawing attention to movements such as Black Lives Matter or protests of undocumented immigrants in the US, which by assembling publicly gain visibility: 'when bodies assemble on the street, in the square, or in the other forms of public space (including virtual ones) they are exercising a plural and performative right to appear, one that asserts and instates the body in the midst of the political field' (Butler 2015: 11).

What is significant in the conception of the space of appearance is that the appearance of the democratic subject is tied to its visibility. Butler's focus on

---

[3] See footnote 2.

the bodies that publicly assemble further emphasizes the aspect of visibility in Arendt's original work: 'our bodies must be viewed and their vocalized sounds must be heard: the body must enter the visual and audible field' (Butler 2015: 86). The argument for configuring democratic subjectivity through visibility is also at the heart of the work on the theatrical nature of democracy (Hénaff and Strong 2001; Parkinson 2012). On the stages of democracy it is the visibility of the actors and the glance of the audience that constitutes democratic subjectivity: 'sight involves us most immediately with other human beings. In seeing someone or something, I create a space that is ours' (Hénaff and Strong 2001: 6). Democracy, according to this argument, requires face-to-face communication with subjects physically present and visible to each other. I deem this exclusive focus on visibility problematic and will return to this point in Chapters 5 and 6.

At this point it is important to note that space provides different identity affordances. Space affects who we are in a given moment. Cornwall claims that the configuration of democratic spaces impacts the roles that participants play and what sides of themselves they express (Cornwall 2004b: 80). Parkinson 'alerts us to the *staging* of democracy: the need for and utility of particular platforms for the performance of particular roles' (Parkinson 2012: 10). In short, space affects identity. As we have seen above, others highlight that subjects create space. Subjects build and arrange physical spaces, generate relations between sentient bodies, and produce discursive constellations. Taken together, we thus see a bidirectional affectivity between space and identity. Identity and space are the product of a dialectical process of co-constitution. The two directions of this dialectical process even converge at times. As Doreen Massey (1995: 285) claims: 'we make our spaces/spatialities in the process of constructing our various identities.'

My argument here is that space and identity function by the same principles. Affective things establish not only the bounds of space but also the lines that demarcate identity. Physical boundaries such as walls and national border crossing points, sentient bodies which carry various identity markers, and performative expressions such as names all simultaneously demarcate space and identity. Butler claims that democracy cannot exist without the demarcation of the demos as subject. In other words, democracy is always based on exclusion through boundary making practices: 'there is no possibility of "the people" without a discursive border drawn somewhere, either traced along the lines of existing nation-states, racial or linguistic communities, or political affiliation. The discursive move to establish "the people" in one way or another is a bid to have a certain border recognized' (Butler 2015: 5).

The demarcations of inclusion and exclusion are simultaneously practices of space making and identity creation. National territories, sentient bodies, and discursive terms are all constituted through exclusion. Linguistic definition and human cognition depend on exclusion per se (Phillips 2010: 48–9). Hence, we can understand identity and the formation of the subject as a process of including affective things within an agentic assemblage. The subject is constituted by its blood flows, skin cells, and muscle fibres, its religion, party affiliation, and opinions, its name, social security number, and signature. The subject emerges as a contingent configuration navigating through a discursive field of concepts, meanings, and identity interpellations. This discursive identity space is intertwined with physical locations of birth, living, and work, and social relations with other humans. The subject as assemblage is not simply the effect of material, sentient, and performative spaces. It is inseparably intertwined with them as their product and their maker.

Spatializing Democratic Subjectivity

So how are the materiality, sentience, and performativity of democratic space intertwined with identity assemblages? The material spaces we inhabit are one of the prime factors defining our identities. Being born or living in a country for a long period of time makes us Australians, Brits, or Nigerians; being at universities makes us students, scholars, or academics; on basketball courts we become basketball players, on shopping streets shoppers, and on dancefloors dancers. The controversy about gender-neutral toilets to break up the male/female binary is a case in point of how material space creates identity (Gershenson and Penner 2009). If you have ever lived abroad for a certain time, you might have experienced the feeling of being someone else. Often the feelings of excitement and liberation in different locations give way to frustration upon returning home when the old environment does not acknowledge the changes so deeply experienced abroad and forces the old self to come out again. The new self appears to be left on the other side of national borders.

The way we experience and express ourselves in different material spaces also plays a crucial role in respect of democratic participation. The internal architecture of Westminster Palace, for example, hails those within it in particular ways. It is characterized by a clear division running through the entire building, separating the House of Commons from the House of Lords. The furniture and decor of the rooms signal a class divide that affects identities expressed within them. The rooms assigned to the Lords convey nobility through their leather benches in royal red and their rich golden decorum covering the walls and ceilings. Not just the chamber where debates take place, which is furnished with three royal thrones, golden clocks, and wooden lions, but all of the rooms, chapels, halls, and lobbies assigned to the Lords display grandeur and nobility. The spaces assigned to the Commons, in contrast, are furnished in a simple style with green benches and plain wooden panels covering the walls. The two realms of the Commons and the Lords are architecturally strictly separated, so that people within these spaces never cross paths except when entering the central lobby that connects the two wings (Dovey 1999: 88; Puwar 2010: 304).

This material assembling of identity can be expression of democratic agency. For example, the Women's Social and Political Union (WSPU) of the UK suf-fragette movement, known for its disruptive action including breaking shop windows and bombing public letter boxes, founded a number of commercial shops. The shops sold the weekly newspaper 'Votes for Women', postcards, tea, and toiletries, as well as a series of other suffrage merchandise in the purple, white, and green colour scheme of the movement. These shops both supported the movement financially and provided meeting spaces for political debate and planning. But the shops did more than this. They publicly constructed an iden-tity of suffragettes as respectable, reliable, and commercially successful women, which counteracted the militant image of the movement. Moreover, the prod-ucts sold in the shop, such as cosmetics and scarfs, connoted with femininity and wealth, constituted an image of domesticity and docility in line with established gender roles (Mercer 2004). By assembling material objects and constructing a particular material space, these suffragettes intentionally assembled a particular identity.

This kind of material identity-making also plays a role for the sentience of demo-cratic space. We can observe how different constellations of sentient bodies and the power relations and emotive bonds between them give rise to different iden-tity performances—think of the empowering effects of the exclusive female bodies constituting the suffragette shops. It is the *betweenness* of human bodies, much in the sense of Arendt's space of appearance, that produces identity (Arendt 1958: 198). In Massey's words: 'the identities, including the political identities, on which the project of radical democracy focuses are themselves formed in a spatialised interlocking of power-filled social relations' (Massey 1995: 285). How participants understand their own identities and how their identities are perceived by others is influenced by the configuration of sentient bodies that constitute a given space, which is in a state of constant flux:

People move between domains of association in everyday life in which the ways they come to be seen by others, and seen themselves, may be strikingly different, with implications for the extent to which they are able to influence and indeed act as agents in particular spaces. Someone who is voluble and assertive in one setting may be silenced in others; someone looked up to with respect in one sphere may find themselves patronized and even derided in another. The mutual impingement of relations of power and difference within and across different arenas conditions possibilities for agency and voice.

(Cornwall 2004b: 80)

Democratic spaces then fulfil a democratic function that is often overlooked. While many scholars ask about the real-world outcomes of democratic innovations, Cornwall and colleagues point to the function of identity constitution of such spaces. Democratic subjects do not enter and leave democratic spaces with predetermined or fixed identities. Rather, they produce, recreate, and alter their identities within the process of participation (Cornwall 2004a: 6; Cornwall and Shankland 2013: 315; see also Lloyd 2005).

This observation draws attention to the performative affordances of democratic space. Here, the democratic subject emerges from the available modes of expression. The names available and the terms that exist to describe democratic subjects bring them into being:

> What 'participation' is taken to mean makes available particular subject positions for participants to take up within particular spaces, bounding the possibilities for inclusion as well as agency. Being constructed as 'beneficiaries', 'clients', 'users' or 'citizens' influences what people are perceived to be able to contribute or entitle to know or decide.
>
> (Cornwall 2002b: 8)

In the same vein, Butler contends that subjects only exist by the terms available to describe them (Butler 2015: 40). Being born into a world of pre-existing patterns of performing the self, spatializing identity means relating discursive concepts and performative expressions that denote identity to each other. These points of identification such as gender, race, profession, class, sexuality, religion, and political affiliation mark different social positions. They mark locations within a web of meaning. Constituting personal identity, then, means navigating within a web of meaning—an identity space—both actively searching for affiliation and being hailed by others. In this process of the spatial constitution of identity, the subject is as volatile as the web of possible identifications it navigates, as the meanings of categories such as 'man', 'lesbian', 'immigrant', 'racist', and 'Catholic' are constantly negotiated and reinterpreted.

These assemblages that constitute the self are not merely discursive. Performance may take a visual form. National parliaments, for example, perform national identity and construct an image of unity and belonging (McCarthy-Cotter et al. 2018: 55). It is not just a national identity that is constructed, but also a democratic identity that invokes citizenship and political rights. Parliamentary buildings as diverse as the traditional neogothic palaces in London and Budapest, the neoclassical US Capitol reminiscent of Ancient Greek democracy, and the modern Parliament of Australia in Canberra all visually express both a national and a democratic collective identity (Parkinson 2012). The example of suffragettes constituting their identities by assembling material objects can also be read as visual performances, which draws attention to the close interrelation between material, sentient, and performative ways of assembling the self.

To conclude, the many identity elements that constitute democratic subjects interact with the many things that constitute democratic spaces in various ways. The red colour of a leather bench cushion may call upon the sentiments of nobility in MPs while historical monuments may prompt a sense of patriotism in citizens. Experts taking part in a citizens' assembly call upon participants as reasoned deliberators, while the exclusion from participating in parliamentary debates may bring out the terrorist in feminists. And for all these identity constructions we depend on the constellation of words that we use to describe ourselves and that are used to hail us. All of these things matter for how subjects assemble. The different material, sentient, and performative arrangements of space resonate with different sides of the multiple self (Elster 1986) from the *homo sociologicus* to the *homo economicus*, from the id, to the ego, and superego, from different desires and impulses to reflected reasons. But the relationship works the other way around too. Closed, invited, and claimed spaces are shaped by human agents who actively arrange material objects, sentient bodies, and performative expressions. Who we perceive ourselves to be and who others perceive us to be within these spaces configures the space itself. The presence of a freedom fighter affects a space differently from the presence of a terrorist. Thus, space depends on the interpretation of identity. This dialectical process, the mutual affectivity of space and the subject, configures different relations of freedom and equality.

Conclusion

This chapter has sought to lay the theoretical groundwork for this book. It conceptualized democratic space and identity as functioning by the same logic. Democratic spaces—be they invited, claimed, or closed—are constituted as assemblages of material objects, sentient bodies, and performative expressions whose relations demarcate an inside and an outside. These relations provide certain affordances both for democratic participation and for performing the self. Hence, democratic space functions as a space of appearance. It provides stages for the democratic subject to become visible to others. The subject is constituted through its corporeal public performance and through the gaze of the audience. Rather than appearing—which would imply a pre-existing subject that only becomes visible through a certain spatial constellation—I argued that subjects actually assemble. Their various parts come together in particular ways both through the affordance structure offered by a given space and through the agency of the subject. Democratic spaces and the subjects that navigate them consist of diverse elements, which explains their volatility.

The various things that constitute such spaces interact with different aspects that constitute the multiple self. Seating arrangements and the size of material space, the combination of sentient bodies present and the social protocols, the terms that describe identities, the embodied performances of participants, and the discursive formations emerging from debate all afford and restrict how subjects see themselves and others. This relationship is not unidirectional, however. The identities that subjects express are, on the one hand, afforded by space, while, on the other, they are constitutive of space. As subjects change, so does space.

When understanding democratic spaces as assemblages, the question arises as to how the subject can gain agency over self-constitution. To what extent democratic subjects can express themselves freely and how they are judged by others within democratic spaces is closely related to their identities. These questions are explored by a feminist discourse in democratic theory identified with the term 'difference democracy'. The next chapter will engage with difference democrats' politics of presence, which seeks to advance inclusion and equality in democratic spaces. The politics of presence, as will become apparent, shares some core features with the space of appearance. It is through the visibility of embodied identities that subjects articulate political claims.

3

Becoming Present

Feminist Interventions

In an early essay entitled 'Throwing Like a Girl', Iris Marion Young discusses the gendered nature of space. She observes that in a Western cultural context, men tend to use their bodies in a more dynamic and uninhibited way. Women, in contrast, tend to make small steps, cross their legs when sitting, and generally try to occupy a smaller space. When throwing a ball, boys tend to use their entire body to achieve maximal momentum while girls tend to stand still, fixed in space, and only use their arms. These gendered behavioural patterns are not rooted in biology, but in the different positions gendered bodies occupy within society. In this gendered matrix, female space appears confined: 'a space surrounds us in imagination that we are not free to move beyond; the space available to our movement is a constricted space' (Young 2005 [1977]: 33). Men tend to perceive their bodies as natural and hardly pay attention to them, which enables their agency. In contrast, 'feminine existence experiences the body as a mere thing— a fragile thing' (39). As objects, female bodies are positioned in space and acted upon by male subjects and masculine power structures. The confinement of female identity space is due to a constant defence against male intrusion. The 'invasion of her body space' (45) always poses a threat to women, of which subtle forms of sexual harassment are a common and rape the most extreme form (see also Phillips 2013).

The space of gendered, racialized, and sexualized groups has markedly increased over the past decades. While Young discusses male sex offenders as intruders, Nirma Puwar turns this observation around and describes those bodies with marginalized identities as 'space invaders' as they push into public democratic spaces. She draws attention to the masculinity of democratic spaces that are commonly perceived as neutral. The normalization of male space as default arenas for public interaction rests on boundary drawing practices that exclude deviant bodies: 'Some bodies are deemed as having the right to belong, while others are marked out as trespassers, who are, in accordance with how both spaces and bodies are imagined (politically, historically and conceptually), circumscribed as being "out of place". Not being the somatic norm, they are space invaders' (Puwar 2004: 8). Puwar describes an incident in which Diane Abbott as the first Black and one of only a few female members of the UK Parliament entered one of the

The Politics of Becoming. Hans Asenbaum, Oxford University Press. © Hans Asenbaum (2023).
DOI: 10.1093/oso/9780192858870.003.0003

smoking rooms of Westminster Palace. The cigar-puffing white men were struck with bewilderment as a person who could only be a cleaner was present among them as their peer. The entering of a Black, female body into white, male space 'represents a dissonance; a jarring of framings that confuses and disorientates. It is a menacing presence that disturbs and interrupts a certain white, usually male, sense of public institutional place' (42).

The invasion of democratic space by bodies with marginalized identities reconfigures the space of appearance. For Arendt plurality is a central precondition for the space of appearance. However, this plurality only concerns ideas. Butler criticizes the Arendtian space of appearance for its unreflected masculine bias, which renders the marginalized invisible (Butler 2015: 73). Arendt's pluralism, in other words, is limited to what Anne Phillips calls 'the politics of ideas'. Phillips argues that liberal theories of pluralist democracy foreground the diversity of competing interests and forget about the diversity of identities. To overcome this omission, she proposes a politics of presence, which gives visibility to the marginalized in the space of appearance (Phillips 1995).

The politics of presence is the central theme of a feminist discourse in democratic theory associated with the term 'difference democracy', which promotes the inclusion of the marginalized in democratic spaces. Through quotas in the closed spaces of parliaments, random selection in invited spaces, and identity politics in claimed spaces, the inclusion of marginalized bodies works as a visible claim for equality. These techniques of inclusion enable a structural interference with the order of things. The politics of presence shifts marginalized bodies from private spaces to spaces of public visibility which contributes to the core democratic value of equality: 'Challenging [power] structures ... acknowledge[s] the group-structured nature of social and political hierarchies, and thereby opens up space for political and policy change' (Phillips 2019a: 182).

This chapter is a celebration of feminist contributions to radical democratic thinking. Although the impact of difference democratic debates on democratic theory is undisputable, comprehensive attempts at mapping difference democracy are scarce and often brief (Dryzek 2000: 57–18; Marx Ferree et al. 2002; Saward 2003: 133–7; Dahlberg 2005). Understanding radical democracy as a project of many voices including participatory, deliberative, and agonistic perspectives, feminist theory and practice should certainly be at its forefront. The chapter argues for difference democracy as a perspective in democratic theory that advances inclusion through three strategies: presence, emotion, and contestation.

As we will see, difference democracy affectively advances equality by means of these three strategies. However, the politics of presence also entails essentializing tendencies that limit the freedom of the democratic subject to change. If the physically embodied identity of the democratic subject stands in the foreground of political engagement, the subject tends to be boxed up, prejudged, and limited in its freedom of expression. This problem is what difference democrats themselves identify as the 'dilemma of difference' (Young 1989). In discussing this dilemma, the chapter presents the core problem this book sets out to tackle.

Feminists Rattling at the Gates

Feminist perspectives had long been kept out of the canon of democratic theory. From the 1980s on, however, the gatekeepers of this canon were challenged. Within a decade, three essays by different feminist scholars appeared with the same title, 'Feminism and Democracy'. The first was by Carole Pateman (1989 [1983]), who sent out a fervent call to no longer ignore the democratic insights feminist theory can offer. Pateman's aim was to instigate a debate about the role of women in democracy and about the refusal to admit feminist scholarship into the canon of democratic theory. Her instigation proved successful, as it was followed by Anne Phillips' 'Feminism and Democracy' (1991), with Jane Mansbridge's (1998) text with the same title following soon thereafter.

These three foundational texts point to significant overlaps between feminist and democratic principles: 'The two traditions [feminism and democracy] have much in common for both deal in notions of equality and both oppose arbitrary power' (Phillips 1991: 1). If feminism, in broad terms, is understood as a movement towards the equality of the sexes by means of the emancipation of women, and democracy is understood as equality and freedom in the political organization of society, their mutuality becomes evident (Pateman 1989: 212; see also Ferguson 2007: 33; McAfee and Snyder 2007: vi). The overlapping core principles of feminist and democratic politics are reflected in the participatory practices of the US women's movement (Pateman 1989: 220; Phillips 1991: Ch. 5; Mansbridge 1998: 154):

> For the women's movement, questions of internal democracy returned to the centre of the stage, this time imbued with an almost anarchist critique of authority, an intensely egalitarian approach. In most of the newly formed women's groups, any kind of hierarchy was automatically suspect. Meetings were informal and only loosely structured.
>
> (Phillips 1991: 121)

To arrange democratic spaces in an egalitarian manner, activists invented new modes of engagement. For example, to facilitate equal opportunity to speak, verbal contributions were limited through an equal number of discs that each participant could 'spend'. Tasks and responsibilities were allocated among the activists by lot.

According to Pateman, participatory democracy is not just about claiming the privatized spaces of work and opening the closed spaces of the state. Her revolutionary fervour goes further: 'democratic ideals and politics have to be put into practice in the kitchen, the nursery and the bedroom' (Pateman 1989: 222). Democracy, then, is not just expressed and practiced in a set of official political institutions. Much rather, it is also a matter of sexual practices, our intimate lives, and even thinking patterns.

Democracy is rooted in the terms we speak and think with. The established terms made to comprehend democracy, however, are made by and for men. By naturalizing masculinist political vocabularies, they tend to make women invisible (see Mansbridge 1998: 142):

The power of men over women is excluded from scrutiny and deemed irrelevant to political life and democracy by the patriarchal construction of the categories with which political theorists work ... The feminist challenge is particularly pressing in the case of radical democratic theory which argues for the active participation of all citizens, but has barely begun to acknowledge the problem of women's standing in political order in which citizenship has been made in the male image.

(Pateman 1989: 14)

This invisibility of women, then, is based on the division of private and public spaces, with the private sphere—the domain of women, reproductive work, and sexuality—left out of sight. While liberal democratic theory, according to Pateman, is based on a contract, in which 'men' consent to being governed, women are seen as naturally subordinate to men as their consent is not sought (Pateman 1988; see also Phillips 1991: 3). 'In sexual relations more generally, a woman's refusal of consent—her utterance of the word "no" or other clear indication of refusal—is systematically invalidated; her refusal is reinterpreted as "yes"' (Pateman 1989: 12–3). While Pateman's observation was made before marital rape was made illegal across the United States in 1993, it still bears relevance today in light of the series of rape and sexual harassment cases being raised in the #MeToo debate. How, then, can a person who is sexually humiliated and abused in the private sphere, and who carries the double burden of housework and professional work, function in the public sphere as an equal and free citizen (221)?

Pateman ends her argument for a feminist democratic theory emphatically: 'The lesson to be learned from the past is that a "democratic" theory and practice that is not at the same time feminist merely serves to maintain a fundamental form of domination and so makes a mockery of the ideals and values that democracy is held to embody' (223).

Internal Exclusion in Democratic Spaces

The feminist response in democratic scholarship that Pateman had hoped for quickly followed. In the same year as Pateman's call to action, Jane Mansbridge's seminal *Beyond Adversary Democracy* (1983) was published investigating race, class, and gender inequalities in townhall meetings and workplace democracy. Throughout the ensuing decade, the feminist discussion associated with the term 'difference democracy' intensified with central publications by Iris Marion Young (1990; 1989), Nancy Fraser (1990), Jane Mansbridge (1993; 1991), Anne Phillips (1995; 1991), and Carol Gould (1996).

The difference democratic perspective provides a vocabulary with which to understand the boundary making practices of inclusion and exclusion *within* democratic spaces. Young differentiates between external and internal exclusion. External exclusion concerns the questions of who is physically present in democratic spaces. Internal exclusion, on the other hand, determines the social standing of participants *within* democratic spaces. Respect and appreciation appear to be distributed just as unevenly as material resources. Internal exclusion, then, draws attention to patterns of devaluation of discursive content uttered by participants whose physical appearance is identified with marginalized social groups (Young 2000). While being physically present, some still remain outside the boundaries of the space of appearance (Butler 2015: 73).

It is not simply the physical body of the marginalized; rather, their socially acquired cultural forms of expression are encoded with inferiority. Thus, it is the manner of expression that signals status. This observation leads difference democrats to criticize the particular forms of expression—namely reasoned, verbal argumentation—that conceptions of deliberative democracy call for:

> Taking deliberation as a signal of democratic practice paradoxically works undemocratically, discrediting on seemingly democratic grounds the views of those who are less likely to present their arguments in ways that we recognize as characteristically deliberative. In our political culture, these citizens are likely to be those who are already underrepresented in formal political institutions and who are systematically materially disadvantaged, namely women; racial minorities, especially Blacks; and poorer people.
>
> (Sanders 1997: 348)[1]

In her extensive study of a New England town meeting and a participatory workplace, Mansbridge (1983) finds gendered and classed patterns of inequality. The town meeting was dominated by the disproportionate participation of large

[1] For further feminist work on the criticism of deliberative democracy, see Fraser 1995; Kohn 2000; Pajnik 2006; Ferguson 2007; Mansbridge 2012; Lupia and Norton 2017.

property-owning men. Only 29 per cent of participants who contributed to the debate were women, who reported that they felt intimidated by the setting. In the participatory workplace, women felt less respected than men. Similarly, Lynn Sanders finds that in US juries men tend to speak more. Moreover, while the juries consisted of two-thirds of women, in 90 per cent of the cases men were chosen to head the jury (Sanders 1997).

The problem of internal exclusion continues to be the subject of ongoing empirical work. A study on deliberative polling found that in the twenty-five discussion groups, women and those with lower income spoke significantly less (Gerber 2015). Another study on parliamentary debates in seven European countries shows that women take the floor less than their male colleagues (Bäck and Debus 2018). The gender gap in traditional forms of political participation, such as voting, indicating external exclusion has closed recently in Western societies (Nancy Burns et al. 2018). Upon closer examination, however, inequality persists. A study of eighteen Western countries found that women are less likely to participate in civil society initiatives and collective action than men (Coffé and Bolzendahl 2010). Another study has found that women in Canada are significantly less likely to participate in small group deliberation (Beauvais 2019). These patterns of self-selection are also mirrored in a dramatic gender gap in ambition to engage in politics among youth (Fox and Lawless 2014).

The extensive work of Christopher Karpowitz and Tali Mendelberg documented in *The Silent Sex* (2014) provides further insight into internal exclusion. The book investigates the effects of the gender composition of deliberative groups in a series of experiments supplemented with data from eighty-seven different school board meetings. The results show that overall women speak significantly less than men; they only speak at equal rates to men if they far outnumber male participants. Women are also interrupted more often than men and report loss of confidence. The authors explain this as a spiral of discouragement due to the lower status society attributes to women so that: 'the fewer women [are] in the group, the lower their status, the less they may speak, and the lower their influence' (Karpowitz et al. 2012: 534). In comparison, men's participation is unaffected by their share of the group. Women also engage in substantive representation and voice women's distinctive concerns, such as family issues, only if they are in the majority. The authors conclude: 'Women are often disadvantaged in speech participation, whereas men are never disadvantaged' (Karpowitz, Mendelberg and Shaker 2012: 544).

I made similar observations in my work on citizens' councils in Austria, comparing two case studies. In the first case, with an equal number of men and women participating, men and women spoke at about equal rates. In the other case, with a majority of women among participants (58 per cent), women spoke 60 per cent of the time, per capita, pointing to a dynamic of peer encouragement (Asenbaum 2016).

Similar exclusionary patterns are observed in non-Western societies. A recent study has shown, for example, that in a Gram Sabha village assembly in India, women only accounted for a third of speaking time and received fewer responses by state officials compared to their male counterparts (Parthasarathy, Rao and Palaniswamy 2019). Internal exclusion is also found in a study on invited spaces in South Africa. Here local authorities set up forums for citizens' discussions, which in the context of a long history of segregation were characterized by deep racial and gendered inequalities. The formalized spatial arrangement instituted by government officials intimidated those in marginalized social positions:

> The public silencing of women such that they are largely passive observers in formal spaces of citizen participation is a spatialized construction of identity since the same women are often very active participants in less formal political spaces, such as street and area committees, savings and housing associations and other community groups.
>
> (McEwan 2005: 982)

Black women, however, reconfigured the spatial ordering to make meetings more inclusive by starting with African greetings, anti-apartheid dances, and resistance and liberation songs. These performances of cultural and political identity, which actively articulated presence, reconfigured the space of appearance.

The Vision of Difference Democracy

To respond to the problem of internal exclusion, difference democrats promote diversity as a democratic value. They understand difference as the essence of democracy and articulate a democratic vision of a plural and inclusive society. This vision makes difference democracy more than just a debate in democratic theory. Difference democracy is a distinct perspective—or a model of democracy as Held (1987) calls it—in its own right. Here, I will engage in model building, sketching out its vision and then moving on to presence, emotion, and contestation as the core elements of difference democracy.

Iris Marion Young formulates her vision of difference democracy in spatial terms and describes the city as the location of an ideal democratic society. This marks a profound break with participatory democratic thought, which is prominent in other difference democratic texts (e.g. Mansbridge 1983; Gould 1996). Participatory democrats focus on small democratic spaces of local communities that facilitate trust and friendship. Young, in contrast, shifts the focus. City life 'is structured by vast networks of temporal and spatial mediation among persons, so that nearly everyone depends on the activities of seen and unseen strangers who mediate between oneself and one's associates, between oneself and one's objects of desire' (Young 1990: 237). What makes the city the ideal place for democracy is its heterogeneity. In contrast with the homogenic tendencies of the local community, the city's sociographic complexity facilitates diversity. The city as democratic space is characterized by the eroticism of unexpected encounters, the accessibility of public places, and the plurality of identities. By articulating difference, various identity groups assemble as the *heterogeneous public.*

The heterogeneous public forms an internally inclusive space of equals. Young starts from the observation of new social movements in the USA from the 1960s into the '80s, which affirm and reinterpret their marginalized group identities in positive terms. The Black Power movement reframed the African American identity with slogans such as 'black is beautiful' and critically distanced itself from the Civil Rights movement's assimilationist strategy. Soon Red Power followed suit, promoting the self-determination of Native Americans. The gay and lesbian movement fought for sexual liberation and promoted alternative concepts of life and family. While one arm of the women's movement advocated a reformist path to equal rights (equality feminism), the other criticized this strategy as conformist and refused to adapt to institutions they had no part in shaping (difference feminism).

The heterogeneous public is realized when these diverse social movements come together in rainbow coalitions, which jointly promote a certain cause, while disagreeing on other issues and thus maintaining their particular identities (Young 1987; 1989; 1990). The street demonstrations of such coalitions reflect this diversity with 'gaily decorative banners with ironic or funny slogans, guerilla theater or costumes serving to make political points, giant puppets standing for people or ideas towering over the crowd, chants, music, songs, dancing' (Young 1987: 75). Drawing on these social movements' experiences, Young claims that difference is to be understood as a resource rather than an obstacle for fruitful deliberation. Young's concept of a communicative democracy actively promotes difference to include a diversity of perspectives and experiences (Young 1989; 1996; 1997b).

From the engagement with these movements, Young derives a vision of democracy that combines equality with difference: 'In this vision the good society does not eliminate or transcend group difference. Rather, there is equality among socially and culturally differentiated groups, who mutually respect one another and affirm one another in their differences' (Young 1990: 163). Young shares the ideal of equality and difference with Nancy Fraser (1990), whose ultimate vision of democracy consists of a classless society that, through its egalitarian economic and social conditions, provides the ground for cultural diversity and creativity.

To realize equality and difference in the heterogeneous public, marginalized groups first need to find their voice. Fraser contends that diversity can best be realized through enclave deliberation. The universality of the Habermasian public sphere is challenged by a long history of counterpublics. Parallel to the bourgeois public clubs, associations, and cafés described by Habermas (1992 [1962]), peasants, women, nationalists, and workers held their own gatherings. Today sub-altern counterpublics claim exclusive spaces, drawing their boundaries along lines of group identification. Counterpublics serve two functions. First, they provide a safe space for members of marginalized groups to reflect their experiences of oppression and form a community free from domination. Second, this safe space serves to reinterpret marginalized identities in positive terms and develop counter narratives and ideas to challenge hegemonic discourses. Mansbridge (1996: 58) elaborates on the functions of counterpublics:

> The goals of these counterpublics include understanding themselves better, forg-ing bonds of solidarity, preserving the memories of past injustices, interpreting and reinterpreting the meaning of those injustices, working out alternative con-ceptions of self, of community, of justice, and of universality, trying to make sense of both the privileges they wield and the oppressions they face, understanding the strategic configurations for and against their desired ends, deciding what alliances to make both emotionally and strategically, deliberating on ends and means, and deciding how to act, individually and collectively.

In line with the difference democratic vision, Anne Phillips' *The Politics of the Human* (2015) stresses that equality as a claim and commitment is compatible with difference. Equality does not denote homogeneity but the recognition of rights and chances. The equality inherent in being human goes along with the diversity of identities. In her earlier work, Phillips (1995) points out that the diver-sity at the heart of the difference democratic vision is not a new concept but has always been a core principle of liberal, and in particular pluralist, democratic thought. However, pluralism was always applied to ideas and not to identities. While the liberal perspective aimed at overcoming inequality by declaring individ-uals equal in rights but indefinitely different—thus perfectly individual—in their identity, it overlooked and obscured structural inequalities.

According to Phillips, pluralism in democratic theory needs to be applied to identities as well as to content. This new perspective on pluralism is promoted by the identity politics of new social movements. These movements claim that while class may be a salient category and the workers' movement has brought about progress, it is time to draw attention to a greater diversity in society consisting not only of capital owners and workers, but also of male and female, Black, white, and brown, gay, lesbian, bi, and transsexual people. This diversity is the foundation of plural deliberation bringing various perspectives together. Such deliberation will and should never result in consensus or unity:

> This is not to say that difference per se will disappear, or that if we only work hard enough on our mutual understanding we will converge on some single set of shared ideals. What distinguishes a radical perspective on democracy is not

its expectation of future homogeneity and consensus, but its commitment to a
politics of solidarity and challenge and change.

(Phillips 1993: 161)

Combining equality with difference is not an easy undertaking. In the context
of capitalist societies marked by drastic inequalities, how can this vision be realized? Difference democrats propose three strategies of inclusion that rearrange
democratic space: presence, emotion, and contestation.

The Politics of Presence

Pateman argues that established democratic theory makes women invisible. The
default citizen is implicitly conceptualized as male: 'There is no set of clothes available for a citizen who is a woman, no vision available within political theory of
the new democratic woman. Women have always been incorporated into the civil
order as "women", as subordinate or lesser men, and democratic theorists have not
yet formulated an alternative' (Pateman 1989: 14).

In response, difference democrats call for increasing the visibility of marginalized bodies through their physical presence in democratic spaces. In *The Politics of
Presence*, Phillips (1995) argues that in democratic engagement it is not just *what*
is said that counts, but also *who* says it. The identified body itself conveys a message. By claiming presence in democratic spaces and drawing attention to social
inequalities represented by their physical bodies and their culturally specific ways
of expression, can members of marginalized groups express their particular experiences, claims, and perspectives. Phillips (1991: 62–6) observes that in liberal
democracies constituencies are represented according to their location of resi-
dence. This partly affords the representation of class and race due to their reflection
in geographic divides, but it entirely neglects gender. Reflecting more recently
on the politics of presence, Phillips upholds her preference for descriptive representation. The goal of descriptive representation is not necessarily substantive
representation, that is, the presence of women need not result in more women-
friendly policies. Rather, 'descriptive representation matters because of what it
symbolizes to us in terms of citizenship and inclusion—what it conveys to us about
who does and who does not count as a full member of society' (Phillips 2012: 517).

Similarly, Mansbridge argues that the attendance of members of marginalized
groups in public assemblies is crucial because their bodies represent identity-
related issues. In relation to parliamentary representation, she argues: 'Even when
the descriptive legislator is silent, his or her mere physical presence reminds the
other legislators of the perspectives and interests of the group of which he or she
is a descriptive member' (Mansbridge 2005: 62). It is the visibility of the physical
body that articulates a political claim.

In the difference democratic perspective, only those with marginalized bodies share particular life experiences and can thus authentically represent them. The politics of presence brings not only a diversity of bodies, but also a diversity of qualities to democratic spaces (Phillips 2019b). Since men and women, hetero-sexual and homosexual, Black and white people are forced into different social positions and are thus socialized in different ways, they also develop different social qualities and character traits. Hence, 'the sexual differentiation in conditions and experience has produced a specifically woman's point of view' (Phillips 1991: 63). Accordingly, women 'have perceived themselves as bringing something new to the political stage. Their much delayed entry will not only add to the dramatis personae, but of necessity alter the play' (3).

The presence of women in democratic spaces is advocated in difference democ-racy by pointing to specific womanly qualities stemming from particular forms of socialization. According to this argument, women tend to be more caring and nur-turing than men. Womanly virtues of mothering could contribute to democratic exchange by focusing on the common good rather than self-interest, persuading rather than forcing, listening carefully, asking questions, moderating and inte-grating rather than competing to win the argument. Mansbridge (1991) discusses the work of difference feminists who speak of women's superior democratic cul-ture. Empathy, sensitivity, and intuition as female characteristics are constitutive of the democratic community as they facilitate social connections of trust, love, and duty (Mansbridge 1993: 345). While Mansbridge does not fully subscribe to the perspective of difference feminists, she takes it as inspiration for her own work. Difference feminist notions are reflected in Mansbridge's (1983) concept of 'uni-tary democracy', which is based on friendship, trust, and agreement within small groups such as the early hunter and gatherer tribes and later the Athenian polis.

In the same vein, Carol Gould argues that women can strengthen deliberative values such as concern for others, reciprocity, and mutual respect. Their nurturing perspective also shifts the focus to the redistributive functions of the state:

> I also believe that the typical concern for providing for the specific needs of others associated with mothering or parenting or with family relations more gen-erally can usefully be imported into the larger democratic community in terms of a focus on meeting the differentiated needs of individuals and not simply protecting their negative liberties.
>
> (Gould 1993: 405)

According to Gould, the best way of ensuring the presence of marginalized groups is by expanding participatory democratic institutions to the workplace, schools, and the social system and linking them to social movements' claimed spaces. This plurality of democratic spaces multiplies the opportunities for the presence of marginalized bodies (Gould 1996: 181).

While difference democrats advocate the expansion of participatory democratic institutions, they also argue that representation is indispensable in modern, large-scale democracies (Phillips 1995: 30; Young 1997a: 352; 2000: 124–5). The politics of presence thus includes not only the presence of the physical body, but also the replication of identity across time and space. Representation gives presence to those not physically present. In Hanna Pitkin's terms, 'representation, talking generally, means the making present in some sense of something which is nevertheless not present literally or in fact' (Pitkin 1967: 8–9). Difference democrats' advocacy for representation focuses on two concepts: mirror representation (also referred to as descriptive representation) replicating the quantitative relations of different groups within society (see debates on minipublics, e.g. Curato et al. 2021) and special representation in the spirit of affirmative action.

For difference democracy, mirror representation in state institutions is crucial. Only members of specific social groups can bring authentic, lived experience and insight from particular social perspectives to deliberation. As mirror representation is not achieved automatically in the face of structural inequalities, quotas along the lines of gender and race are necessary (Phillips 1991; 1993; 1995; Mansbridge 1999b; 2005). This calls for a redefinition of the use of power in democracy. The use of power is coercion as a necessary evil to counter injustice. Besides quotas, facilitation through moderators in democratic spaces can be seen as the coercive redistribution of speaking time. Thus, coercive power secures equal presence, while it also infringes on personal freedom (Mansbridge 1996b: 46; Mansbridge et al. 2010: 82).

Special representation of disadvantaged groups, who suffer from the effects of historical oppression, is another central feature of difference democracy. Disadvantaged groups need to receive economic and social resources to self-organize, such as dedicated airtime on public media. The current system of party representation is to be supplemented by a structure of self-organized associations of marginalized groups. Special representation also needs to come into effect in the democratic spaces of schools, workplaces, and neighbourhood communities. Furthermore, in decisions which directly affect these communities, they need to wield veto power. These measures need to be accompanied by affirmative action in education and employment and the expansion of bilingual and bicultural education and state services (Young 1989; 1990; 1992; 1997a; 2000).

Expressing Emotions in Democratic Spaces

A second way to facilitate the inclusion of marginalized bodies in democratic spaces is through emotions, passion, and affect. According to difference democrats, emotions are undermined in deliberation by a focus on dispassionate, impartial reasoning: 'When deliberation turns into a demonstration of logic, it leaves out many who cannot work their emotionally felt needs into a neat equation' (Mansbridge 1991: 130). Embracing emotions in participatory processes can contribute to inclusion because not everything can be put into words. The grief of parents who have lost their child, for example, can be described in words, but seeing their tears speaks a different language. Emotions go beyond impartial reasoning as they enrich the experience of perspective-taking: 'Solutions often require the emotional capacity to guess what others want ... [E]ngaging the emotions helps create the self-transformations necessary to think "we" instead of "I"' (Mansbridge 1998: 151). Both reason and emotion are essential elements of democratic deliberation (Mansbridge 1993; 1999a).

Cheryl Hall investigates the exclusion of passion in democratic theory (Hall 2007). She argues that emotion and reason are dependent upon each other. For every emotion—be it grief, anger, or joy—there is a logical reason. Emotions can be reasonably explained. Deliberation as a process of reasoning, on the other hand, is always driven by passion. Deliberation is based on emotional resources to engage in debate. Thus, emotion and reason are dialectically interrelated. Emotions are based on reasons and reasoning is motivated by emotions.

To facilitate the expression of emotions in democratic spaces, difference democrats turn to modes of expression beyond rational argumentation. This expansion of communicative modes enhances inclusion as it acknowledges the diversity of expressions of marginalized groups who may not articulate their claims in the manner of verbalized argumentation (Pajnik 2006). Young draws attention to the diverse communication techniques of carnivalesque protest movements: 'Liberating public expression means ... affirming in the practice of such discussions the proper place of passion and play in public' (Young 1987: 75). Today's age of communicative plenty, in which different media channels provide a broad variety of means of participation, may contribute to the inclusion of disadvantaged groups (Ercan, Hendriks and Dryzek 2018).

Young (2000) suggests supplementing rational arguments with greeting, rhetoric, and storytelling. Greeting encompasses not only short phrases such as 'Good morning!' and 'How are you?' but also compliments and bodily gestures such as handshakes, hugs, nods, and smiles. Greeting serves the expression of mutual respect and trust and aims at making participants feel appreciated. The traditional greetings and anti-apartheid dances in the invited spaces in South Africa mentioned earlier are a good example of the powerful impact of greeting. Greeting can be more than a gesture of sympathy; it can formulate political claims for inclusion and express cultural identity (McEwan 2005: 978). Rhetoric in speech consisting of word play, jokes, flirtation, and metaphors is often denigrated in democratic theory. Yet, Young argues that rhetoric provides a specific channel to introduce affective, intuitive, and situated knowledge into democratic spaces. Storytelling entails the narrating of certain events without necessarily transmitting an argument. Stories aid mutual understanding as they make specific social perspectives comprehensible through their affective qualities. They afford listeners the time to become immersed in others' points of view and ways of thinking. Stories can give expression to emotions as they are told from a personal perspective without requiring objectivity or impartiality (Young 1996: 129; Young 2000: 57).

Sanders highlights the inclusive impetus of giving testimony through storytelling: 'Instead of aiming for a common discussion, democrats might adopt a more fundamental goal: to try to ensure that those who are usually left out of public discussions learn to speak whether their perspectives are common or not, and those who usually dominate learn to hear the perspectives of others' (Sanders 1997: 372–3). Rather than engaging in a conversation, one person at a time gets to share their perspective. An example of testimony can be found in US-American rap culture, in which young people of marginalized class and race backgrounds find a critical voice. In contrast to a hierarchy of knowledge in a rational discourse, '[t]estimony is also radically egalitarian: the standard for whether a view is worthy of public attention is simply that everyone should have a voice, a chance to tell her story' (Sanders 1997: 372). In comparison to common conversational modes, testimony allows speakers to narrate without interruption. Some versions of testimony have been realized in invited spaces through particular facilitation techniques whereby moderators focus attention on one participant at a time with others listening (Asenbaum 2016). Testimony also plays a central role in community conferences, where victims and the accused of a crime come together with the local community. Around the circle, each participant gets to tell the same story from their personal perspective (Dzur 2019: 77).

By focusing on the democratic contributions of everyday talk, Mansbridge (1999a) adds another mode of communication that enhances the role of emotions. Rather than focusing on reasoned arguments, democrats should acknowledge the contribution of mundane verbal exchange that is often deemed unpolitical. Everyday talk, however, always entails a political component. Since it emerges in the context of everyday life rather than in the political sphere, it is more intimate and more closely connected to emotions.

The difference democratic debate about an expansion of modes of communication is extended today. The unspeakable has moved the centre of democratic theory. Nicole Curato asks how those who have suffered extreme loss in the face of a natural disaster can contribute to deliberation. In these situations, '[e]xpression through voice is not only cognitively challenging, it is also emotionally strenuous' (Curato 2019: 14). Overwhelmed and numbed by emotions, victims often go silent. Silence in democratic exchange is not nothing. It can express a refusal of taking part in deliberation (Rollo 2017). It can also express suffering. It articulates the unspeakable. The unspeakable is necessarily expressed nonverbally. We need to expand the deliberative repertoire to include nonverbal expressions. Beyond greeting, rhetoric, storytelling, and everyday talk, which still rely on words, we need to include visuals, sound, and physical presence into democratic exchange (Mendonça, Ercan, and Asenbaum 2020).

Contestation and Marginalized Interests

Difference democrats stress the role of conflict and even competition in democracy. The argument for conflict is linked to the argument of emotion. Instead of suppressing anger, it needs to be vented. Allowing for conflict in democratic spaces can contribute to equality as anger often arises in response to oppression:

> Both in a public forum and in everyday talk, there are justifiable places for offensiveness, non-cooperation, and the threat of retaliation—even for raucous, angry, self-centred, bitter talk, aiming at nothing but hurt ... These uncivil forms of talk are also often necessary as means to the end of approaching both liberty and equality in deliberation. Sometimes only intensity in oppositions can break down the barriers of the status quo ... So subordinates sometimes need the battering ram of rage.
>
> (Mansbridge 1999a: 223)

Like agonists (e.g. Wenman 2013: 45–57), difference democrats not only favour contestation that challenges domination, but also display some affinity for competition. Fraser (1990: 68), for example, speaks of the 'contestation among competing publics'. Likewise (1997a: 359), Young highlights the value of competition for democracy when she calls for the 'contestation of the constituency with itself about the content of a decision-making agenda'. And Mansbridge sees elements of adversary democracy, such as voting and party competition, as an essential part of participatory societies. She argues that these competitive modes are necessary to overcome the conformist tendencies of consensus decision-making. Where no consensus can be reached on the grounds of fundamental disagreement, majority rule through voting needs to be employed to break the deadlock (Mansbridge 1981; 1983; 1990; Mansbridge et al. 2010). In line with agonists (Mouffe 1999), Mansbridge contends that consensus can mask conflict. This is corroborated by an empirical study comparing a consensus-orientated and a contentious democratic space. In the consensus-orientated participatory planning process, conflict was supressed and dissenting voices marginalized. In the contentious public hearings, citizens aired their anger and conflicts took centre stage (Karpowitz and Mansbridge 2005).

Young (2001) engages in a fictive dialogue between an activist engaging in contentious politics and a consensus-seeking deliberative democrat. While the deliberative democrat strives to change the system from within by persuading those in power to take a path of progressive reform, the activist calls for disruptive action. In conclusion, Young calls for a critical theory of democracy, encompassing both cooperation and conflict. Elsewhere she argues:

> Especially under circumstances where there are serious conflicts that arise from structural positions of privilege and disadvantage, and/or where a subordinated, less powerful or minority group finds its interests ignored in public debate, members of such groups do not violate norms of reasonableness if they engage in serious disruptive actions, or express their claims with angry accusations. Disorderliness is an important tool of critical communication aimed at calling attention to the unreasonableness of others.
>
> (Young 2000: 48–9)

By calling for confrontational politics, difference democrats promote the recognition of the self-interest of the marginalized. While in conceptions of deliberative democracy the focus on the common good restricts members of disadvantaged groups to challenge inequality, in difference democracy the subject is legitimately self-interested: 'Women, for example, have often been socialized to put the interests of others ahead of their own in ways that interfere with understanding their own interests. The articulation of self-interest has a legitimate role in democratic deliberation, particularly in discussions of fair distribution' (Mansbridge 1999a: 226). In the context of the unequal distribution of resources along the lines of sex, race, and class, difference democratic contestation explicitly includes *material* self-interest (Mansbridge 1990; 1991: 126; 1996b: 49, 57; 2012: 797; Mansbridge et al. 2010; Young 1997a: 362–3): 'Because of their materially different position in society, women have objectively different interests from men' (Phillips 1991: 70).

Subjects in democratic spaces need the freedom to articulate their own particular needs while also taking the common good into account. Acknowledging self-interest contributes to transparency as the aim of the common good often functions as cover for private interests. The freedom to openly articulate self-interests thus promotes more honest political debate. Moreover, identifying a multiplicity of self-interests contributes to democratic pluralism. It 'embraces the diversity of human objectives as well as the diversity of human opinions' (Mansbridge et al. 2010: 73).

The Dilemma of Difference

Difference democrats have repeatedly pointed to a conundrum that emerges from the politics of presence: the strategy of including the marginalized through physical presence within democratic spaces achieves visibility and thus furthers equality, but at the same time this strategy entails essentialist tendencies. It affirms existing identity constructions along with their limitations, confinements, and stereotypes (Young 1990: 172; 1994: 714; 1997a: 350f; 1997b: 389; Mansbridge 1993: 371; 1999b: 637–8; 2005; Gould 1996: 182; Phillips 1996: 146; 2009; 2010; 2019a). Young calls this the 'dilemma of difference' (Young 1989: 268). While identity politics through social movements such as the Black Power movement or feminist groups might be successful in reinterpreting their identities in positive terms, in doing so they recreate the limitations inherent to all identities. Labels such as woman, man, gay, lesbian, Black, Asian, Jewish, and so on always create confinements of self-expression and self-definition, no matter if they are connoted positively or negatively. This is even more problematic considering intersectionality. Within Western societies, identity categories such as 'woman' mostly emerge in discourses produced by white, heterosexual, able-bodied women with higher education and incomes and rarely reflect the experiences of LGBTIAQ, non-white, poor women or those with disabilities (Fraser 1996; Mansbridge 2003: 357; Wojciechowska 2018; Phillips 2019b).

Mansbridge acknowledges that descriptive representation in parliaments through quotas entails essentializing tendencies:

> One broad cost derives from focusing citizens' attention on their own and legislators' background characteristics rather than the capacity and desire of those legislators to promote effective public policies ... [A]ny proposal to select some characteristic for conscious representation has the potential for encouraging a kind of essentialism in identities ... As a specific identity becomes the focus, the identity of citizen may be lost.
>
> (Mansbridge 2015: 261, 267)

Such essentialist tendencies in descriptive representation are problematic because they reify and fix identification and thus curtail the freedom of the democratic subject. Instead of increasing diversity through inclusion of multiple identities, the politics of presence might actually *undermine* diversity as it creates rigid identity categories and homogenizes multiple and intersectional identifications:

> Essentialist beliefs reinforce stereotypes, trap the individuals in the group in the images traditionally held of the group, make it hard for those individuals to treat their identities flexibly and performatively, de-emphasize lines of division within groups to the advantage of dominant groups within the group, and harden lines of division between groups.
>
> (Mansbridge 2005: 623)

The problems of essentialism through the politics of presence that Mansbridge observes in closed spaces, Phillips discusses in relation to claimed spaces: 'The irony, as many feminists and critical race theorists acknowledge, is that movements to combat the hierarchical structure that generate and sustain these stereotypes often invoke a collectivity that itself seems to presume a unified, perhaps essentialised, group' (Phillips 2010: 54–5). In reference to feminist movements, Phillips goes on to argue: 'The "women" brought into existence through this politics may, moreover, obscure many differences between women along axes such as class, sexuality, race, nationality, or religion.'

In her early work, Young (1987; 1990) discusses the 'logic of identity'. While Young uses this concept to draw attention to the workings of domination, in my reading it also aptly explains the confining tendencies of the politics of presence: 'The logic of identity also seeks to reduce the plurality of particular subjects, their bodily, perspectival experience, to a unity' (Young 1990: 99). However powerful the unifying move of the logic of identity, it is bound to fail. Identity can only be constructed in demarcation to difference (see Connolly 1991: 64; Butler 1993: 3; Mouffe 2005 [2000]: 21). Ultimate unity is impossible. The failed attempt at unification results in binary identity constructions, which are, however, not perceived as equal in value. Those racial, sexual, and gendered identities perceived as inferior are expelled from the public and banished to the private sphere (Young 1987: 62–3; 1990: 99).

These identities, however, do not entirely disappear in privacy. Young identifies a paradox: marginalized identities are both made invisible and stereotyped at the same time. They are made invisible as democratic subjects, as agents in the public realm, but concurrently they are constructed as the Other, the embodied deviation from the norm. Young describes this kind of stereotyping as confining marginalized subjects to their bodies. Inferior identities are linked to 'ugly, fearful, or loathsome bodies' (Young 1990: 124). Their realm of creative self-realization is limited by narrowly defined stereotypes. The identities of those who dominate, in contrast, remain largely undefined. White, upper class men are immune to stereotyping and perceived as impartial and universal—as the norm (100, 125).

While Young herself does not make a link between the logic of identity and the dilemma of difference, the connection is apparent. It is not just the problem of hierarchization between different identity groups, the identities themselves bear problematic tendencies. As Young explains: 'The unifying process required by group representation inappropriately freezes fluid relational identities into a unity, and can recreate oppressive segregation' (Young 1990: 350). I agree with Young that the confining tendencies of identities come into effect to a different degree for those born into positions of marginalization and those in positions of domination. Maleness, whiteness, able-bodiedness, and heterosexuality are indeed established as the norm and undergo far less scrutiny. The fundamentally confining nature of identity nevertheless comes into effect even for those with privileged identities. Exposed to the gaze of others in the space of appearance, even they are not free to change. The logic of identity curtails freedom for all.

Conclusion

Difference democracy suggests reconfiguring the order of things that constitute democratic space by including marginalized bodies, suppressed emotions, and neglected interests. The visible presence of the marginalized changes the dynamics of the assemblages that constitute the space of appearance. Here, Butler goes along with difference democrats who explain even the silent democratic subject as expressing content through the body:

> it matters that bodies assemble, and that the political meanings enacted by demonstrations are not only those that are enacted by discourse whether written or vocalized. Embodied actions of various kinds signify in ways that are, strictly speaking, neither discursive nor prediscursive. In other words, forms of assembly already signify prior to, and apart from, any particular demands they make.
>
> (Butler 2015: 8)

The body, then, functions as an affective thing equipping the democratic subject with agency. As difference democrats acknowledge, however, the politics of presence also entails limitations to freedom of expression. The marginalized body becomes not only an agentic subject, but also an object of prejudice and stereotyping. In Young's study on gendered spaces discussed in the introduction to this chapter, she claims: 'To the extent that a woman lives her body as a thing, she remains rooted in immanence, is inhibited, and retains a distance from her body as transcending movement' (Young 2005 [1977]: 39). I believe that the confinements described by Young do not only concern women but affect everyone to a certain degree, as identities have an inherently limiting effect.

One way of dealing with the dilemma of difference is to simply reject the affectivity of the body and focus on the content that subjects utter rather than on their appearance. Michael Saward, for example, counters the claim of the agency of silent bodies: 'There is no self-presenting subject whose essential character and desires and interests are ... evident enough to be "read off" their appearance' (Saward 2010: 77). But looking beyond difference not only threatens to obscure inequalities, as difference democrats rightfully argue, but also overlooks the nuanced ways in which our corporeal identity performances indeed affect democratic participation.

The question that arises then is: how can identities in democratic spaces be acknowledged, while at the same time affording the subject a greater degree of freedom in exploring and expressing the multiple self—the freedom for the subject to change? The next chapter will seek ways out of the dilemma of difference by exploring democratic theory's conceptions of self-transformation. It will enrich democratic theory with intersectional and Black queer theory in order to develop the concept of disidentification. The resulting politics of becoming does not replace but rather augments the politics of presence.

4
Becoming Multiple
Identity, Interrupted

> Democracy is that which dissolves the power of the identities used to discriminate between us, that differentiate and hierarchise ... Democracy is the possibility to build better worlds which will no doubt comprise new identities, but that can overcome the inequalities of today.
>
> *Clare Woodford 2018*

This chapter turns to the ability to self-identify in participatory processes, to wield agency in the construction of one's own identity, and to have the freedom to change how we are identified by others. This notion of the democratic subject as *subject to change* responds to the dilemma of difference discussed in the previous chapter. The difference democratic politics of presence calls for the public visibility of marginalized identities to advance equality, but at the same time curtails the freedom of the democratic subject to express its multiple self.

This is an important point for this book where its scope is extended beyond the question of the marginalization of disadvantaged groups in democracy. Democratic freedom, which is the topic of this chapter, directly affects all members of society. It is the question of how the perception of our selves limits or expands the scope of self-expression and self-realization. Recall Mansbridge's (2005: 62) claim that through descriptive representation even silent subjects communicate political claims through their identified bodies. While this strategy successfully draws attention to marginalized bodies and perspectives, it also entails reducing the democratic subject and confining it to a particular identity:

> The silent body speaks, whether it wills that speech or not. It speaks of its place in the social order: of race, sex, age. The black man must speak as a black man, the white woman as a white woman. The old speak from the shell of age. Some speak from the haze of beauty. The text written on the body, read from the body, may amplify or mute what the speaker says, but it cannot be easily silenced ... We have spoken before we speak, we have been read before we write.
>
> (Lupia and Norton 2017: 68)

The Politics of Becoming. Hans Asenbaum, Oxford University Press. © Hans Asenbaum (2023).
DOI: 10.1093/oso/9780192858870.003.0004

This is the first of three chapters that each seek ways out of the dilemma of difference and explore the personal freedom to express the multiple self in democratic spaces. This chapter will lay the theoretical groundwork that will be substantiated through an investigation of its practical relevance in the following two chapters. To develop these theoretical foundations, this chapter will draw on several perspectives in radical democratic thought. First, it will consult difference, participatory, deliberative, and agonistic perspectives with regard to their conceptions of self-transformation. As all four approaches only generate limited accounts of freedom for the subject to change, a fifth perspective in democratic theory that focuses on societal transformation will be introduced. Through the lens of the transformative perspective, the politics of presence will be re-read as part of a politics of becoming, which focuses on identity disruption through disidentification. Disidentification entails the rejection of hegemonic identity ascriptions and the articulation of alternative identities. Disidentification in transformative democratic theory, however, only explains radical democratic subjectivization on a collective level, so that the democratic subject is caught up in the group dynamics of social movements. To tackle this problem and explore disidentification on a personal level of democratic subjectivity, the politics of becoming will be further enriched with insights from queer theory, and in particular intersectional and Black queer theory, which explains identity via the concepts of performativity and masquerade and develops strategies of resignification and abolition as ways forward. This results in an ideal of democracy as the condition for self-transformation. It is not an ideal of overcoming identity, but one that sets free the multiplicity, plasticity, and transformative potential of identification.

Self-transformation in Democratic Theories

The question at hand is how the confining tendencies in the politics of presence can be tackled and how the successful advancement of inclusion of such identity politics can be made compatible with strategies of self-transformation. In accordance with the perspectival approach adopted by this book, it will consult four perspectives in democratic theory in pursuit of ways out of the dilemma of difference. The obvious first port of call for this undertaking is difference democracy itself. As will be seen, difference democratic strategies to overcoming the dilemma of difference, while generating promising approaches, remain limited by and in conflict with essentialist tendencies. Hence, three other radical democratic perspectives—namely participatory, deliberative, and agonistic democracy—will be consulted with regard to their approaches to self-transformation.

Essentializing Constructed Identities: The Difference Democratic Perspective

As discussed in the previous chapter, identity fulfils a positive function in difference democratic strategies for inclusion. Nevertheless, difference democrats also point to the problematic role of identity, limiting democratic agency. Young describes marginalized identity as a confining space that restricts physical motion and personal expression. The freedom of marginalized groups is bound by hegemonic spatiality as gendered, raced, sexed, and classed codes suggest how to act and what to say. While 'some women escape or transcend the typical situation and definition of women in various degrees and respects' (Young 2005 [1977]: 33), overall women are like objects that are placed into and confined by a web of social relations. The logic of identity described by Young (1990) that reduces plurality to unity and supresses diversity—as I have argued in the previous chapter—limits not just the freedom of those with marginalized identities, but that of everyone. We are all limited by our stable identity constructs and others' expectations of identity continuity and integrity. This critical view on the confining function of identity, then, raises the question as to how the fixities of the spaces that bind identity can be loosened.

To counter the confining tendencies of the politics of presence, difference democrats propose that the strategies of a politics of presence, most notably quota regulations, are not incompatible with an understanding of contingent identity construction. In various texts, difference democrats develop performative accounts of identity that are compatible with a politics of presence. Understanding identity in constructivist and performative terms opens up identity spaces to potential transformations of the self.

Mansbridge (2003: 358), for example, argues that although focusing on identity categories 'is dangerous, not only because it exaggerates reality but also because it underlines the very stereotypes that have been used to keep women in their place, the existence of danger does not mean that we should forswear [quota strategies].' In order to counter essentializing effects, the introduction of quotas needs to be justified by a public debate explaining gender identities as relational and a product of a history of subordination (Mansbridge 2005). The category 'women' is to be understood in terms of positionality. Women are a product of specific, gender-coded experiences, which are distributed unevenly among humans (Mansbridge 1991: 133). Acknowledging different social positionalities and particular experiences does not rule out an understanding of identities as fluid (Phillips 1996: 142).

Young's work goes the furthest in outlining an approach to thinking identity in contingent terms (Young 1987; 1989; 1990; 1997b; 2000). She employs the concept of seriality, which Jean-Paul Sartre used to describe class, to understand the category 'women'. While the term 'group' is commonly used to describe people with the same identity markers, it is misleading as it implies direct interaction between its members. In a group, people know each other and gather consciously for a specific reason. In contrast, a series puts individuals in a similar structural position defined by specific material objects, practices, routines, and cultures. Women, understood as a series rather than a group, are individually unknown to each other. Nevertheless, they identify with one another as they are socialized within the same material milieu marked by heterosexuality and a gendered division of labour. They employ the same material objects such as specific clothing, cosmetic products, and toiletries. However powerful the structures confining seriality, they do not ultimately define each individual woman; they only enable and constrain certain actions (Young 1994). Identity as a series can be understood as spatial assemblage as discussed in Chapter 2 with culturally-coded objects, human bodies, and social constructs interwoven in a terrain that constitutes and binds identity expression. A series marks a spatial order in which one follows the other. This also suggests that one can stop following, step out of the series, and break new ground.

In order to break out of such identity space, Young (1990: 124) calls for 'a revolution of subjectivity. Rather than seeking a wholeness of the self, the subjects of this plural and complex society should affirm the otherness within ourselves, acknowledging that as subjects we are heterogeneous and multiple in our affiliations and desires.' This revolution of subjectivity is realized by the identity politics of social movements who reclaim the definition of their own identity. The newly generated identifications are not stable; rather, they overlap with other identities which are part of a process of continuous redefinition.

These approaches of difference democrats to overcome the dilemma of difference are promising. Understanding identity as contingent construction opens up the potential for self-transcendence and greater freedom of identity articulation. Difference democratic approaches are, however, hampered by some essentializing tendencies that run through their work. In making the argument for a politics of presence, difference democrats repeatedly fall back into essentialist thinking. Young, for example, describes the liberating effects of reclaiming and affirming one's marginalized identity:

> I am just what they say I am—a Jewboy, a colored girl, a fag, a dyke, or a hag—and proud of it. No longer does one have the impossible project of *trying to become something one is not* under circumstances where the very trying reminds one of *who one is.*
>
> (Young 1990: 166, emphasis added)

In response to constructivist notions of identity, Young states: 'it is foolish to deny the reality of groups' (47). Similarly, in reference to the abstract individualism of

Enlightenment thought, Phillips (1993: 95) warns of the 'distorting consequences of trying to pretend away group differences'. And Mansbridge describes the process of socialization in essentializing terms: 'Because *healthy people want to be who they are*, children usually value being a boy or a girl long before they understand the full social connotations of this identity' (Mansbridge 1993: 344, emphasis added).

The argument that particular gendered or racial qualities stem not from a biological core but from socialization only provides a partial remedy to this problem. The stabilization of identity constructions in a politics of presence remains. When a person is approached with the expectation of being particularly good at listening because of her gender, or dancing because of her race, this always limits the freedom of that person to express and explore their multiple self, no matter what explanation underlies this assumption. From this point of view, the call of Phillips (1995) and Young (2000) for citizens to place special trust in representatives who share the same corporeal identity features based on similar positions in society is problematic. So too is Mansbridge's (1991) and Gould's (1993) call for introducing womanly qualities into the polity. Here women are called upon to embrace their socialized nurturing and mothering qualities. However positive the interpretation of these features, they nevertheless limit the possibilities of self-definition. Positive identity affirmation always entails confinement by identity.

We have seen that while difference democrats extensively problematize the dilemma of difference and elaborate ways to overcome its essentialist tendencies, they are only partially successful. Despite the rich potential of the constructivist notions that call for a revolution of subjectivity and understand gender as seriality, difference democrats forgo the exploration of what this means for changing identity and exploring the multiple self. The question thus remains as to how the freedom of the democratic subject to change can be advanced within democratic spaces.

Shaping Enlightened Subjects: The Participatory Perspective

In contrast to liberal conceptions of democracy that locate participation in the institutionalized closed spaces of the state and restrict citizens' engagement to the voting booth (Schumpeter 1947; Downs 1957), theories of participatory democracy emerging in the 1960s and '70s relocate democracy to new democratic spaces from self-managed workplaces (Dahl 1986; Gould 1988), to neighbourhood associations (Barber 2003 [1984]), and sites of self-organization of education and public services (Hirst 1994). Theories of participatory democracy see participation as self-realization and an antidote to alienation from politics. Democratic spaces function as schools in which democratic subjects learn about various issues and enhance empathy with others (Pateman 1970). This educative process in democratic spaces entails deep personal transformation.

Participatory democrats take their inspiration from the republican tradition and particularly from Rousseau (1998 [1762]: Book 1, Ch. 8) who argues that 'The passage from the state of nature to the civil state produces a very remarkable change in man ... [H]is faculties are so stimulated and developed, his ideas so extended, his feelings so ennobled, and his whole soul so uplifted' that he is transformed from 'a stupid and unimaginative animal' into 'an intelligent being and a man'. In the same vein, participatory democrats understand democratic spaces as educational institutions which facilitate personal development, self-expression, and self-discovery (Pateman 1970; Macpherson 1977).

The notion of self-realization in participatory democracy can be traced back not only to the humanist and republican tradition (Dacombe 2018), but also to socialist thought (Held 2006 [1987]; Asenbaum 2012, 2013), and particularly utopian socialism (Taylor 2016 [1982]). Utopian socialists developed detailed conceptions of future societies with the goal of achieving liberation and self-realization. Such ideas often opposed the professional specialization imposed by emerging capitalist societies and advocated instead the cultivation of multiple talents and inclinations which give expression to the multiple self. Although Marx and Engels harshly rejected such utopianism in the name of scientific socialism, it is clearly reflected in their writings. In contrast with the capitalist division of labour ...

in communist society, where nobody has one exclusive sphere of activity but each can become accomplished in any branch he wishes, society regulates the general production and thus makes it possible for me to do one thing today and another tomorrow, to hunt in the morning, fish in the afternoon, rear cattle in the evening, criticise after dinner, just as I have a mind, without ever becoming hunter, fisherman, herdsman or critic.

(Marx and Engels 1998 [1845], Vol. 1)

The Marxian argument, inspired by early utopian socialists, challenges the fixity of identities and calls for a multiplicity of the self. Such an approach is also reflected in current pedagogics which emphasize practical experiences in art, handicrafts, theatre, and intercultural exchange over the knowledge of facts (e.g. Miller, Irwin and Nigh 2014). Yet, the notion of personal development through education has also inspired the authoritarian strands of socialist thinking, resulting in conceptions of the 'new man' in Marxist and Soviet texts. Here, educational institutions in particular and social and political institutions more generally are used to shape a specific subject from above. This idea runs counter to participatory democratic thinking, where self-development is instituted outside of state influence. Referring to civil society's democratic spaces, Schmitter and Karl (1991: 79–80), for example, write: 'The diverse units of social identity and interest, by remaining independent of the

state, can also contribute to forming better citizens who are more aware of the preferences of others, more self-confident in their actions, and more civic-minded in
their willingness to sacrifice for the common good.'

However, theories of participatory democracy do not manage to completely rid
themselves of their authoritarian legacy. A compulsive undertone can be detected
in their call for collectivity: 'Strong democracy creates the very citizens it depends
upon ... because it mandates a permanent confrontation between the me as citizen and the "Other" as citizen, *forcing us to think in common and act in common*'
(Barber 2003 [1984]: 153, emphasis added). The compulsion expressed by Barber
echoes Rousseau's argument, to wit: 'man, who so far had considered only himself, finds that he is *forced to act* on different principles, and to consult his reason
before listening to his inclinations' (Rousseau 1998 [1762], Book 1, Ch. 8, emphasis
added). Participatory democracy thus produces particular subjects. The outcome
of this transformative process is to a certain extent predetermined. In many ways,
the subject is seen as a product, an object of creation, rather than an autonomous
self-explorer.

Creating Better Citizens: The Deliberative Perspective

In contrast with participatory democrats, thinkers in the deliberative tradition
bring a whole new set of expertise to the discussion. Rooted in the linguistic turn
with structuralism and later poststructuralism becoming the dominant paradigm
in the social sciences, deliberative democracy draws on notions of discursive identity construction (e.g. Mansbridge et al. 2010: 79). They take inspiration from
Habermas' (1992 [1962]: 1996 [1992]) discourse theory and its ideal of personal
autonomy and freedom from domination, which provides a promising outlook
for democratic self-transformation. John Dryzek and Simon Niemeyer explore the
constructivist potential of deliberative democracy. They define identities not only
or even primarily as embodied, but as produced through communicative interaction and hence as the result of discursive representation (Dryzek 2000; Dryzek
and Niemeyer 2008).

Upon closer examination, however, constraints similar to those in participatory
democracy become apparent. Simone Chambers (1996: 103), for example, elaborates: 'Our inner selves (who we are and what we want) are shaped through the
communicative relationships we enter into. Practical discourse rationalizes this
process by asking participants to reflect upon and evaluate their needs and interests rationally from the point of view of their generalizability.' Chambers insists
that the freedom of self-expression lies in these modes of communication: 'deliberative democracy, because it asks participants to examine, justify, and deliberate
about their preferences and interests, gives the individual the opportunity to shape
her preferences and interest autonomously' (189). The element of compulsion

identified in both Rousseau's and Barber's writing, however, is also reflected in Chamber's text:

> Citizens themselves *come under a publicity requirement* in deliberation such that they *must offer reasons* for their positions and claims. Reason giving initiates a learning process in which participants acquire discursive skills. Participants are asked to defend their preference in terms that others could find convincing. They are asked to look at their preferences from both the partial and the impartial point of view.
>
> (Chambers 1996: 190, emphasis added)

These are exactly the tendencies of compulsion criticized by difference democrats. The requirement of reasoned argumentation produces specific democratic subjects. They are not only recreating a masculinist, Eurocentric subject, as difference democrats argue. More importantly for the question of freedom in self-definition, the subjects created in deliberative democracy appear to be restricted in the development of their personality. The logic of deliberation dictates that subjects need to be reasoned, open-minded, other-regarding, and so on.

Similar to Chambers, Mark Warren (1992: 8) states that through deliberation citizens 'become more public-spirited, more tolerant, more knowledgeable, more attentive to the interests of others, and more probing of their own interests.' Warren's account generates further insights as to why deliberative identity construction increases freedom and autonomy. First, deliberation induces self-reflection and makes subjects more aware of their own interests which is liberating in itself (Warren 1996: 254–5). And second, conflict is to be understood as limiting freedom because it entails confrontation which constitutes relations of domination. When conflict is diminished through deliberation and mutual understanding, this increases freedom. Yet, he remains critical of the notion of consensus to which many deliberative democrats adhere. He distances himself from Rousseau's conception of the subordination of all individual wills under the general will (Warren 1992: 11). In 'the process of self-discovery (or self-creation)' (12), conflict cannot always be transformed into mutuality, hence there need to be spaces for conflict and confrontation that do not require identity change (9).

Even in a nuanced account such as Warren's, which allows for conflict and contestation, deliberative identity construction remains limited by its norms. Such a conception of self-transformation is particularly worrying when objectivist assumptions about knowledge are employed. Some studies in deliberative democracy have been particularly keen to point to knowledge gain through deliberation: 'Deliberative institutions in this mode should offer training and education to *create informed participants*' (Fung 2003: 345, emphasis added). And in an empirical study, the authors observe: '[participants'] knowledge about the issue, as well as their capabilities to engage in political debates, increased. In this sense, deliberation *created "better" citizens'* (Andersen and Hansen 2007: 552, emphasis added; see also Newton 2012). This evaluative tone which gauges the 'quality' of citizens is indicative of a top-down approach to shaping democratic subjects.

To conclude, while deliberative conceptions of democracy provide notions of self-transformation that try to strengthen individual autonomy, these attempts are only partly successful. Although Warren and Chambers point to some important gains in personal autonomy through deliberation, this does not overcome the inherently limiting paths of self-transformation laid out in the deliberative perspective. Democratic spaces for deliberation are constructed with the purpose of producing 'better' (empathetic, public-spirited, knowledgeable) citizens. Thus, democratic subjects are not free to change, but instead are subject to particular transformations designed by others.

Articulating the Tormented Self: The Agonistic Perspective

Warren's argument linking the reification of identity to confrontation finds support in the agonistic perspective. Agonists conceptualize the formation of alternative collective identities as a precondition to any challenge to the neoliberal order. Firmly rooted in the linguistic turn, agonistic thinkers explain identities as the product of discursive contestation with subjects at the margins of society developing aversive identities to challenge domination (Connolly 1991; Norval 2007). The self in the agonistic perspective is conceptualized in anti-essentialist terms as multiple, contingent, and fraught with inner contradiction (Honig 1994; Connolly 1995). This opens up new potential for self-transformation.

Chantal Mouffe (1995a) directly responds to the difference democratic politics of presence. She fervently argues against any kind of essentialism which she detects in the work of Pateman (1989) and Young (1987; 1989). While sympathizing with these feminist approaches, which contest the universal construction of the citizen in the image of men, Mouffe (1995: 322) criticizes their fixed conceptions of (gender) identity: 'I do not believe, however, that the remedy is to replace [the modern category of the individual] by a sexually differentiated, "bigendered" conception of the individual and to bring women's so-called specific tasks into the very definition of citizenship.' Instead, Mouffe argues for a radical constructivist position. In this view, identities are constituted through discursive articulation. Based on the work of the psychoanalyst Jacques Lacan who points to the vast field of the unconscious which indicates the decentred nature of human identity, Mouffe argues that the core of human identity, on which subjectivity is based, consists of a lack, nothing, an empty space. Attempts at permanently reifying identity through the articulation of nodal points in a web of discourses are bound to fail due to the lack upon which they are built. Identity, then, emerges through a continuous dialectical process of fixity and mutability (Mouffe 1995b). The understanding of lack at the core of the subject opens prospects of *de*construction. What is crucial is that the de-articulation of identity is not an end in itself. The disentanglement of discursive constructs always has to go hand-in-hand with the rearticulation of new identities (Mouffe 2006: 5–6).

In terms of Mouffe's response to the politics of presence, this means that there is no essential core on which a feminist claim for a female identity can be based: 'we no longer have a homogenous entity "woman" facing another homogenous entity "man", but a multiplicity of social relations in which sexual difference is always constructed in very diverse ways' (Mouffe 1995a: 319). Sexual difference would not disappear in a pluralist conception of radical democracy, but it would lose its significance in political interaction. The de-identification with sexual constructs needs to be followed by a rearticulation of an identity as radical democratic citizen, which is open enough to allow for various identifications while still orientating the subject towards freedom and equality.

Mouffe's anti-essentialist conception of democratic subjects who are defined by their lack of a foundational core provides new fertile ground for the exploration of the freedom of the subject to change. The notion of the plural and contradictory self also resonates with the work of other agonists (Honig 1994; Connolly 1995) and echoes Young's call for a revolution of subjectivity that embraces the otherness within the self (Young 1990: 124). Despite this promising outlook, the liberating potential of the agonistic perspective remains unfulfilled for three reasons. First, the tragic horizon of agonism thwarts any substantive self-transformation. Second, the inherent conservativism of the agonistic perspective constructs a subject of submission rather than a subject of emancipation. And third, the notion of a hegemonic struggle suggests a top-down construction of democratic subjectivity.

As agonistic democracy is defined by conflict, there can never be a final resolution. The end of conflict would mean the end of democracy. This is the tragedy of agonistic democracy (Wenman 2013: 33; Tambakaki 2017: 581). Mouffe (2013: 84) clarifies that there is no such thing as radical democracy: 'the extension and radicalization of democratic struggles will never have a final point of arrival in the achievement of a fully liberated society.' The social structures surrounding and constituting the subject can be contested, but its hierarchical relations and competitive principles cannot be overcome (Tambakaki 2017: 581). This tragic view also stifles any real self-transformation. The perpetual conflictuality that positions different actors and different discourses in society in constant confrontation with each other is mirrored within the self (Honig 1994). Helen McManus explores the agonistic self in political participation. The contradictory self needs democratic spaces to release the tension of constant inner conflict that it endures:

> it is precisely in the experience of inner conflict as 'torment', as something that needs to be addressed and yet can never be entirely resolved, that individuals find themselves compelled to act ... The individual knows that the exhilarating

'release' of action will in turn bind her up in another set of torments, another set of excesses along with the attendant perturbation and relief of acting on those excesses.

(McManus 2008: 525)

This tragic horizon of agonistic democracy is owed to an inherent conservativism that stands in contrast with its emancipatory impetus. Since a true alternative to the ruling order can never be achieved, improvements within the liberal order are the best that agonistic contestation can hope to achieve. Mark Wenman points to the agonistic conservativism within Mouffe's work. The fear of fascist tendencies in the surge of right-wing populism leads Mouffe to develop 'a model of agonistic democracy built around the need to construct order, unity and authority' (Wenman 2013: 182). In this context, Mouffe's call for constructing an identity of radical democratic citizenship primarily serves to fulfil the function of maintaining the liberal order: 'To belong to the political community, what is required is to accept a specific language of civil intercourse ... Those rules prescribe norms of conduct to be subscribed to in seeking self-chosen satisfaction and in performing self-chosen actions' (Mouffe 1992b: 77). And elsewhere democratic citizenship is described as 'a common political identity of persons ... who accept submission to certain authoritative rules of conduct' (Mouffe 1992a: 30–1). Mouffe (1995b: 264) also calls for a '"civic" nationalism'. Such civic nationalism is not to be understood as homogenous, but rather as a plural and open category. However, this pluralism serves as a tool for diverting potentially destructive energies. Multiple identifications within the civic national identity disperse potentially destructive energies. Rather than one antagonistic relationship, Mouffe (1994: 111) advocates many agonistic identifications.

It becomes apparent that Mouffe's theory is driven by a fear of destructive forces that make conserving the status quo more appealing than risking upheaval in the name of substantive change. Wenman is right to liken Mouffe's later texts to the contractual theory of Thomas Hobbes (1968 [1851]), who pitted the monstrous Leviathan against the monstrous wolf in all of us. Mouffe's criticism of essentialism in difference democracy ultimately fails to afford any perspectives for self-transformation.

Finally, it is the notion of hegemony that limits the freedom of the agonistic subject to change. Understanding identity as the product of collective contestation limits personal freedom as the subject appears to be constructed from the top down as a subject to leadership. Mouffe's recent work on populism makes clear that the actors who articulate new identities are political parties and their charismatic leaders who vie for attention in a competitive corporate media environment (Mouffe 2018). Although the goal of left populist movements is to increase freedom and equality, processes of identity construction are advanced by leaders rather than the grassroots, which is in line with the Gramscian thought on which

Mouffe builds and which partly overlaps with Leninist conceptions of a vanguard leadership. In a similar vein, Kioupkiolis (2017: 42) criticizes Laclau's conception of hegemony, in which 'the people are an "amorphous mass" that need to be educated, moulded, and directed by enlightened leaders.' As long as agonistic democracy is limited by its tragic horizon that disallows fundamental change, and the fear of upheaval results in aspirations of social conservation, theories of identity construction inevitably wind up as tools in the hands of elites who lead the masses. Ironically, in a similar way as in theories of participatory and deliberative democracy, identities are shaped by enlightened, intellectual elites and paths of self-transformation are predetermined.

To conclude, agonistic conceptions of the democratic subject as a contingent identity construction offer great potential to explore self-transformation in democratic spaces. Yet, this potential remains unrealized on account of the tragic horizon of agonism, its conservative outlook that maintains the liberal, capitalist order, and the notion of hegemonic identity construction as a top-down process.

Transforming Systems and Selves: A New Perspective in Democratic Thought

While the different radical democratic perspectives discussed so far provide promising approaches to performative identity constitution through embodied presence (difference democracy), participatory self-development (participatory democracy), autonomous self-constitution (deliberative democracy), and the construction of new collective subjectivities (agonistic democracy), they all fall short of realizing freedom within these processes. The limited societal change advanced in these theories is reflected in the bound and channelled transformations of the subject. The particular self-transformations outlined here appear to be advanced from the top down, by enlightened academics, intellectual leaders, and populist parties. What is needed, then, is a perspective in democratic theory that provides the grounds for freedom in identity construction, freedom for the subject to change.

To this end, another perspective in democratic thought that emerged in the wake of the new millennium offers fruitful ground. What I call transformative democracy was entangled with the agonistic perspective in the early writings that identified with the term 'radical democracy', but it has developed its own distinctive features in recent years. In critical response to and clear demarcation from earlier agonistic approaches, texts on post-hegemony aim to overcome the tragic perspective of agonism (Beasley-Murray 2011). Although this literature, despite its partial theoretical complexity, is very well received publicly, it has yet to be acknowledged in the texts defining the canon of democratic theory. This chapter provides one of the first attempts at outlining this perspective and relating it to other theories of democracy (see also Wenman 2013: 89–92; Tambakaki 2017: 578).

What most clearly distinguishes transformative democracy from the other radical democratic perspectives discussed so far is the bold articulation of systemic alternatives. In contrast with the discourse on the revitalization of democracy in the participatory, deliberative, difference, and agonistic perspectives, it puts societal transformation at its centre. This is aptly illustrated by its use of the spatial concept of utopia. In the literal translation from Greek, utopia denotes 'no-place', a space that is 'nowhere' or 'elsewhere'. Transformative democrats use the notion of utopia not only for the imagination of systemic alternatives, but also as a way to point to 'real utopias' that establish alternatives in the here and now. The founding of collective alternatives, such as cooperative modes of production, occupied buildings, and self-managed spaces, are not just insular phenomena but form part of a transformative movement. Erik Olin Wright argues that at times there is only a thin line between reformist and transformative strategies. Yet, the transformative perspective always keeps the systemic alternative in clear sight: 'Real utopias, in contrast [with reformism], envision the contours of an alternative social world that embodies emancipatory ideals and then look for social innovations we can create in the world as it is that moves us towards that destination' (Wright 2013: 17).

The notion of utopia is also central in post-anarchism, which enriches traditional anarchist work of the nineteenth and twentieth centuries with post-structuralist and post-foundationalist thinking. Post-anarchism entails 'a utopian moment of rupture and excess which disturbs the limits of politics' (Newman 2010b: 7). This transformative divergence from the presence of domination consists of a reconfiguration of space. The project of transforming social relations on a macro level is pursued by reconfiguring democratic space in various sites on a micro level; it hence entails a series of uncoordinated interruptions of the dominant order. Post-anarchism is aimed 'at fostering the emergence of new autonomous political spaces, where communal and free relations can develop. This would involve an experimentation with new ways of living' (128). Post-anarchism reinterprets the term of design, central to democratic design thinking (Saward 2021) and democratic innovations (Smith 2009), and describes it as 'forms of autonomous self-ordering from below' (Newman 2011: 355) through the formation of 'insurrectional spaces'.

As creators of insurrectional spaces, social movements and autonomous collectives become the central agents of transformative democracy. They fulfil a double role. They are both agents striving towards democracy and sites of the lived experience of democracy. Different from agonistic approaches, it is not conflict, but the experience of commonality in collective struggle that defines democracy. Democracy is 'a rebellious moment' (Wolin 1994: 23)—a subjective state of mind. In contrast with agonistic tragedy, the transformative perspective opens prospects for systemic change. This change is sometimes referred to as transformation, revolution, insurrection, or rebellion. What is crucial is that democracy does not just lie beyond this process; democracy is realized within it:

> Democracy is not about where the political is located but how it is experienced. Revolutions activate the demos and destroy boundaries that bar access to political experience. Individuals from the excluded social strata take on responsibilities, deliberate about goals and choices, and share in decisions that have broad consequences and affect unknown and distant others. Thus revolutionary transgression is the means by which the demos makes itself political.
>
> (Wolin 1994: 18)

In contrast with the radical democratic perspectives discussed so far, which all see the necessity for both representative and direct democratic institutions, the transformative perspective collapses this division and understands democracy in its original sense as self-rule. Hardt and Negri (2017: 247) describe what they call absolute democracy as the 'rule of everyone by everyone'. This form of self-rule is constituted by *the common*. The transformative democratic concept of the common bears some resemblance to participatory democrats' notion of democratic community. In contrast to the participatory democratic spirit of communal organization, however, transformative democracy directly addresses the question of property. Rancière (2014 [2005]: 57) argues that while capitalist forces of privatization aim to constantly expand the commercial sphere, democratic forces expand the common as public sphere including everyone.

Hardt and Negri, like Rancière, use the term 'common'. The commons (in plural) as originally discussed by Garrett Hardin (1968) and later Elinor Ostrom (1990) are common-pool resources including land, water, public places, and knowledge. The concept of the commons thus addresses the question of property ownership and develops an understanding of communal self-management. Many insist, however, that the commons are never owned, but only preliminarily used. They function as hosts to their users. Commons (as subjects) then create a community of commoners. Commons are defined by the interactive process of *commoning*—the creation and recreation of resource (Deleixhe 2018).

This notion of cooperative production also plays a crucial role in the current freedom of information and the open-source movements, which confront the capitalist drive towards the commercialization of knowledge. In the digital age, the logic of commoning through sharing knowledge online challenges the capitalist logic of property rights enforced through online paywalls that confine digital knowledge space (Beyer 2014b). Wikipedia is a particularly illustrative example of how common-based knowledge production can work (Konieczny 2010). And the concept of liquid democracy as practiced by Pirate Parties shows how open-source principles and wiki technology can be used to produce collective decisions, texts, and even laws (Blum and Zuber 2016).

Considering the immateriality of digital objects and the discursive nature of knowledge, Hardt and Negri (2012) develop the understanding of the commons further and define the common (in singular) as the outcome of any social and communicative interaction. Hence, any linguistic or performative articulation is part of the process of commoning.

To conclude, the transformative perspective outlined above differs from other radical democratic perspectives in advocating fundamental systemic change. The constitution of insurrectional spaces is part of a deep reconfiguration of demo-cratic space through an interruption of domination. This outlook provides fresh and fertile ground for the self-transformation and self-explorations of the demo-cratic subject. So, how can democratic subjectivity be re-imagined through a trans-formative democratic lens, and what possibilities can it provide for democratic self-constitution?

From the Politics of Presence to the Politics of Becoming: Disidentification as Radical Democratic Practice

The freedom for the subject to change in the transformative perspective is based on a different conception of democratic space. The difference, participatory, delib-erative, and agonistic perspectives understand space as stable and only partly changing. The rearrangement of spatial assemblages for democratic participa-tion they recommend is limited by the liberal, capitalist context in which they are produced. The transformative perspective, in contrast, explains space itself as morphological. The transformation of the self goes along with the transformation of space as two dialectically intertwined assemblages, as discussed in Chapter 2. Transformative democracy, building on post-anarchist theory, 'conceives of a political space which is indeterminate, contingent and heterogeneous—a space whose lines and contours are undecidable. Postanarchist political space is, in other words, a space of *becoming*' (Newman 2011: 355). In contrast with the Arend-tian space of appearance in which the gaze of spectators actualizes the subject, the space of becoming constitutes morphological subjectivities. Self-transformation is, of course, not an entirely autonomous process. The subject always depends on the interpellation of others. But this interpellation, as will become clear, is interrupted by freedom and equality enlarging the identity spaces through which the subject moves. Exploring freedom in democratic self-constitution, I will augment the pol-itics of presence with a politics of becoming. In this section, I will first recount the transformative democratic critique of identity politics and develop the notion of a fugitive self, whose essence can never be captured. Second, I will draw on William Connolly's original concept of a politics of becoming, which I will, third, enrich with the Rancièrian notion of disidentification before engaging with queer theory in the following section.

The transformative perspective challenges the core assumptions of identity politics. It criticizes the essentializing elements of the politics of presence that erects boundaries and divides the demos. 'Postmodern cultural politics follows in the footsteps of nationalism in insisting upon boundaries that establish differences (as in gender or racial politics) but proclaims identities as well. Here, too, the political becomes associated with purification' (Wolin 1994: 12). The division of the demos into group identities impedes a common democratic project:

> A politics that is based around the assertion of an identity, or seeks an institutional recognition of a specific difference ... [is] confining itself to a certain particularity, thus closing itself off from struggles and identities outside itself. What is foreclosed is an egalitarian, collective, democratic dimension which embodies a necessary openness to the other.
>
> (Newman 2010a: 8)

This democratic dimension that overcomes division is reflected in Hardt and Negri's multitude, which they describe as 'the *living flesh* that rules itself' (2004: 100). The multitude emerges as a new democratic subjectivity with a mosaic-like character: 'The multitude is an internally different, multiple social subject whose constitution and action is based not on identity or unity (or, much less, indifference) but on what it has in common' (Hardt and Negri 2004: 99).

The notion of a transformative and internally diverse collective resonates with Sheldon Wolin's call for 'heterogeneity, diversity, multiple selves' (Wolin 1994: 24). Wolin's aversion to the boundaries that fix identity is constitutive of his conception of fugitive democracy. He claims that democracy can never be captured and institutionalized. Institutionalization eradicates the spirit of democracy, which can only live in the moment of deeply experienced mutuality. Applying Wolin's notion of democracy to the self, I suggest that we speak of a fugitive self, whose reification through identification equates to its death. Attempts to capture the self can produce continuous identity performances of the legally identified persona in the public sphere, but, as I will argue later, this is only a form of masquerade (Butler 1990). The self can never be captured in its multiplicity.

Wolin's fugitivity that equates the confinement of state boundaries with the confinement of identity boundaries is further developed by Marquis Bey, who engages the history of US slavery with identity formation. From this perspective, state boundaries denote the imposition of human life as property, legally defensible by torture and death. Fugitivity, in this context, stages both a revolt against a violent boundary regime and at the same time against the imposition of the identity of 'the slave'. Through this mutiny, the formerly enslaved *becomes* '[t]he runaway, the subject engendering another iteration of themselves, transing themselves, quintessentializing the tenor of fugitivity: a perpetual, fishy, escape-ful slitheriness that power's hands cannot contain' (Bey 2022: 16). The violent racial regime did not only regulate human bodies as property but also the identity performances these bodies were allowed to engage in. Some US states legally pro-hibited Black people from wearing expensive fabrics irrespective of freedom and financial funds. State power, then, prescribed and fixed classed identities. Gender crossdressing was forbidden in some US states for reasons of indecency, and Black people in particular were forbidden from using any type of disguise. Disguising as the opposite gender, however, was a frequently used strategy for escape. Crossing gender and class lines functioned as an inherently revolutionary act against both slavery and the nation state (Bey 2022: 15–22). Resonating with the post-anarchist space of becoming, Bey (2022: 27) calls for 'an indeterminate, nonfixed space' that resists the 'retroactive installment of ourselves and others in the paradigmatic (racialized, gendered) grid'.

These nonfixed spaces of becoming situated in the transformative perspec-tive constitute morphological subjectivities that experience greater freedom of self-constitution. To best capture such identity reconfigurations, I will build on William Connolly's notion of a 'politics of becoming'. Interestingly, Connolly uses the term to describe exactly the same phenomena that in the difference demo-cratic perspective are associated with the politics of presence. He argues that the women's, the anti-slavery, and the gay/lesbian rights movement all engage in a politics of becoming, not by reifying their identities through physical pres-ence, but through pursuing an agenda of identity change. They aim to *become* citizens with equal rights deserving of equal respect: 'The politics of becoming occurs when a culturally marked constituency, suffering under its current social constitution, strives to reconfigure itself by moving the cultural constellation of identity/difference then in place' (Connolly 1996: 255–6). While participants in these claimed spaces often define their identities in essentialist terms, the lack of a natural essence of their identities allows them to engage in a transformative politics.

This perspectival shift offers a complete reinterpretation of identity politics. It allows us to understand an aspect of identity transformation that is already inher-ent in the politics of presence. The confinements of the dilemma of difference can partly be tackled by a focus on the contingency of identity constructions *cre-ated through identity politics*. Paradoxically, physical presence is a performative act of becoming. Participants in these movements are always becoming; they always strive to be what they are currently perceived not to be. Young (1990 124: 169) hints towards such an understanding when she calls for a revolution of subjectivity and explains the self-definitions of the marginalized as contingent constructions. Even in its physically embodied form, the subject is always subject to change.

In the perspective I am suggesting, the politics of becoming does not replace the politics of presence. The two concepts are rather in a relation of augmentation. The politics of becoming suggests that presence is not fixed in time and space. Rather, presence itself needs to be understood as a transformative performance. The identity claimed through presence in democratic spaces is a becoming identity, one that claims a future self. Suffragettes, for example, did not take a stance as housewives but as future voters and politicians. They emerged in the space of appearance as who they aspired to be. In that brief moment of experiencing democracy, they became equal citizens. Thus, the concept of the politics of becoming allows us to rethink the politics of presence.

The understanding of a politics of becoming and its compatibility with a politics of presence can be further developed through the work of Moya Lloyd (2005). According to Lloyd, instead of perceiving identity as pre-political, so that the politics of presence can represent the category 'women' in democratic spaces, identity needs to be understood as created *within* democratic spaces. The democratic subject is a subject-in-process. This does not preclude the strategic use of essentialism (Spivak 1988). Rather, democratic spaces need to express diversity through the presence of the marginalized. However, at the same time, they need to function as the sites of critiquing and deconstructing essentialism. Even when engaging in strategic essentialism, the performative nature of identities must be foregrounded: 'even when an essence becomes hegemonic, it is never simply locked down. It remains performative ... For this reason, performative identities are always susceptible to subversion, transgression and even transformation' (Lloyd 2005: 67).

Understanding the self as inherently fugitive—as that which tries to escape reification through identification and representation—we can see that a politics of presence temporarily stabilizes identity through embodied performance. The self, however, remains fugitive. The subject to change keeps transforming in different spatial contexts. Its identity assemblage is altered as it interacts with different things in other spaces, which are themselves in constant flux.

I propose to take the meaning of the politics of becoming beyond identity politics to include all aspects of self-transformation in democratic spaces. Beyond Connolly's original notion, which focuses on claimed spaces, this also includes identity transformations in invited and even in closed spaces. More importantly, however, by overcoming the agonistic constraints of tragedy and a continuous struggle for hegemony of both Connolly and Lloyd, I will investigate the politics of becoming through the transformative perspective to explore a democratization of subject constitution.

Rancière's work on subjectivization and in particular on the concept of disidentification provides a promising outlook. To understand the meaning of disidentification, let us start with its opposite: identification. Rancière explains the established political order as consensus or post-democracy, which is governed by the police. The police rests on the logic of identification. Moved by an impetus of control and conservation, it names its subjects and assigns them a place and a part. This logic of control and conservation aims at eradicating democracy: 'Postdemocracy ... is an identifying mode, among institutional mechanisms and allocation of the society's appropriate parts and shares, for making the subject and democracy's own specific actions disappear' (Rancière 1999: 102). Thus, 'little by little the identity of the whole with the all is obtained' (124).

This process of homogenization through identification advanced by the police is disrupted by processes of subjectivization. Subjectivization consists of the collective creation of new identities that contest the police order through acts of *disidentification*. Disidentification is the political act of disrupting the identificatory processes of the police by rejecting the names it assigns. Instead of creating another identity, which would, again, comply with the logic of police, disidentification creates an improper identity, a wrong name (Rancière 2007: 561).

The disidentifying subject is an outcast, a nobody, somebody who does not count and is not assigned a share in the social order. Between this nowhere, where nobody is located, and the precisely localized position controlled by the police, emerges a new ground through disidentification. It is the gap between identification and nothing where subjectivization through disidentification occurs. Through this 'identification with an anybody that has no body' (Rancière 1992: 62), new collective subjectivities arise which cannot be controlled and administered.

Rancière explains disidentification using various examples. In the early nineteenth century, those who, in the eyes of the police, merely served the production of offspring, but did not count as individuals in the liberal-capitalist order, were named after their most valuable attribute. While the police hailed them as proletarians (proles, Latin 'offspring'), many workers rejected this ascription. Their disidentification consisted of a rejection of the class system altogether by promoting a classless society, in which neither capitalists nor proletarians would exist. Rancière (1992: 61) notes that in this case 'a process of subjectivization is a process of disidentification or declassification.'

According to Rancière (2007), the position of the outcast earlier occupied by proletarians is now the place of immigrants. Engaging with the immigration debate in Australia, Rancière asks, what it means to be 'un-Australian' and *un-* itself. He argues that the appropriation of the racist slur of un-Australians residing in the imaginary place of un-Australia by immigrants does not simply create a positive counter-identity in opposition to a nationalist Australian identity. The positionality of un-Australians between an individual identity produced and administered by the police and the location of the unnamed immigrant as an outcast and a nobody creates an *un*-identity, a purposefully wrong name that neither signifies a 'real' identifiable person, nor a nobody: 'politics as such', Rancière (2007: 562) notes, 'rests on the anarchic power of the ... un-identified'.

Finally, Rancière uses the example of the phrase 'We are all German Jews' to illustrate the reappropriation of a derogatory term as an improper name. When the conservative mainstream opposing the student demonstrations of May 1968 in France tried to discredit the student leader Daniel Cohn-Bendit by pointing to his German-Jewish roots, protesters engaged in subjectivization by chanting 'We are all German Jews!' These German Jews neither denoted countable and nameable people, nor were (at least the vast majority of) the protesters actually German or Jewish. Rather, they purposely employed a wrong name, creating an improper identification to express their political convictions (Rancière 1999: 126).

Rancière's notion of improper names is further developed in the work of Marco Deseriis, who explores these novel collective identities as the actualization of Hardt and Negri's multitude. Improper names bring together individuals who form agentic assemblages as a *condividual*. In contrast with the individualistic subject of liberal theory, the condividual is based on a shared identity. The human bodies that form the collective subject interact with the discursive articulations they produce, forming a space of becoming. In doing so, they reject the individual names assigned to them and create an improper name: 'Although these aliases retain the formal features of a proper name, their multiple and unpredictable iterations in the public sphere put into crisis the referential function of the proper name' (Deseriis 2015: 4–5).

Improper names can take two forms: multi-user names and collective pseudonyms. The latter are exemplified by the hacktivist collective Anonymous, which reifies its improper identity through the Guy Fawkes mask, both in its physical version in street demonstrations and its digital version in online protest (Asenbaum 2018). The improper face of Anonymous belongs to a proper historical figure. Guy Fawkes is known for his role in the failed Gunpowder Plot of 1605. Similarly, in the late eighteenth century, the popular folk tale of Ned Ludd breaking a stocking frame in anger was taken up by a political movement protesting the devaluation of special skills in the industry that were outdated by industrial machinery. Declaring the mythical Ned Ludd their leader, the Luddites signed proclamations and letters with his name, thus assuming an improper identity. In contrast to collective pseudonyms, multi-user names can be exemplified by Robin Hood, a name that was used by different people to steal and redistribute property (Deseriis 2015).

The use of improper names is explained by Deseriis as a spatial practice. Improper names disrupt the spatial order of the police: 'Because the state apparatus produces the subject as a political, epistemological, and biological unit that is always fundamentally *in place*, those subjectivities that cannot properly be located pose a fundamental threat to state power' (Deseriis 2015: 24). By breaking down established boundaries and introducing a disorder of things, improper names create new spaces of becoming:

Because they are open to unforeseen appropriation, improper names imply an opening of closed spaces and a constant subversion of fixed relations ... [B]y making themselves available to unforeseen appropriations, they let the outside slip into the inside, and vice versa. This means that improper names do not designate fixed identities. Rather, they are heterogeneous assemblages in which the whole (the ensemble of an improper name's iterations) is unable to unify and totalize the parts, among which, nevertheless, it establishes relationships and paths of communication.

(Deseriis 2015: 6, 18)

Modes of disidentification through improper names that disrupt the established order generate new potentials of freedom for the democratic subject to explore its multiple self.

However, as the notion of improper names makes clear, the transformative perspective as discussed so far only explains the becoming of *collective* subjectivities. One potential problem in understanding the democratic subject primarily as condividual or multitude rather than as individual is that it presupposes submission to group identity. While the democratic subject is thought here in more morphological terms than in other radical democratic theories, the individual subject has to adjust and adapt to the dynamics of swarms and networked flows. Understanding identity as a product of commoning limits the freedom for the individual subject to self-identify.

The post-anarchist conception of democracy cautions against this danger: 'the revolution against power and authority must involve a micro-political revolution which takes place at the level of the subject's desire' (Newman 2010a: 6). Yet guidance on how to achieve such micro-political revolutions is scarce. I suggest that debates in intersectional and Black queer theory generate fertile ground for a micro revolution that addresses personal desires and identity change. Of course, the democratic subject can never simply constitute itself independently. The whole notion of identification rests on networked affiliations through cognitive associations with other humans, objects, and concepts. In contrast with the notion of subjectivization in the transformative perspective that explains the individual as a part of swarms, collectives, and multitudes, queer theories allow for a focus on individual agency in disidentification. How can hegemonic identity interpellations be rejected in everyday interaction? And how can those identities that define us on a personal level be reworked?

Queering Democratic Subjectivity

Feminist thought has undergone profound changes in the last few decades. This shift is often described as the move from second to third wave feminism. While feminists from the 1960s into the '80s engaged in a fight for sexual liberation through concepts of the female body and female experience as particular (and sometimes superior), from the 1990s onwards feminist debates shifted to poststructuralist concepts that understood identity as a volatile construction. This transition can also be observed in academic labels turning from 'women's studies' to 'gender studies', not only including queer, trans, Black feminist, and intersectional thought, but also broadening their scope through the lenses of masculinity, critical whiteness, and disability studies. Notions of identity politics of second wave feminism were contested by third wave notions of performativity, which describe gender as an active process of doing rather than a fixed state of being.

While second wave feminism has made its way into democratic thought in the debates of difference democrats, third wave feminism and queer and gender studies have hardly been acknowledged by democratic theory (an exception is Lloyd 2005; 2009). In the final section of this chapter, I will employ queer theory, and in particular intersectional and Black queer theory, to explore its transformative potential with two aims in mind. First, I intend to enrich democratic theory with the specific expertise of queer theory in relation to identity change. The radical democratic concept of disidentification will be deepened through an intersectional and Black queer lens and, moreover, supplemented with the notions of masquerade and resignification. Second, queer perspectives will be employed to focus on the micro level of democratic subjectivity to explore the revolution on the level of desires that Newman (2010a) calls for.

Hardt and Negri (2004) acknowledge the potential contribution of queer theory, and particularly the work of Judith Butler, to democratic thought. They position the conceptions of gender performativity in opposition to identity politics to illustrate the multitude as transformative subjectivity: 'Queer politics ... is not really an affirmation of homosexual identities but a subversion of the logics of identity in general. There are no queer bodies, only queer flesh that resides in the communication and collaboration of social conduct' (200). The authors are right in pointing to the subversive potential of queer politics, which goes beyond gay and lesbian liberation. Queering identity denotes an understanding of the self as fugitive, escaping and subverting the heterosexual matrix. However, I disagree with Hardt and Negri's claim that queer politics stands in opposition to identity politics. I rather go along with Butler who suggests that queer morphology and (feminist) identity politics are compatible:

> Although the political discourses that mobilize identity categories tend to cultivate identifications in the service of a political goal, it may be that the persistence of *dis*identification is equally crucial to the rearticulation of democratic contestation. Indeed, it may be precisely through practices which underscore disidentification with those regulatory norms by which sexual difference is materialized that both feminist and queer politics are mobilized.
>
> (Butler 1993: 4)

With Butler, I will argue that it is not about taking sides with either a politics of presence or a politics of becoming, but about their mutual enrichment. If the politics of becoming is understood as the contingent enactment of future selves

(Connolly 1996), as continuously rearticulating a subject-in-process through embodied performances (Lloyd 2005), then there is nothing that makes a politics of presence incompatible with a politics of becoming.

As discussed above, Rancière explains disidentification as the rejection of a name assigned by the police order, as 'an impossible identification' (Rancière 1992: 61). Queer theorist José Esteban Muñoz (1999) conceptualizes disidentification in similar terms, albeit on the level of personal identity. He describes various personal stories of different people located at the intersectional position of queer people of colour struggling to identify as they are being hailed by different identity categories. Disidentification occurs when dominant interpellations fail, which, according to Muñoz, are part of heteronormative, sexist, and racist discourses that stabilize state power and conserve established hierarchies.

Cuban born and raised in the US, Muñoz recounts several incidents when he was drawn to the identity performances of others not associated with his identity group. Transsexual, gay, and female identity performances had an enticing effect. Disidentification, thus, consists not just of the rejection of dominant interpellations, but also of accepting alternative interpellation: 'To disidentify is to read oneself and one's own life narrative in a moment, object, or subject that is not culturally coded to "connect" with the disidentifying subject. It is not to pick and choose what one takes out of an identification' (12). Rather than freely constructing one's own identity at will, the disidentifactory modes of becoming depend on alternative interpellations. This signifies a democratization of identity construction as subjects gain a greater degree of freedom in articulating their multiple selves.

> Disidentification is about recycling and rethinking encoded meaning. The process of disidentification scrambles and reconstructs the encoded message of a cultural text in a fashion that both exposes the encoded message's universalizing and exclusionary machinations and recircuits its workings to account for, include, and empower minority identities and identifications. Thus, disidentification is a step further than cracking open the code of the majority; it proceeds to use this code as a raw material for representing a disempowered politics or positionality that has been rendered unthinkable by the dominant culture. (31)

Marquis Bey's call for *Black Trans Feminism* (2022) opens a more radically transformative perspective. Bey combines blackness as 'a force of transfiguration, of being and becoming otherwise-than' (21) with transness that describes 'gender-self-determination [as] movement toward dissolving given gender ontologies' (24). The Western liberal democratic regime champions transparency. Transparency, however, demands the legibility and surveillance of identity. Identity needs to be made comprehensible, articulated in established terms and expressed through established performances. It needs to be simplified and reduced in order to be read, traced, and recorded by those in power. In contrast, Bey engenders

the democratic potential of opacity. Opacity blocks the dominant gaze and eradicates imposed identities along with the hegemonic structures that conserve
power asymmetries. Without using the term 'disidentification', Bey (2022: 24)
argues for the rejection of hegemonic identities: 'black trans feminist gender self-
determination avows a subjective cultivation of ways to do illegible genders... it
means we advocate for the ethical requisite to say "No"—or better, to decline to
state—with regard to the imposition of gender.' Rejecting assigned identities opens
paths towards the self-determination as 'we, too, *become* through abolishing the
ways we ourselves have been formed' (25).

That disidentification is relevant not just for marginalized people but for everyone becomes clear in the work of Judith Butler. She points to the potential failure
of interpellations of broad categories such as 'woman' or 'man'. Binary gender categories do not acknowledge the wide variety of internal differences within these
groups, so that even those who clearly identify as either of the sexes might feel
unease about the package of preconceptions and expectations that accompany
these categories. In other words, even those who express their identities within
categories of the heterosexual matrix of masculinity, femininity, and attraction to
the opposite sex might disidentify to a certain extent.

In Mouffe's (1995a) terms, one could argue that closure of identity is never
possible because consensus with one's own self about who one is can never be
achieved. The boundaries of personal identity space cannot be closed because the
self remains fugitive. With regards to disidentification, Butler (1993: 219) states:
'it may be that the affirmation of that slippage, that the failure of identification,
is itself the point of departure for a more democratizing affirmation of internal
difference.' Here it becomes clear how queer theory can contribute to a democratization of subjectivity on the individual, rather than a collective level. It advances
the freedom to rework or decrease the significance of collective identities with their
confining tendencies and promotes freedom for the individual subject to live its
inner multiplicity.

> Paradoxically, the failure of such signifiers—'women' is the one that comes to
> mind—fully to describe the constituency they name is precisely what constitutes
> these signifiers as sites of phantasmatic investment and discursive rearticulation.
> It is what opens the signifier to new meanings and new possibilities for political
> resignification. It is this open-ended and performative function of the signifier
> that seems to me to be crucial to a radical democratic notion of futurity. (191)

It is thus not always necessary to create new terms to signify new identities. Rather,
new identities can be expressed through the resignification of established categories. Such practices of resignification can be understood as part of a politics of
becoming. To make sense of resignification, we need to take a step back and look
at the foundations of Butler's work.

While Butler is not a democratic theorist and only occasionally refers to scholarship on democracy, her work on performativity has much to contribute to democratic thought (Lloyd 2005; 2007; 2009; Schippers 2009). Butler's approach is based on a radical deconstructivist ontology, articulated in her famous claim that there is no difference between biological sex and social gender. Rather, sex is constructed, from the moment of the doctor's exclamation: 'It's a boy!' The discourses through which identities are performed depend upon citation and recitation. Subjects can only express themselves in the terms that are already established. Because there is no pre-discursive subject, hegemonic discourse has no origin. Identity, then, is the product of discursive formations, which subjects are born into and constantly reproduce (Butler 1990).

The term 'performativity' draws attention to the naturalized effort it takes to reproduce identity. Butler explains all gender identities as parody and drag. By studying the gender crossings of travesty, she points to the citationality of gender performances. To indicate the imperceptible artificiality of all identity performances, Butler employs the concept of masquerade as a mode of recitation: 'The mask is taken on through the process of incorporation which is a way of inscribing and then wearing a melancholic identification in and on the body, in effect, it is the signification of the body in the mold of the Other' (Butler 1990: 50).

When understanding identity performance as masquerade, what is of interest is how the mask is produced and which freedoms exist or could be expanded in its creation. As the theory of performativity conceptualizes citationality as a pre-established process with no original author, the freedom to author identity seems to be fairly limited. And indeed, Butler clearly rejects interpretations of her work that suggest one is freely able to choose a gender. However, the recognition that performative structures are the product of human interaction also opens up perspectives on the remaking of such structures, which has great significance for democratic theory: 'The terms by which we are recognized as human are socially articulated and changeable ... [They] have far-reaching consequences for how we understand the model of the human entitled to rights or included in the participatory sphere of political deliberation' (Butler 2004: 2). Thus, while the performative structures of citationality in which subjects navigate are limiting, they also provide a space for renegotiation: 'The "I" that I am finds itself at once constituted by norms and dependent on them but also endeavors to live in ways that maintain a critical transformative relation to them' (3).

Through intentional attempts at resignification, the masks that reify identities can be remoulded. This can be exemplified by the reappropriation and positive connotation of derogatory terms originally intended to demean marginalized identities. The term 'queer' is exemplary, which from its original pejorative intention in the late nineteenth century was redefined in activist and academic discourses over the last few decades. Such resignification fulfils its democratic potential if it is the product of an open and participatory process. If so conducted, 'resignification challenges and contests linguistic norms in an everyday setting, opening up a new terrain for transformative struggles and participatory democratic practices' (Schippers 2009: 84).

Butler further argues that the potential for personal autonomy to decide over one's own identity depends upon the institutional settings that facilitate such identity expression:

> Indeed, individuals rely on institutions of social support in order to exercise self-determination with respect to what body and what gender to have and maintain, so that self-determination becomes a plausible concept only in the context of a social world that supports and enables that exercise of agency ... [C]hanging the institutions by which humanly viable choice is established and maintained is a prerequisite for the exercise of self-determination. (Butler 2004: 7)

Here Butler evidently refers to legal arrangements that afford, for example, the registration of a third sex in official documents. When such institutional arrangements are understood in terms of performativity themselves, and thereby as spatial assemblages as suggested in Chapter 2, then we can see how the theory of citationality can explain identity change and institutional change in the same vein. The perpetuation of political institutions, such as the US presidency or the UK Parliament, can be understood in terms of recitation and their reforms and changes as partial resignifications.

In strategies of resignification, the overlaps between difference democratic and the transformative perspective become apparent. The politics of presence stands for the reappropriation and reinterpretation of the terms that denote marginalized identities. What is more, physical presence in the space of appearance goes beyond the reinterpretation of words and reconfigures meaning through the corporeal performance of marginalized identities. The politics of presence, hence, is always part of a politics of becoming.

While Butler's work provides valuable concepts of remaking identity, her affinity with agonistic democracy and its tragic outlook departs from the transformative angle we are interested in here. If the remaking of identity is confined by narrow discursive limits, there is little leeway for democratic transformation. Bey (2022: 12), in contrast, gestures towards: 'an other world that harbors otherwise states of becoming.' Bey responds to Butler's confinements with the concept of abolition. Rather than focusing exclusively on abolishing prison and racial injustice in the incarceration system, abolition more broadly signifies the overcoming of a prison *mentality* that rests on a logic of discipline and punishment. Abolition, then, entails the eradication of all discursive violence that identity imposes. Ultimately, this means overcoming identity as we know it today: 'If we want freedom, we need to free ourselves, too, of the things with which we capture ourselves' (Bey 2022: 12). As the state itself facilitates and is the product of the logic of identitarian violence, abolition calls for the overcoming of state power (22–7). Identity transformation, then, is not an individual or isolated endeavour. The personal disruption of the self, as I will argue in the final chapter, seeds societal transformation.

Conclusion

This chapter has set out to tackle the confining implications of the politics of presence. The dilemma of difference reifies hegemonic identity constructions, impedes self-transformation, and stifles the exploration of different aspects of the multiple self. Difference, participatory, deliberative, and agonistic perspectives provide promising conceptions of self-transformation. However, all of these radical democratic approaches tend to imagine identity change as a guided process that is advanced by elite actors in society. Their transformative potential, moreover, is restricted by the limited societal change that they envision. The chapter suggested a transformative perspective in democratic theory that provides a new vantage point with a focus on systemic transformation. Enriched with queer and gender theories, the transformative perspective articulates a politics of becoming that allows for the imagination of the democratic subject in transformative terms. According to Butler (2004: 4), 'to remake the human' requires an 'interrogation of the terms by which life is constrained in order to open up the possibility of different modes of living.'

Employing a politics of becoming situated in the transformative perspective does not entail opposing the practical mechanisms proposed by difference democrats to realize the politics of presence. Rather, both quotas and identity politics need to be rethought from a perspective of performative identity construction (Mansbridge 2005). By understanding presence as a performative act of becoming, the transformative aspects inherent in the politics of presence become apparent. The Arendtian space of appearance is reconfigured as a space of becoming when situated in the context of transformative democracy. This convergence becomes apparent when Butler (2015: 87) asks: 'is appearance not necessarily a morphological moment ... ?'

But the politics of becoming developed here needs to be interrogated about its own limitations to facilitate freedom for the subject to change. These limitations are due to the poststructuralist ontology that some queer theorists employ. Situating the subject within a tight corset of discursivity only allows for limited stretching, reinterpreting, and rearticulating. The transformative concepts of interruption and disidentification can help to alleviate this problem. The Rancièrian rupture affords a radical break. The fugitive self that always escapes permanent reification through identification and representation expresses different sides of its inherent multiplicity in moments of rupture. The reach of rupture can be further extended by the concept of abolition which seeks to overcome all forms of structural domination, including discursive, identitarian, and state structures (Bey 2022).

Situating these concepts in the spatial theory based on new materialist thinking outlined in Chapter 2 further emphasizes the democratic impetus of the transformative perspective. Understanding spaces and subjects as assemblages allows for thinking rupture as a radical democratic intervention in the order of things. Rather than in the claustrophobic notions of hegemonic discourse that also create the tragic horizon of agonistic democracy, the politics of becoming operates in terms of assembling and reassembling the things that constitute reality. These things are seen not as simply being acted upon as objects, but as agentic products in the making that are themselves continuously becoming (Barad 2008). Their agentic nature constantly reassembles the space of appearance that produces subjects and is produced by subjects in different ways. Instead of navigating through the thicket of discursive structures, we move in spaces constituted by things that can be realigned and remade. This does not denote a break with discursive theory by all means; rather, it denotes a different angle that emphasizes the agency of the subject.

The politics of becoming provides a valuable outlook for rethinking democratic subjectivity in performative terms. However, the question of how disidentification can be engaged with on a practical level remains unanswered. Some fruitful answers can be found in the debates on transformative democracy in terms of critique and deconstruction. Critical discourse analysis of identity constructions can contribute to their denaturalization. While this is a promising approach, Rancière (2007: 569) rightly notes that '[i]t is not so easy to be *un*'. After pointing to the many academic tools of discourse analysis available for deconstructing identity, he asks: 'Are we framing a world of idiots where we play the part of the smart guys?' While deconstruction can also be understood as everyday practice rather than as academic exercise, Rancière makes a valid point. Whether through psychotherapy, meditation, or artistic engagement, gaining a critical distance and decoding everyday identity performances requires resources and effort. So, which practical tools are available that may help to realize radical democratic practices of disidentification? And how can the arrangement of democratic spaces afford such disidentifactory practices?

We find some hints in Rancière's work. Recall that with disidentification Rancière describes how those who do not have a part form a visible collective subject. Subjectivization resulting from disidentification is defined by not having a proper name: 'The name of an injured community that invokes its rights is always the name of the *anonym*' (Rancière 1992: 60, emphasis added). Disidentification produces intentionally wrong names, not with the purpose of deception but as evidently artificial constructs. Hence, in the next chapter I propose anonymity as a potential practice of disidentification. An improper name, a mask, a pseudonym, an online avatar, or even a blank space where a name would be expected evoke alternative democratic subjectivities on both an individual and a collective level. Anonymity interrupts established modes of identification and at the same time creates new improper identities. Such improper identities often afford the expression of otherwise hidden aspects of the multiple self. Anonymity as the disruption of continuous identity performances is often employed to counter surveillance and control by the established order, particularly in the digital age, which I will discuss in Chapter 6. Anonymity reconfigures identity assemblages by bringing things into disorder, altering the configuration of the multiple self. While anonymity should not simply be understood as the realization of disidentification, I propose that it has the *potential* to function as a practical strategy of a politics of becoming.

5

Becoming Anonymous

Absence as Presence

I need to become anonymous. In order to be present.
The more I am anonymous, the more I am present.

Tiqqun 2008

Reflecting on her activity as a guerrilla fighter during the military dictatorship in Brazil from the 1960s into the '80s, the former president of Brazil, Dilma Rousseff, says: 'There is a huge freedom in being anonymous. Immense. Which we had when we were in hiding. That's the thing. The immense feeling of freedom, which I never had again. For a short time.'[1] Rousseff's reflection exhibits several core features of anonymity. Anonymity's main effect is a deeply felt sensation of liberation, a freedom for the subject to change, which is, however, temporarily restricted. In the case of Rousseff, anonymity transformed a faceless, supressed citizen into an empowered freedom fighter. Anonymity can work to make the absent present. This is achieved through an interruption of modes of identification that stabilize the dominant order—whether this order takes the form of a brutal military dictatorship, a neoliberal surveillance state, or the discursive networks of disciplinary identity interpellations we navigate every day. As one strategy of a politics of becoming, not only can anonymity contribute to contesting the political order, but it also liberates the fugitive self. By challenging the integrity and uniformity of the public persona, anonymity sets free inner multiplicity:

In providing the means to belong, simultaneously, to several mental universes, [anonymous action] enables the possibility of playing them out against each other and, in this way, to put to work a process of dis-identification and de-simplification of oneself vis-à-vis institutions: to promote practices that are freer and more selective—more and more emancipated from the psychic hold of external and arbitrary constraints. Thus, we could consider 'anonymity' the term for a technique of desubjugation.

(de Lagasnerie 2017: 72)

---

[1] Interview with Dilma Rousseff in the film documentary *The Edge of Democracy*, 2019, by Petra Costa, Busca Vida Filmes.

The Politics of Becoming. Hans Asenbaum, Oxford University Press. © Hans Asenbaum (2023).
DOI: 10.1093/oso/9780192858870.003.0005

The subversive forces of anonymity as described here rest on modes of identity negation. Anonymity is commonly understood in terms of concealment—as a negative act of detracting or eradicating identity, as effacing the democratic subject. In the established interpretation, anonymity is framed as the opposite of identity. It negates the legally identified, officially registered, and physically embodied persona. It is in this sense that Bey (2022: 10) draws our attention to the radical democratic workings of opacity as 'a tactical evasion that eludes medicalized, biometric, and regulatory frameworks of "knowing" a subject,' as discussed in the previous chapter.

Anonymity, then, appears deeply at odds with the politics of presence as continuous identity articulation in the space of appearance. And indeed, while in some places difference democrats are sympathetic towards anonymity and acknowledge its liberating effects for marginalized groups (Mansbridge 1983: 60–1; Young 1990: 238) and its advancement of meritocracy (Phillips 2015: 35; 2019b: 5), overall they appear sceptical of concealing identity: 'Women should *not* have to present themselves as disembodied abstractions—from behind a curtain that conceals their bodily peculiarities—in order to claim their equal status in the world. Those with dark skins should *not* have to insist on us all being the same "under the skin"' (Phillips 2015: 36). Rather than anonymous participation in voting booths or behind computer screens, the difference democratic perspective calls for corporeal engagement through the physical appearance of diverse bodies (Phillips 1991: 11, 130, 132; 1995: 150).

The sceptical position of difference democrats is also reflected in Butler's discussion of the space of appearance. Butler (2004: 3) acknowledges that concealing identity may have liberating effects for marginalized groups: 'There are advantages of remaining less than intelligible ... [I]f I have no desire to be recognized within a certain set of norms, then it follows that my sense of survival depends upon escaping the clutch of those norms.' This kind of being 'under the radar' denotes a state of not appearing in the public sphere. Butler's space of appearance is demarcated by a clear boundary regime separating a sphere of visibility from a sphere of invisibility. Geoffroy de Lagasnerie pushes this interpretation even further. For him, anonymity is diametrically opposed to the space of appearance. Anonymity breaks with the public sphere. It enacts a secession from the public: 'Anonymous subjects are not subjects who appear. On the contrary, they dissolve as public subjects and organize their own invisibility ... Anonymity, then, enables the field of politics and democracy to be disconnected from the public sphere' (de Lagasnerie 2017: 62–3).

In this chapter, I will oppose this interpretation of anonymity. This understanding of anonymity rests on a long history of public misconception, which stems from a lack of theorization of the term. There are hardly any coherent explanations of anonymity in academic discourses (Gardner 2011; Ponesse 2014). This is particularly evident in democratic theory. It is surprising that while anonymity plays a crucial role in the various modes of democratic participation, such as secret voting, campaign funding, textual political debates in newspapers, manifestos, pamphlets, online political engagement, graffiti, and masked protesting, there is to date no coherent explanation of anonymity in democratic theory. In contrast to this omission (with Moore 2018 and Forestal and Philips 2020 being recent exceptions), there is a plethora of diverse, empirically driven literature discussing anonymity in various forms of democratic engagement. This literature, however, suffers from a lack of theoretical attention to its main subject of research. Eric Barendt's *Anonymous Speech* (2016), for example, discusses anonymity in various forms of political participation but fails to provide a definition of anonymity. The traces of definitions that are to be found in this literature are lacking in crucial respects. Firstly, they fail to acknowledge the complexity of the phenomenon. Many scholars treat the concept of anonymity as simple and self-explanatory. They state, for example, that 'anonymity means that it is impossible to determine who sent which message to whom' (Jonker and Pieters 2010: 216). Secondly, and more importantly, anonymity is often equated with privacy. For instance, when the only definition of anonymity consists of the sentence: 'As a concept anonymity is closely related to free speech and privacy' (Akdeniz 2002: 224). These two interrelated shortcomings—the oversimplified definition of anonymity as privacy—result in a lack of theoretical attention to the complexity of anonymity in a democratic context.

De Lagasnerie's understanding of anonymity as secession from the public sphere thus rests on an understanding of anonymity in negative terms as identity negation and restriction to the private sphere. This is in line with Butler's understanding of the space of appearance as defined by the physically embodied subject stepping into a sphere constituted by the gaze of its spectators. In short, if the subject remains invisible, it does not appear. I contend that this is a misled conclusion. In contrast, I argue that anonymous subjects *do* appear even when their physical bodies remain invisible. Anonymity reconfigures presence as a mode of becoming and, in my reading, is compatible with the difference democratic perspective. What is more, this appearance is public. In contrast to privacy, which demarcates a spatiality shielded from public view, anonymity depends on communication and is thus inherently public. Anonymity, then, is not at all equivalent to privacy. Ponesse claims that 'Anonymity and other techniques of nonidentifiability function as the gatekeepers of the boundary between our private selves and the public domain' (Ponesse 2014: 351). But we need to go further. Anonymity does not only open the door to privacy while leaving the spatial boundaries separating the private and the public sphere intact. It reconfigures the boundaries between public and private spaces by channelling private sentiments into the public sphere. It affords a performance of the private self in public space.

The interpretation of anonymity as identity negation that effaces the subject emerges from an emphasis on public *visibility* as the prime mode of identification. Public identity performance, however, consists of more than the visibility of the physically embodied persona. For instance, it might also entail the perception of sounds, written or spoken words, images, avatars, and blank spaces (see Mendonça, Ercan, and Asenbaum 2020). To be clear, I am not arguing that anonymity is not *also* about (in)visibility. I contend that the visibility of the physically embodied persona is not a condition for appearing in public. Rather than focusing solely on the visibility of the body, to properly understand anonymity we need to focus on the 'sensible manifestation of things' (Dikeç 2015: 2). Instead of mere vision, a focus on *experience* is needed. It is not only through the presence of the visible body but through communication more generally, of which corporeal presence is one mode among many, that subjects appear. This opens up a perspective for understanding presence as a mode of becoming. Presence is actualized through the multimodal expressions of the subject.

The oversight of anonymity's inherently public character is due to the common interpretation of anonymity that focuses on the negative moment of effacing the subject. And indeed disidentification, which is potentially realized through anonymity, does entail rejecting the names assigned to the subject. As the notion of improper names demonstrates, however, disidentification always also entails identity creation. Thus, what is needed is a focus on the constructive moment of anonymity as public articulation. In Mouffe's words: 'to construct oppositional identities it is not enough to simply foster a process of "de-identification" or "de-individualization". The second move, the moment of "re-identification", of "re-individualization" is decisive' (Mouffe 2006: 5). Anonymity's double move of identity negation and creation is well explained by the concept of representation. As mentioned in Chapter 3, representation, according to Hanna Pitkin (1967: 8–9), makes present what is physically absent. I will argue that anonymity as an interruption of the dominant spatial order takes this logic further. This can also be explained with Laclau and Mouffe's (1985) concept of the constitutive outside discussed in Chapter 2. The definition of the inside by the absence of the outside makes the outside present (see Butler 2015: 4–5). Woman is defined as 'not-man' and straight is defined as not queer. In this sense, anonymity makes present what is absent. It affords experiences of sides of the multiple self that are not represented in the official version of the self. Anonymity enlarges the identity space, in which the democratic subject navigates a set of possible identifications.

While it may appear that this assessment adopts an overly optimistic view on anonymity, this chapter will also account for the undemocratic aspects of anonymity in democratic spaces. Owing to the inherently contradictory character of anonymity's core functions of identity negation and identity creation, and its quality of reconfiguring private and public space, anonymity causes deeply ambivalent effects for democracy. Exploring the workings of anonymity in various democratic spaces will show that anonymity affords both inclusion and exclusion, subversion and submission, and honesty and deception. While anonymity thus has both democratic and undemocratic effects, all of these effects, I will argue, are liberating for the democratic subject. John Suler (2004) describes anonymous online communication as inherently disinhibiting, freeing the subject of social constraints—for better or worse. Even if the subject engages in exclusion, submission, and deception, the subject itself does so because anonymity loosens its constraints. In the words of Paulo Freire, anonymity affords 'the "freedom" to oppress' (Freire 2005 [1907]: 46). In this way, anonymity always enlarges the free space in which the democratic subject can act. I arrive at this understanding by conceptualizing anonymity not in terms of negative liberty, which protects individuals from unwanted intrusions. It is this negative understanding of freedom that goes along with a focus on identity negation, equating anonymity with privacy. Rather, freedom needs to be understood as the positive liberty to act. Freedom enables action (Fromm 1941; Berlin 1969 [1958]) with both positive and negative consequences for others.

I develop this concept of anonymity and elucidate its affordances in two steps. First, I review etymologies and conceptualizations of anonymity and their relation to privacy in various academic disciplines. Both their merits and shortcomings provide inspiration for the new definition of anonymity rooted in democratic theory to be developed here. Second, the chapter turns to empirical studies on anonymity in democratic spaces. It briefly describes anonymity in voting, campaign funding, textual political discussions, and masked protesting. It then identifies anonymity's three sets of contradictory freedoms, offering illustrations from the empirical literature on democratic engagement. The section thereafter explores the context of anonymous engagement. The form that anonymity takes, I will argue, depends on the materiality of the communicative infrastructure, the power relations between participants, and the constellation of identity knowledge. In the conclusion, I deepen the theoretical conceptualization of anonymity in contrast to privacy.

What is Anonymity?

The etymological development of the term 'anonymity' is characterized by a continuous expansion of meaning. To trace this development, I bring together three sets of literature, moving from literary studies to computer science—which each describe anonymity in a specific context—and finally to more general elaborations of anonymity in communication studies, sociology, political science, and philosophy. The same expansionary development of meaning can be observed in the use of the term 'privacy'. The expansions of both 'anonymity' and 'privacy' coalesce with the development of new communication technologies, resulting in their overlapping and partial convergence. The task undertaken here of developing a definition of anonymity rooted in democratic theory consists of disentangling anonymity and privacy.

The term 'anonymous' entered the English language in the late sixteenth century, referring to publications whose authors remained unknown. While the meaning of the Greek original, which translates to 'nameless', is already quite confined, its meaning in English became even more narrow: 'Anonymity [was] defined broadly as the absence of reference to the legal name of the writer on the title page' (Griffin 1999: 882; also see Kopley 2016: 2). 'Anonymity' thus did not refer to any kind of unidentified communication, but solely to nameless textual publications (Ferry 2002). The practice of anonymous publishing was common even before this time. It was only then, however, that the blank spaces on pamphlets, poems, and books were replaced by the word 'Anonymous'. The question arises as to why the blank space was not simply left blank but filled with the name-like 'Anonymous'. This move appears to be a collective effort to draw attention to the author's unknown identity and their conscious decision to remain unidentified. In the linguistic establishment of 'anonymity' we thus find the first traces of identity creation rather than solely identity negation. Here 'Anonymous' begins to function as an improper name (Deseriis 2015), as a nascent form of identity rearticulation (Mouffe 2006), which, as I will argue later, is a core element of anonymity.

Current conceptualizations of anonymity in computer science and technology studies illustrate the significant qualitative shift that the term has undergone through the emergence of digital communication. The nameless author now becomes the unidentified communicator. The recipient of a message perceives 'all subjects in the anonymity set as equally probable of being the originator of a message' (Diaz et al. 2003: 57). This literature acknowledges the complexities of anonymity as part of a communicative process that goes beyond textual publication. Moreover, it insists on the scalability of anonymity. Anonymity is not a state that is present or not, but a matter of degree to be measured on a scale between two opposing poles: anonymity and identity. To acknowledge the different degrees of anonymity, this literature introduces not only quantitative measures, but different types of anonymity, specifically insisting on its demarcation from 'pseudonymity': the use of pseudonyms in contrast with communication without any identifier (Pfitzmann and Hansen 2010).

This qualitative shift in anonymity's meaning, expressed in quite technical terms in computer science and technology studies, is also recognized in sociology, political science, communications studies, and philosophy. Exceeding definitions of anonymity in literary publications and online communication, the humanities and social sciences generate more complex understandings of anonymity as a social phenomenon both online and offline. Anonymity is defined not as an objective state, but as a matter of degree that depends on subjective perception and intersubjective communication (Scott 1998; Thiel 2017). In contrast with the established perception of the anonymous individual as coherent unity, the humanities and social sciences draw attention to the plethora of identity markers that define a person (G. Marx 1999; Nissenbaum 1999; Wallace 1999; Véliz 2018). While for anonymous textual publishing the name was the sole identifier, in today's information age and in light of increasingly complex understandings of anonymity, factors such as location (address), social security numbers, looks, identity categories (race, class, gender), profession, family relations, etc. comprise a set of highly diverse identifiers that constitute a person. Accordingly, anonymity is defined as the non-identifiability of one or several of these traits (Marx 1999), 'the noncoordinability of traits' (Wallace 1999: 24), and the inability to 'join the dots' (Véliz 2018: 2).

Nissenbaum (1999: 143) describes anonymity as unreachability: 'Deepening our understanding of the issue of anonymity in an information age ... requires an appreciation of what it takes to be "unreachable" or "out of grasp" in a world where technologies of knowledge and information are increasingly efficacious at reaching, grasping, and identifying.' In a similar vein, anonymity is defined as 'a suite of techniques of nonidentifiability that persons use to manage and protect their privacy. At the core of these techniques is the aim of being untrackable' (Matthews 2010: 351). And Moore (2018) names a lack of traceability as one core dimension of anonymity.

But if anonymity means unreachability, untrackability, or untraceability, how is it different from privacy, which can be broadly understood as a personal sphere protected from external intrusion? In the information age, the meanings of anonymity as one's personal identity being undetectable in a communicative network and privacy as personal information being undetectable in a communicative network become virtually indistinguishable. The term 'privacy' has undergone an expansion similar to that of anonymity (see Westin 1984). Its original meaning in the work of Ancient philosophers such as Aristotle and Plato referred to private property as objects under personal control (Papacharissi 2010: 27). In its modern sense, the term 'privacy' was first used by Warren and Brandeis in 1890 as 'the right to be let alone'. When newspapers—at the time of the emergence of the printing press in Europe and the US—started publishing details about the lives of public persons, this was perceived as an intrusion into their personal affairs. This notion of privacy, thus, constitutes a sphere that is shielded from outside intervention. Privacy in this version has not lost its original meaning of ownership, as the private sphere is characterized by its control by the individual subject (Reiman 1976). It relies on a physical demarcation of space, distinguishing between private locations (such as the home) and public locations (such as cafés, squares, etc.). It is this demarcation of private and public space in the context of patriarchal modes of domination that has been aptly criticized by feminist scholars (Wagner Decew 2015).

This physical geography is upset by new forms of communication. The public/private dichotomy appears to be collapsing as new online spaces are both 'privately public and publicly private' (Papacharissi 2010: 142). Public digital communication relies on websites run by private companies, with participants located in private homes. To grasp this new hybridity, Nissenbaum (1997; 2010) develops the concept of 'privacy in public'. The individual's control over who has access to personal information is compromised by governmental surveillance and commercial data mining. This new understanding of privacy still contains original elements of personal control and the demarcation of a sphere to be left alone. It is uprooted, however, by the physical dislocation of this sphere. Privacy becomes mobile.

This brief review explains why and how the terms anonymity and privacy overlap. Their parallel expansion in meaning has peaked following their digitization, resulting in overlapping and blurred understandings. Hence, a new understanding of anonymity has to not only overcome this amalgamation, but also confront several other key challenges.

Current discussions successfully deepen the understanding of anonymity by explaining it as subjective, a matter of degree, depending on various identifiers, and resulting in several types of anonymity. However, these definitions suffer, first, from their conceptualization of anonymity as mere identity negation, neglecting the possibilities of identity creation. This is observable in the use of terms such as unidentifiability, unknowability, undetectability, unreachability, untrackability, untraceability, and noncoordinability. These terms suggest that anonymity marks the impossibility of communicators being identified by the audience, rather than as an action undertaken by communicators themselves. The sole focus on identity negation is also evident when anonymity is defined as the opposite of identity. This is another reason why anonymity and privacy appear to be so closely related. When anonymity is conceptualized as concealing identity and privacy is seen as restricting access to personal information, they are hardly distinguishable. Second, the terms employed to describe anonymity do not coincidently share the suffix -ity, which indicates that they are conceptualized as a state rather than as a process. And third, the differentiation of types of anonymity is helpful to a certain extent. But terms such as 'pseudonymity', 'physical anonymity', 'discursive anonymity', 'offline anonymity', 'online anonymity', 'self-anonymity', 'other-anonymity' (Scott 1999), 'agent anonymity', 'recipient anonymity', and 'process anonymity' (Wallace 1999) can lead to confusion and overcomplication. A new definition of anonymity must provide clarity and, at the same time, encompass these various subtypes.

I generate this new definition of anonymity by employing the concepts of democratic space and positive freedom. First, current understandings of anonymity as closely related to privacy emerge from concerns over the infringement of civil rights. The association of anonymity with privacy results in defensiveness. Anonymity is related to the private spaces that shield one from public intrusion. A focus on the spaces that form the context of anonymity, however, makes clear that anonymity does not describe a sphere shielded from engagement with others. On the contrary, anonymity is inherently communicative. It is not primarily a matter of hiding in isolated spaces, but rather one of showing, exchanging opinions, and creating identities in common spaces. *Anonymity is a mode of presence.* It articulates the self in the public sphere. Anonymous identity performances cross the boundaries between public and private, channelling content from the private into the public sphere. The anonymous subject steps into the space of appearance by making itself perceptible through an aesthetic self-formation in vocalized or written words, through physical body language or digitized symbols and images.

Second, the inherently liberating effects of anonymity as unidentifiability have been conceptualized as negative freedoms, freedoms to be protected from external intrusion. Again, the overlap with privacy is all too apparent. However, I suggest that we also need to take into account positive freedoms, freedoms to act: 'anonymity functions to increase an individual's agency ... Being anonymous widens the sphere of possible action' (Ponesse 2014: 312). Thus, while privacy is closely related to negative freedoms protecting from intrusion, anonymity also relates to positive freedoms of expression and identity creation.

Since the original conceptualization of negative and positive freedoms by Erich Fromm (1941) and later Isaiah Berlin (1969 [1958]), critics have contended that the two cannot be easily demarcated, since every freedom contains both positive and negative aspects (MacCallum 1967; Blau 2004). I agree with and build upon this critique by drawing attention to the positive freedoms of anonymity that add to its negative freedoms of concealment. Thus, while anonymity in current debates is conceptualized as the impossibility of interlocutors to identify the subject, I define anonymity as the self-expression of the democratic subject. Anonymity is not the opposite of identity; it is a precondition for creating identity in a freer manner, drawing on both positive and negative freedoms. Anonymity allows the subject to assemble in new ways.

In my view, the established definition, which understands anonymity in purely negative terms—as a technique to protect privacy—misses the point. Here Moore's (2018) work is helpful since it defines anonymity not only in terms of lacking traceability but also in positive terms of durability and connectedness, which points to newly created identities. But I also believe that there is indeed a negative moment in anonymity. This moment of dissociation constitutes an interruption of established modes of identification. The interruption that facilitates the negative freedom not to be detected by dominant forces, however, can only be understood in direct relation with the positive freedom of exploring the multiple self. Our understanding of anonymity, as Mouffe (2006) aptly points out with regard to disidentification, should not linger in the moment of disarticulation; rather, it needs to focus on rearticulation. It is the interruption of identification that frees the fugitive self to explore its multiplicity. The gap that this interruption opens up provides an empty space that enables the experience of lack at the core of the subject (Mouffe 1995b). On the basis of this lack, new identities are articulated in anonymous engagements that afford presence in the space of appearance.

I therefore define anonymity as follows:

Anonymity is a context-dependent mode of presence. It enables the subject to express private content in the public sphere by negating some aspects of the legally identified and/or physically embodied persona.

Unlike previous definitions, the above definition gives priority to the creative and constructive aspects of anonymity, while not neglecting its negating aspects. Moreover, it defines anonymity as a public, communicative process, rather than as a private state, stressing its performative and agentic nature. And finally, it is broad enough to encompass various subtypes, both providing unity and allowing for differentiations, which will be further elaborated in the final section of this chapter. The following sections will investigate the workings of anonymity in various democratic spaces and illustrate how its positive freedoms both advance and undermine democracy.

Anonymity in Democratic Spaces

Anonymity plays a key role in different modes of democratic engagement. In what follows, I briefly outline anonymous (a) voting, (b) campaign funding, (c) textual political discussions, and (d) masked protest. In comparison with the democratic spaces discussed so far, anonymous spaces have a more decentred character. The interruptive moment of anonymity mediated through interfaces such as computer screens, avatars, sheets of paper, and walls often entails asynchronicity. Anonymous textual discussions via political pamphlets, letters to the editor, graffiti, or online forums connect participants by providing a common forum for content, but without assembling them physically at the same time in the same place. Synchronous anonymous interaction, on the other hand, entails the geographical separation of interacting participants, for example in online chats. Whether synchronous or asynchronous, anonymity does not depend on a common physical location but creates a common discursive space. Through anonymous participation, then, decentred kinds of democratic spaces emerge. Anonymous democratic spaces are more amorphous. As spaces of becoming, they free the fugitive self.

Voting as the central mode of participation in representative democracies is in its current form strongly linked to the notion of anonymity. However, the correlation between anonymity and voting is a relatively recent phenomenon. Open voting either by voice, raising of hands, or on a visually identifiable ballot provided by different parties in different colours was the common practice in the US for more than 100 years from its constitutional founding in 1789. Under these circumstances, political parties heavily influenced voting behaviour either by threat or patronage. This was the reasoning behind introducing the secret ballot in the

US and the UK in the late nineteenth century (Gardner 2011: 942; Barendt 2016: 156). The opposite legal trend to voting procedures, from anonymity to public identification, occurred in the case of private campaign contributions. In the late twentieth century, the US introduced requirements for the mandatory disclosure of financial contributions to candidates and political parties that exceeded a certain threshold (Gardner 2011: 944). Nevertheless, anonymity is still in place in most countries for donations below a certain amount.

Anonymity in textual political discussions as mode of democratic participation takes at least three forms: the publication of political texts, graffiti, and online communication. First, anonymity played a crucial role in circulating political pamphlets and articles as exemplified by the political controversy between Federalists and Anti-Federalists in the debate over the US Constitution in 1787. The use of pseudonyms was essential in this debate and built on a long European tradition of anonymous publishing (Smith Ekstrand and Imfeld Jeyaram 2011). Second, anonymity is a core feature of graffiti and street art. Studies of one American and one Australian university campus (Rodriguez and Clair 1999; Butler 2006) demonstrate that bathroom graffiti appear as extensive dialogues between students who negotiate their gender, sexuality, race, and political views. Third, the medium of bathroom walls is surprisingly comparable to online forums. Participants post messages and check back at a later date to see if someone has responded. With the advent of the internet, textually anonymous discussions have become more prevalent, with increasing publication speed and reach, as well as reduced costs (Akdeniz 2002; Woo 2006; Gardner 2011; Leitner 2015). While asynchronous posts in online forums are reminiscent of anonymous political writings from the eighteenth century and bathroom wall graffiti, real-time chats make political writing more akin to live discussions.

Masked protest used by both progressive and reactionary social movements is another mode of anonymous participation. Progressive movements use masking to turn demonstrations into street parties with clownesque performances, street theatre, and carnivalesque tactics of disguise (Bruner 2005; Morris 2012; Ruiz 2013; Spiegel 2015). An example can be seen in the Russian feminist collective Pussy Riot, who performed their 'Punk Prayer' at Moscow's Cathedral of Christ the Saviour in 2012. Three of the five women, who used colourful balaclavas to mask their faces, were arrested and jailed. A global movement in solidarity with Pussy Riot re-enacted the mockery of authority, taking on the colourful balaclavas as their symbol. This form of democratic participation builds on carnival traditions that date back to Ancient Rome. Medieval carnival was more political than its commercialized reprisals today. The tradition of people taking to the streets in disguise was used to challenge authorities through mockery and to enact a reversal of social hierarchies (Bruner 2005). Similar practices of masking are used in online protest by hacktivist groups such as Anonymous who uses online anonymity to promote freedom of speech and social justice (Coleman 2014; Asenbaum 2018). The Black

Lives Matter movement uses the guise of hoods to enact solidarity with victims of hate crimes and police brutality who are criminalized because of wearing hoodies. The 'Million Hoodie March' can be read as a proud reclaiming of a marginalized race/class identity (Nguyen 2015; Kinney 2016). On the other side of the political spectrum, the Ku Klux Klan uses anonymity to enact white racial homogeneity through uniform white hoods. Emerging in 1865 in the US South, the KKK fast became the largest and most influential white supremacist movement (Blee and McDowell 2013). This example also illustrates that anonymous hate crimes predate the internet. The connectivity and reach of the KKK is, however, amplified today by the use of online communication (Schmitz 2016).

While anonymous voting, campaign funding, textual political discussions, and masked protest appear as quite distinct forms of participation, the discussion of the freedoms afforded by anonymity in the following section reveals some surprising similarities. Despite their diversity, all of these modes of political engagement form democratic spaces. They are configured differently by the different constellations of material objects, sentient bodies, and performative expressions which constitute democratic space.

Anonymity's Contradictory Freedoms

The starting point for developing a more complex understanding of anonymity, one that goes beyond merely equating it with privacy, is the observation that anonymity not only facilitates identity negation, but also affords identity creation. Sociologists such as Erving Goffman (1956) pointed out decades ago that new identities are constructed on the foundation of the identity hidden through anonymity. Goffman explains these identity performances in spatial terms. Subjects act on front stages and back stages. Through this terminology, we can observe how anonymity channels private selves from the backstage to the public front stage. The mask—be it physical or virtual—serves both the negation and creation of identity.

In democratic engagement, identity negation appears necessary in the face of various repressive forces in society. Anonymity affords negative freedom—it serves as a means of becoming invisible and avoiding detection. In online communication 'anonymity enables users to prevent surveillance and monitoring of their activities on the internet from commercial companies and from the government' (Akdeniz 2002: 233). Yet, identity negation protects not only from interference by state and economic actors, but also from peer pressure by family, friends, and colleagues. The secret ballot was introduced in the late nineteenth century in the US and the UK not just to protect workers from their employers; the voting booth also proved especially important to women gaining suffrage in the early and mid-twentieth century as it shielded them from the influence of husbands and fathers

(Barendt 2016: 156). This negative moment inherent to anonymity interrupts identification. It protects the subject from external interference through a reconfiguration of space by employing physical things such as voting booths, masks, and computer screens, or discursive things such as pseudonyms, improper names, and blank spaces.

The moment of identity negation in democratic spaces is followed by a creative moment in which new imaginaries and alternative personae emerge: 'the mask does not negate identity; instead it signifies the possibility of a multiplicity of identities ... It suggests a way of thinking about blankness as a means not only of erasing difference but also as a means of articulating difference' (Ruiz 2013: 2275). Anonymity bestows democratic subjects with the ability to reinvent their appearance and thus to influence their perception by others, be it through wearing a mask, creating a pseudonym, designing an avatar, or narrating the self through text. Masked protest in claimed spaces, for example, often has liberating effects and enables a playful experimentation with a diversity of identities. As Mikhail Bakhtin puts it, 'The mask is connected with the joy of change and reincarnation, with gay relativity and merry negation of uniformity and similarity; it *rejects conformity to oneself*' (Bakhtin 1968: 39, emphasis added).

Based on this core contradiction of identity negation and creation as anonymity's founding elements, three sets of contradictory freedoms emerge, each consisting of one element advancing and the other undermining democracy. Anonymity in democratic spaces serves (a) inclusion and exclusion, (b) subversion and submission, and (c) honesty and deception.

Inclusion and Exclusion

Nowhere is the ambivalent character of anonymity so clear as in the discussion of inclusion and exclusion. On the one hand, anonymity reconfigures democratic spaces by levelling the playing field. It strips away identity markers, thus flattening hierarchies and generating more inclusive democratic spaces. On the other hand, anonymous interaction often exhibits attacks on marginalized social groups in an attempt to exclude those deemed as inferior. This exacerbates internal hierarchies and bolsters the boundaries of democratic spaces.

Inclusion. The common argument for the equalizing effect of anonymity claims that social hierarchies are suspended—or at least that their effects are mitigated—by concealing visible markers of gender, race, class, sexuality, disability, age, and so on, thus contributing to inclusion. Because of its inherent anonymity, cyberspace, for example 'represents a sphere of existence free from (or at least freer from) socio-economic inequalities and social constraints. Without the ex-ante requirement of self-identification, individuals can equally share in the personal freedom to choose how to express themselves, including whether and how to self-identify' (Leitner 2015: 167).

Similarly, among those who participate in bathroom graffiti, anonymity structurally impedes discrimination along visual identity markers. While identity clues might persist in writing, physically embodied signifiers of social status are suspended: 'graffiti level the playing field by getting past all of the factors—such as social status, hierarchical position, education, access, familiarity with rules, expertise, communication competence—that advantageously privilege and benefit certain members against others' (Rodriguez and Clair 1999: 2). The same argument is made by activists in the Pussy Riot movement who cover their faces to enact equality: 'We are anonymous because we act against any personality cult, against hierarchies implied by appearance, age and other visible social attributes. We cover our heads because we oppose the very idea of using female faces as a trademark for promoting any sort of goods or services' (cited in Groeneveld 2015: 10).

These equalizing effects of anonymity result in meritocracy. While in non-anonymous settings identity markers indicating the status of the speaker influence the perception of what is said, anonymous communication can only be judged by the value of its content. Anonymity also blinds the Greek goddess Justicia so she cannot discriminate between subjects and all are equal in front of the law. A student participating in bathroom graffiti explains: 'I like toilet walls because there's no identity. Because if you knew who wrote it, you could think "oh, I don't like that person, I'm not going to respond well to what they said", but if you don't know who wrote it, you're going to respond with whatever you think is the best response' (cited in Butler 2006: 23). This argument is curiously echoed in the US constitutional debate. Melancton Smith, writing under the pseudonym Plebeian, claimed that arguments should be judged 'on their own merits. If it be good, it stands not in need of great men's names to support it. If it be bad, their names ought not to sanction it' (cited in Smith Ekstrand and Imfeld Jeyaram 2011: 46).

The principle of meritocracy is also at the centre of both the ideology and practices of Anonymous. The hacktivist collective originated on the image board 4chan and its sub-board /b/, where mostly young North Americans share and discuss digital images with complete anonymity. 'With no method of individual identity verification, /b/ becomes a community made up of non-persistent individual identities. When you post on /b/, nobody can prejudge you based on your looks, age, wealth, status, or style. They only have your words' (Wesch 2012: 92–3). The ephemerality of the site, with every post expiring as new posts appear, can be interpreted in terms of a critique of digital archiving and monitoring. Anonymous functions as antitheses to the Facebook culture of naming, liking, and tagging, which connects value to the persona and not the content, and creates an archive easily abused for surveillance (Cambre 2014: 305; McDonald 2015: 979). Hence,

'Anonymous ... is an ontological shift on the terrain of identity at the very moment that identity has become the highest form of selection and exploitation in cognitive capitalism, the first glimpse of life without identity on the Internet' (Halpin 2012: 19).

Anonymity's ability to destabilize capitalist hierarchies by countering personality cults is also reflected in masked protest (Morris 2012; Ruiz 2013). Social movements' claimed spaces position themselves in opposition to capitalist inequality as places of horizontality, reciprocity, and solidarity. The movement itself appears as a democratic utopia, as in the transformative perspective outlined in the previous chapter. This inclusive agenda is expressed in inclusive identity frames as expressed by the slogans of the Occupy movement 'We are the 99%', Anonymous 'We are Anonymous, We are Legion', the Pussy Riot movement 'We are all Pussy Riot', the Black Lives Matter movement, 'We are all Trayvon Martin', and the Zapatistas 'We are you'. All these slogans begin with self-definitions rather than political claims. They rearticulate a common identity based on the de-articulation of individual identity (Mouffe 2006) and engage in modes of subjectivization through improper names (Rancière 1999; Deseriis 2015). The identification 'We are' is then followed by a broad, inclusive term. The 'We' is constructed as an inclusive space for (almost) everyone. Thus, not only the negation of hierarchizing identity markers, but also the creation of new collective identities in insurrectional spaces (Newman 2011) can lead to inclusion: 'the mask creates a space that can be occupied by those who perceive themselves to be excluded' (Ruiz 2013: 274).

Exclusion. The freedom to dominate, oppress, and exclude is facilitated by anonymity when identity negation is used to avoid accountability and discriminate against those whose positions are marginalized within society resulting in both internal and external exclusion (Young 2000). Internal exclusion within democratic spaces through a devaluation of participants with marginalized identities results from disinhibited misogynist, racist, homophobic, or other discriminatory utterances. Although all are unknown to each other within anonymous democratic spaces, insults automatically find their addressees as social hierarchies existing outside the discursive setting are replicated and potentially exacerbated.

The phenomena of hate speech and 'flaming', which are largely discussed today in the context of online anonymity, were also well known to participants in the US constitutional debate. Addressing insults to each other's pseudonyms, Federalists and Anti-Federalists used terms such as 'ignorant loggerhead' and 'ungrateful monster' to degrade their opponent: 'An onslaught of sparring and often libellous remarks appeared in newspapers and pamphlets ... The absence of an author's true identity, however, did not spare anonymous authors from attack and may have indeed made such attacks easier' (Smith Ekstrand and Imfeld Jeyaram 2011: 39, 43).

Hate speech is also a central feature of bathroom graffiti on university campuses. Graffiti is often used as an outlet for suppressed anger by those on the top of social hierarchies: 'dominant groups—especially white heterosexual men—use the open nature of graffiti to intimidate and "discipline" minority groups'. Graffiti may 'establish or reinforce the privileging aspects of patriarchal practice, thus, supporting the hegemonic order' (Rodriguez and Clair 1999: 3).

The Ku Klux Klan represents a telling example of external exclusion through anonymity. Here, anonymity is used in an attempt to cast those with marginalized identities out of democratic spaces in order to construct a homogenous cultural and racial space. The most appalling use of anonymity can be observed in racist hate crimes and the murder of African Americans in the 1920s (Blee and McDowell 2013). In these cases, masking was used in public lynchings to avoid detection. Today the KKK disseminate their ideology of white supremacy via social media (Schmitz 2016). The goal of propagating hate is to expel particular ethnic groups who are perceived as a threat to the white culturally cognate community. The example of the KKK illustrates not only how identity negation can be used for exclusion, but also identity creation. The ghost-like figures created on the basis of anonymity are meant to intimidate their victims. Moreover, this attire also establishes internal hierarchies. While collective actors such as Occupy, Pussy Riot, and Anonymous use the mask to enact internal equality, the KKK employs a system of attire that expresses difference in social status between Klan members (Blee and McDowell 2013). The equalizing effects of the hood are countered by different coloured robes, stripes, and decorations enacting hierarchy.

The freedom to exclude facilitated by anonymity does not always take the form of discrimination of marginalized groups. It can also be observed wherever those in privileged social positions, such as economic elites or state actors, employ anonymity to amplify power imbalances. In many countries, riot police concerned with maintaining public order at demonstrations and protests increasingly appear masked. While these black masks, either in the form of balaclavas or gas masks, serve physical protection, they also fulfil the dual function of anonymity: negating and creating identity. First, by concealing identity police evade personal identification and avoid public scrutiny. This is accompanied by trends of police refusing to wear their badge numbers and restricting civilians from filming their actions, which is most frequently observed in the context of police brutality against ethnic minorities (Spiegel 2015). Second, anonymity also allows police to construct menacing personae. Riot police uniforms are akin to soldiers' military gear, evoking the image of an army at war. While the camouflage of military uniforms is meant to allow soldiers to disappear, the black police uniforms signal presence, threat, and unity.

The power imbalance between anonymous police and demonstrators in claimed spaces is amplified by bans on face coverings in public gatherings. The Canadian federal ban on masks of 2012, for example, punishes mask wearing with up to ten years' imprisonment. Here the original logic of liberal democracies making state actors identifiable to be held accountable and simultaneously upholding citizens' right to privacy is inverted:

> In the United States, cases of individuals arrested and charged for filming police officers multiply, while high-profile cases such as those of Chelsea Manning and Edward Snowden, both charged with breaching national security for exposing to the American people state documents concerning American government activity, further anchor the asymmetrical logic of coding and surveilling individuals while *obscuring* the actions of public forces that, in principle, serve and answer to these same individuals.
>
> (Spiegel 2015: 791–2)

The internet amplifies the possibilities of surveillance as Woo elaborates: 'users' identities have become increasingly exposed, while the subject of surveillance and their activities have become less identifiable. Therefore, the major impetus for the power imbalance between the subject and the object of surveillance in the network is their differences in identifiability' (Woo 2006: 961).

This imbalance of invisible power holders and the identified citizens can also be seen when economic actors influence the legislative process through lobbying, corruption, and campaign and party funding. Where there are no transparency laws in place requiring the identification of donors, anonymous financial contributions establish secret connections between the donor and the candidate or party. Although the donors are known to the beneficiary, they remain unknown to the public. While in clear cases of corruption the donation is tied to explicit political demands, in less explicit cases the beneficiary might act in the donor's interest in the expectation of further donations. Such concerns were raised in 1997 when the British Labour government proposed to exempt motor racing from a ban on tobacco advertising shortly after the Labour Party received a £1 million donation from business magnate and Formula One chief executive, Bernie Ecclestone (Barendt 2016: 163). Thus, anonymous party financing can distort democratic legislative processes, which translates economic inequality into political domination.

Subversion and Submission

By allowing dissidents and marginalized groups to avoid detection (identity negation) and to form new collective identities through improper names (identity creation), anonymity facilitates the contestation of hegemonic power structures. Simultaneously, however, anonymity evokes conformist tendencies when anonymous participants give up individual beliefs and critical thinking in exchange for a feeling of belonging to a community. Anonymity, thus, facilitates both subversion and submission.

Subversion. Some of the most influential texts contesting political power relations that are today clearly attributed to their authors were originally published anonymously, such as Thomas Paine's *Common Sense* attacking the English government published in 1776 by 'an Englishman'. *The Communist Manifesto* by Karl Marx and Friedrich Engels, calling for a proletarian revolution, was first published anonymously in 1848 and only attributed to its authors more than two decades later.

The importance of anonymity for subversion has remained ever since. Neoliberal developments of commodification and surveillance create a political context in which anonymity becomes an empowering tool:

> Anonymity is not only a politically-motivated response to the encroachments of data-gathering devices and the bioinformatics that underwrite the impersonal efficiency of contemporary biopolitical control societies. It is also an aesthetic revolt against the era of navel-gazing narcissism that has hypnotized the subject of these regimes ... A form of resistance to the State, then, is to eliminate its access to its economic subjects by scrambling the informatics networks it uses to delineate, organize and manage them, effectively de-activating oneself as a political subject.
>
> (Morris 2012: 110)

Whistleblowing, for example, is a subversive practice in which individuals 'leak' information about illegal or immoral actions from an insider perspective (Barendt 2016: 75). WikiLeaks, one of the most prominent examples, provides a website for the anonymous publication of information on US governmental wrongdoings. In 2010, Bradley/Chelsea Manning, a soldier in gender transition, leaked to the public the largest amount of classified military and diplomatic material in US history via WikiLeaks and other channels, exposing human rights violations such as the purposeful killing of civilians by the US military in Iraq and Afghanistan (de Lagasnerie 2017). The story of WikiLeaks appears at the centre of a global cultural rupture of identity reconfigurations. The anonymity of its whistleblowing practices contrasts dramatically with the celebrity status of Julian Assange, its public face overshadowing the drama of Manning, a young person searching for a new gender identity between army barracks and prison walls.

WikiLeaks is part of a broader 'freedom of information movement' (Beyer 2014b; McCarthy 2015; Coleman 2019), evolving from the hacker counter culture that upholds the principle of free speech and open source. Political groups such as the Pirate Party derive their name from the notion of online piracy, consisting of stealing and publicly sharing digital private property. Anonymous is another actor in the freedom of information movement that engages in the practices of hacking and leaking. It is most notorious for its Distributed Denial of Service Attacks (DDoS), making their opponents' websites inaccessible by flooding them with access requests. This tactic is often equated with analogue forms of claiming space such as sit-ins or occupations. Anonymous illustrates how employing anonymity enables some 'computer nerds' to inflict serious harm on powerful institutions such as the Church of Scientology, Visa and MasterCard, and governments around the world (Asenbaum 2018).

The mask becomes a common focal point of diverse movements contesting practices of identification and surveillance. What the Guy Fawkes mask is for Anonymous, the colourful balaclava is for the Pussy Riot movement. In contrast to the white-faced, bearded man who is associated with the digital culture of disembodiment and Western reason, the hand-knit balaclavas in different colours enact physical embodiment, femininity, cultural diversity, and passion much in the spirit of difference democracy (see Chapter 3). This contrast between Pussy Riot and Anonymous shows how Pussy Riot's performative interventions are deeply rooted in a feminist contestation of patriarchy. Pussy Riot's 'Punk Prayer' directly attacked Vladimir Putin's government and the Russian Orthodox Church—the two centres of patriarchal rule in Russia. This act of anonymous subversion aims to reappropriate established spaces of power:

> The spectacle of brightly colored balaclavas on the five women standing on the altar of a sacred but also fraught religious space not only occupies space but offers an example of the new kinds of bodies and sensations that can take place in a public space. They open up room to consider the cathedral otherwise.
>
> (Bruce 2015: 52)

The global movement in support of Pussy Riot reinterprets their political objectives and resituates them in a Western context, not as protest against dictatorship but as protest against state surveillance and police brutality. While the Western and Eastern perspectives differ in certain respects, they both focus on the balaclava as a subversive object that thwarts identification. The balaclava circulates as a physical object in street protest and as a digital object in online discourses (Bruce 2015).

It is no coincidence that Pussy Riot staged their 'Punk Prayer' protest in February—the carnival season. Medieval carnival provided a temporary chance to enact the inversion of social hierarchies as 'the lower classes had an opportunity to dress up as the ruling classes and mock their power' (Spiegel 2015: 808). Political dissidents and disenfranchised groups 'used carnival festivities to critique government officials and state institutions and demand significant political reform' (Bruner 2005: 139). For example, in 1580 Romans-sur-Isére, a small town in France, the gap between the rich and the poor widened as the ruling elite exempted themselves from paying taxes. In response, the carnival festivities organized by the common people ran under the theme 'eat the rich'. The crowd in disguise held mock armed military parades, marched with rakes and brooms to sweep away the rich, and enacted selling the meat of the rich at a market. This fictive performance had real consequences as the mock rebel leaders were prosecuted, tortured, and hanged (Bruner 2005: 142).

The parallels with Pussy Riot's 'Punk Prayer' are apparent: 'Medieval carnival is known to have included mockery of church authorities, even swearing and indecent behaviour from pulpits and altars' (Steinholt 2013: 123). While both Pussy Riot and medieval carnival encompass elements of humour, they combine these with serious threat. The threat 'eat the rich' is echoed by the chorus of the Punk Prayer 'Virgin Mary, chase Putin away'. The Punk Prayer consists of aggressive rock music and swear words. The balaclava itself, however colourful, contains aspects of threat: 'the circulatory power of the balaclava means that such endless reproduction can become monstrous and terrifying' (Bruce 2015: 49). This can also be observed in black bloc techniques in anti-capitalist demonstrations. Hiding their faces behind black balaclavas, scarves, and hoods, the creation of a menacing persona is not an unintentional side effect, as one anti-globalization protester explains: 'part of the effectiveness of our mass mobilizations rest on this threat of implied violence' (cited in Ruiz 2013: 269).

Hiding faces in hoods is also practiced by the Black Lives Matter movement. The hood affords a performance of defiance through its association with youth riots, gang wars, and anti-capitalist insurgency. In the 'Million Hoodie March', protesters took to the streets of New York City in hoods in response to the killing of Trayvon Martin, a 17-year-old African American, whose killer, white neighbourhood watchman George Zimmerman, walked free. As the anonymity of Martin's hood was blamed for creating a threat which justified Zimmerman's actions, Black Lives Matter activists wear hoodies to perform solidarity with the victim and claim their race/class identity (Nguyen 2015). 'But even when, and sometimes because, authorities brand the hood as criminal or illegitimate, people keep wearing their hoods for resistance, revolution, and transformation. For self-expression, defiance, and play' (Kinney 2016: 71).

Finally, the subversive freedom of anonymity can be illustrated by the controversy surrounding the veiling of Muslim women. In her book *Veil*, Rafia Zakaria (2017) contends that in the context of the enforcement of burka bans and Islamophobic media discourses, the practice of publicly wearing the veil becomes an act of democratic contestation. The veil functions as a tool for subversion, confronting Islamophobia and claiming diversity in the public sphere. The state, or, in Rancière's terms, the police, demands access to the individual person's face as prime identifier. The veil interrupts identification just as the hood does. The forced unveiling of Muslim women in schools and courts by the state and the politically motivated hate act of other citizens pulling a headscarf off a woman's head is echoed in media threats addressed to Black youth to unhood, not to become the next shooting target. The disciplinary power that confronts anonymous subversion takes the form of a physical threat to life and freedom of the defiant subject.

Submission. From the 1930s on, studies in social psychology have tried to find explanations for the strong group dynamics of crowds, particularly regarding the emerging fascist movements in Europe. They discovered that individuals appeared to give up or lose their individuality in groups and tended to follow group dynamics and leadership. An explanation for this deindividuation was found in the anonymity of the crowd. Perceiving themselves as unidentifiable, individuals not only felt less accountable for their actions, but were also swayed by emotive group dynamics (e.g. Le Bon 2009 [1896]). Current models of deindividuation clarify that it is not just that negative behaviour is emulated, or that crowds are always deindividuating; indeed, they can have the opposite effect. Whether individuals conform to group dynamics under the condition of anonymity depends on the salience of certain features of identity that are shared between both the individual and the group. In other words, anonymity leads individuals to submit to a group, if that group is defined by a strong group identity that individuals share in. The salient collective identity amplifies those aspects that the individual shares with the group (Reicher 1984). The identity of the assemblage gains control over individual action. The individual subject is free from making decisions, free to submit to the group, and free from the constraints of accountability: 'The mob has all the power of its aggregate of members, who, embedded as they are in the group, are virtually invisible as individuals; they feel liberated from responsibility, and thus the chain of personal accountability is all but destroyed' (Boyd and Field 2016: 340).

The most horrendous consequences that submission to the collective through anonymity can have can be illustrated by the racially motivated lynchings that occurred in the US in the nineteenth and twentieth centuries. Lynching as a political hate crime against Black people was used by groups such as the KKK, as discussed above. In these hate crimes, individuals' submission to a group identity of terror played an important role. The affectivity of hate that spreads through groups is partly facilitated by the anonymity of its participants who negate their individual identity through the group identity of the crowd. In contrast with the KKK, who actively seek anonymity through the physical object of the hood, lynch mobs do not need guises; they simply depend on the multiplicity of their members to hide individual identity: 'One form of anonymity has been substituted for another: unmasked, the lynch men can both claim public credit for their reign of terror and dodge legal responsibility' (Boyd and Field 2016: 341).

The freedom to submit to collectivity does not always come in such appalling forms. More subtle forms can be observed in current political collectivities such as Anonymous, who, as discussed above, create inclusive collective identities. Individuals included in the collective not only occupy equal positions in the social hierarchy, but also submit to a commonly constructed persona. They tend to adjust their modes of expression to collectively perform and reinforce this improper identity. Gabriela Coleman (2012: 86), for example, claims that 'donning the Guy Fawkes mask associated with Anonymous ... entails trading individualism for collectivism.' The absence of individual identifiers on discussion boards such as 4chan and its forum /b/ results in mutual mimicry. A sort of group think emerges: 'After a certain amount of time, one loses one's individuality and enters the "hivemind" of "/b/"' (Halpin 2012: 22). The use of the Guy Fawkes mask can be understood both as facilitating inclusion as well as a performance of deindividuation: 'an Anonymous twitter user claimed: "*Today I took off my face*". Whereas many activist movements have used carnivalistic components as part of a strategy of resistance and embraced masking, others have emphasized the removal or erasure of the human face, the defacement of the subject' (Cambre 2014: 316). In her analysis of images generated and circulated by Anonymous activists, Cambre shows a picture with a man taking off the Guy Fawkes mask with no face behind it. Another image bears the caption: 'It is time to leave behind your names. It is once again time to become Anonymous' (Cambre 2014: 316–7).

This inclination towards homogeneity can be witnessed in other movements too: 'a trend shared in twenty-first century protest from Tahrir Square to Occupy is the refusal to have a representative *face* come forward as the avatar of the revolution ... Anonymous protest ... asserts the protesting body as *collective* and *depersonalized*' (Spiegel 2015: 795, emphasis added). According to Forestal and Philips, anonymity fulfils an associational function: 'anonymity works to draw individuals out of their singular perspective and forces them to engage in public debate from an alternative, collaborative position' (Forestal and Philips 2020: 515). In the protests in Hong Kong in 2019, many protesters wore the Guy Fawkes, Joker, or other masks to shield their public identities from government persecution. This leads to a decrease in subjectively perceived individuality: '[E]ach member withdrawing one's individuality in the moment ... The mutual beckoning among those who wear the same mask also encourages them to model one another, enabling them to develop intersubjective bonding' (Pang 2021: 3 and 12).

What appears to be happening here is that participants in these movements more or less consciously give up their individuality to a certain degree so as to form an unassailable unit, while, with the same move, adhering to the ideology of equality. In addition to these strategic and ideological motives, this unity of equals also satisfies a psychological function: the yearning for belonging. Building a community that accommodates a feeling of belonging, mutual appreciation, and acceptance is an important aspect of inclusion. If belonging and acceptance is the participants' main motive, their political beliefs might prove flexible. This is particularly relevant in the context of the increasing openness—and at times emptiness—of the content of current social movements engaging via social media, in which anonymity plays a central role. Concepts such as networked social movements (Castells 2012), connective action (Bennett and Segerberg 2012), and cyborg activism (Asenbaum 2018) point to an increasing eclecticism and even nihilism in the content of these movements. When political causes and content become less important and increasingly vague, deindividuation through anonymity can contribute to submitting to group dynamics.

Moreover, there is a practical reason for tendencies of conformity in anonymous protest. Improper names exemplified by the Guy Fawkes mask, the Pussy Riot balaclava, and the pseudonyms in the US constitutional debate entail that different people can take on the same anonymous persona (Deseriis 2015). To the many arrests of hacktivists, Anonymous responds: 'You can't arrest an idea.' This implies that participants within movements or civil society organizations need to adhere to a common ideology or set of ideas even if these diverge from their individual political beliefs. While in non-anonymous movements, individual participants can be authorized to speak for the group and held accountable, in collectives such as Anonymous this is hardly possible due to the unidentifiability of participants. This leads to intense controversies within Anonymous, with sub-groups accusing one another of being inauthentic or individual participants being 'doxed'—expelled and publicly shamed by finding and publishing their legal identities (Dobusch and Schoeneborn 2015). In the case of sharing a pseudonym, such as Publius used by Alexander Hamilton, James Madison, and John Jay, the pressure to stick to a consistent line of thought might be even stronger as participants try to 'pass' as the same person.

Honesty and Deception

Finally, accounts of anonymity in democratic spaces describe how anonymous subjects are more willing to reveal their true beliefs and selves. Identity negation helps to avoid peer pressure which in turn leads to more sincerity in public discourse. Others, however, point to anonymity's affordance of lying as it allows for the construction of fake identities and deceit through a lack of accountability. Thus anonymity contributes to both honesty and deception in democracy.

Honesty. Oscar Wilde famously wrote: 'Man is least himself when he talks in his own person. Give him a mask and he will tell you the truth' (Wilde 1968 [1861]: 389). These words were based on nineteenth century practices of masked balls allowing for sexually frivolous behaviour and anonymously published novels that often contained strong political undertones (Barendt 2016: 14). The same can be observed today in all modes of anonymous participation discussed here: escaping domination through anonymity—be it from state institutions, economic actors or peers—contributes to a diversity of opinions in the public sphere:

> There are certain unpopular positions which some people might want to explore, but not if they know they will be exposed to ridicule and perhaps even physical

harm if they are tied to such views in public. To completely forbid anonymity would therefore result in no unorthodox views ever reaching the public sphere of debate.

(Hunter 2002)

Through the secret ballot in elections and referendums, voters can uninhibit-edly express their personal interests. Similarly, anonymity is used in polling to detect the electorate's true preferences on various political issues (Kuran 1993). Anonymity's freedom to speak the truth also plays into the freedom of subver-sion as dissidents including Pussy Riot and Anonymous reveal their true beliefs when shielded by anonymity. Anonymous media channels are established as truth-promoting institutions, such as WikiLeaks' whistleblowing website or Anonymous' independent media platform anonews.co that challenges mainstream media nar-ratives (McDonald 2015). However, honesty does not just contribute to subver-sion; it can also aid exclusion and submission. Aggressive and derogatory speech directed at marginalized groups is an expression of true sentiment. Thus, Gard-ner's (2011: 929) two sides of anonymity might actually be seen as one and the same: 'anonymity has been both praised for freeing citizens to vote and speak their true beliefs, and condemned for providing convenient cover to harmful or democratically undesirable behavior.'

In anonymous dialogues through bathroom graffiti on university campuses, for instance, students verbalize political opinions that are deemed inappropriate in classroom discussions and student newspapers. Thus, the more formally regulated public sphere has exclusive effects: 'Graffiti allow the key benefit of anonymity, that is, protection against any form of retribution. All can say whatever, however, and whenever, to whomever' (Rodriguez and Clair 1999: 2). The bathroom stall functions as a kind of confession booth where social identities and political views are expressed and negotiated. One might add the comparison to a voting booth, also serving the expression of true beliefs. The study of bathroom graffiti at a US university with predominantly African American students in the late 1990s illus-trates how, under conditions of anonymity, taboo topics such as homosexuality could be addressed. As the following dialogue shows, both sides of the argument—those defending and those opposing homosexuality—expressed their opinions in a candid and unrestricted manner:

(D) I really don't understand how a woman could be attracted to another woman and I agree with the sister girl to the left of me. Homosexuality is very unnatural and since God says its wrong in the bible I don't [think] he would create a human being that way. It's a learned behaviour.

(E) You have to learn to interpret the bible. King James was a racist woman hater. Reading is Fundamental. You also think God is a HE. Question everything that contradicts your Freedom and liberty.

(A) African American women. Look! Don't judge people. You don't understand homosexuality at all! If it was a choice I wouldn't choose it because of all the abuse. Why can't I just be myself in this world? (cited in Rodriguez and Clair 1999: 6–7)

This genuine dialogue would most likely not have taken place without an anonymous medium. The question A poses at the end is especially telling: 'Why can't I just be myself in this world?' implies that she can only express her real self publicly under conditions of anonymity. Both freedoms of subversion of hegemonic identity constructions and internal exclusion within a peer group resulting from frankly speaking one's mind can be observed in the dialogue.

The case of bathroom graffiti illustrates that anonymity is particularly important to marginalized social groups in allowing them to publicly express their identities. Anonymous online channels provide another outlet to articulate queer identities. In South Korea, for example, LGBTIAQs often face stigmatism and social ostracism: 'many persons identifying with a homosexual (or other non-heterosexual) identity find an anonymous Internet to be the only recourse for open expression ... A lack of expressive opportunity deprives homosexual persons of reasonable opportunities to develop their identities' (Leitner 2015: 2010). In countries with more accepting cultures towards queer sexualities, anonymity nevertheless plays an important role. Annual LGBTIAQ Pride parades are characterized by carnivalesque identity performances enacting gender changes and fusions through masks, makeup, and disguise (Baxter 2015).

Deception. Although enabling a more honest discourse by concealing identity is an undisputed feature of anonymity, facilitating deceit appears just as plausible. In stark contrast to Oscar Wilde's assessment of the mask as facilitator of truth, Leonardo da Vinci wrote: 'the mask [represents] lying and falsehood which conceal truth' (da Vinci 2005: 684).

While today hiding one's identity when casting the ballot in elections is perceived as a core political right, the role of the secret ballot was far more contested in nineteenth century Britain: 'secret voting was contrary to the English cultural traditions of honesty and openness; it would lead to habits of falsehood and deception' (Barendt 2016: 157). A proper citizen was expected to vote in accordance with the common good. The secret ballot, however, gave the opportunity for selfish voting, either concealing or even lying about one's decision. Voting based on the common good was particularly important in the face of exclusion of certain social groups from the franchise—most prominently women. Thus, John Stuart Mill argued that men had to reveal their voting behaviour not only to a wider public, but specifically to their wives and daughters whose interests they were supposed to include in their considerations.

In contrast to single voting acts, online communication provides multiple and continuous opportunities for deception. The case of *A Gay Girl in Damascus* is a telling example. In the wake of the uprisings in many Arab countries in 2011, the blog *A Gay Girl in Damascus* told the personal story of the Syrian LGBTIAQ activist Amina, resisting the ultra-conservative Syrian regime from within. Amina's blog posts were promoted by *Lez Get Real*, a US-based LGBTIAQ news website run by Paula Brooks. After the blog rapidly rose in popularity in just a few months, news spread that Amina was abducted, causing her loyal community to spring into action under the hashtag #FreeAmina. However, it soon turned out that Amina was really Tom MacMaster, a 40-year-old, white, heterosexual, US-American. Paula Brooks, who had promoted Amina's blog and engaged in private and allegedly romantic contact with Amina, later turned out to be Bill Graber, a 57-year-old, heterosexual US-American. Both men claimed to have invented fictive personae to more credibly rally for a social group that they were not part of (Cardell and Maguire 2015).

Conscious deceit is also used to troll or infiltrate political opponents and to spread fake news. Anonymous, for example, employed deception facilitated by anonymity to attack the white supremacist Hal Turner. Turner propagated racist views via his radio show and website. Anonymous activists flooded the radio show with anonymous prank phone calls and the website with prank comments (Coleman 2014: 19–20). This is not an isolated case. The group Expose documents the illegal activities of extreme right-wing groups online and reports them to the police. While this is not the official policy of the group, some members create fake accounts on social media—so-called 'sock puppets'—and post racist comments, add right-wing individuals as friends, and 'like' right-wing groups in order to gain the trust of the online community. When they are ultimately invited to secret chat rooms where strategy and future actions are planned, they gain access to valuable information (Bartlett 2015: 62).

More sophisticated forms of deception are employed when anonymous programmers design social bots to present themselves as human social media users. On Twitter, bots posing as political supporters or activist groups tweet and retweet political content, heavily influencing which political messages are read online and potentially having an impact on the results of elections and referendums. Donald Trump's presidential campaign in 2016 and the campaign for Brexit in the UK's 2016 referendum were both heavily supported by artificial agents whose puppeteers remained in the dark (Bessi and Ferrara 2016; Bastos and Mercea 2017).

Anonymity in Context

As the discussion above has shown, anonymity is inherently ambivalent and facilitates democratic and undemocratic freedoms. How, then, can democratic spaces be assembled and designed employing anonymity? How do the democratic and the undemocratic freedoms relate to each other? Can the structural settings of democratic spaces favour democratic over undemocratic freedoms? I believe that a clear-cut separation of the two can hardly be realized. Rather, the two always go together, in varying constellations and intensities. This becomes clear when we observe both democratic and undemocratic freedoms in the same space. In the anonymous discourses scribbled as graffiti on bathroom walls, for example, subjects challenge power asymmetries by venting honest sentiments, but at the same time they engage in exclusion by disciplining marginalized groups. Anonymous prank phone calls to troll white supremacists and the social media sock puppet accounts of Expose entail both deception and subversion. Anonymity's freedoms always both undermine and advance democracy and, thus, remain contradictory.

Often even the two opposing freedoms of one binary (e.g. inclusion and exclusion) are at work simultaneously. Anonymous, for example, engages in subversion confronting social inequality, while at the same time exhibiting internal tendencies of submission. The inclusive, levelled playing field in the debate about the US Constitution is characterized by a highly exclusive language of personal insult. The same can be observed regarding honesty and deception. Hubertus Buchstein argues in an essay on online deliberation: 'the network presents an unreal world which allows all of us to create one or even more virtual identities ... In most cases people pretend to have those positive characteristics they feel they lack' (Buchstein 1997: 258–9, emphasis added). The literature on masked protest offers a different explanation. It interprets identity creation as revealing aspects of the multifaceted self: 'The mask is related to transition, metamorphoses, the violation of natural boundaries, to mockery and familiar nicknames. It contains the playful element of life' (Bakhtin 1968: 40). While this chapter has compared cases of deception with cases of honesty for the purpose of analytical clarity, in practice all cases contain both aspects as the boundaries between reality and fiction are blurry. Referring to the Guy Fawkes mask (V-mask) employed by Anonymous, Cambre (2014: 318) states: 'The generative trait of the V-mask, as Deleuzian multiplicity, like the quality of undecideability, ensures resistance to representation because it provides a riddle rather than a clear relationship, it is a non-identity acting as if an identity, but instead of choosing one or the other it oscillates between them. It rejects dominant "either/or" alternatives.' Rather than viewing the contradictory freedoms as mutually exclusive, I suggest that we understand them as interacting dialectically.

The dialectic of anonymity's contradictory freedoms is further complicated by a normative aspect. While the division in the dichotomies of freedoms advancing and undermining democracy might be a helpful heuristic, it is also necessary to think about the positive and negative effects within each freedom. Exclusion, for example, can contribute to democracy, as the access of privileged groups needs to be restricted in public decision-making (Dovi 2009). While Forestal and Philips' concept of associational anonymity aptly illustrates how anonymous subjects forgo their individual opinion and give into group dynamics, the authors stress how anonymity furthers solidarity and cooperation among activists (Forestal and Philips 2020, also see Pang 2021). In short, exclusion, submission, and honesty can have democratic effects, and inclusion, subversion, and honesty may have anti-democratic effects.

One further step is necessary to fully understand anonymity in democratic spaces. As discussed above, the academic debate on anonymity provides several suggestions as to how to differentiate particular types of anonymity. Authors speak of pseudonymity, physical anonymity, discursive anonymity, offline anonymity, online anonymity, self-anonymity, other-anonymity (Scott 1999), agent anonymity, recipient anonymity, and process anonymity (Wallace 1999). The definition developed here, in contrast, is broad enough to encompass all of them, but in turn loses the sharp distinctions offered by these terms. Instead of developing complicated terminologies of subtypes, clarifying the context of anonymous engagement can help to sharpen our view of different forms of anonymity, while not losing the macro view afforded by the definition of anonymity advanced here. To understand specific manifestations of anonymity, we need to take into account the materiality of the communicative infrastructure, the power relations between participants, and the configuration of identity knowledge.

The materiality of the communicative infrastructure plays a crucial role in what form anonymous engagement takes. The material objects that mediate anonymous participation include pens and paper, marker pens and bathroom walls, keyboards and computer screens, typewriters, masks, hoods, veils, voting booths, and even human bodies (when they are so numerous that they become indifferentiable). All these things constitute new interfaces. What is curious about these interfaces is that they both mediate communication and interrupt identification. This interruptive mediation allows for the constitution of new self-reifications through which the subject exerts presence. The specific materiality of the things that interrupt and mediate identification plays an essential role. The socio-cultural identity of the speaker is constructed differently if a political message is written on a bathroom wall or as a letter to the editor. This is well illustrated by the hood that came to represent the murdered Trayvon Martin: 'Because clothing is both contiguous and not contiguous with what it covers—skin, flesh—it is a mutable boundary that asserts itself within a field of matter, forcing us to confront the intimacy between bodies and things, and the interface between their amalgam and the environment' (Nguyen 2015: 792). The raced and classed object of the hood articulates a representative claim (Saward 2010) making the absent Martin present. A special case among the things that interrupt and mediate identity are large assemblages of human bodies. Here it is the quantity of bodies that impedes individual identification and thus interrupts the continuous identity performance of the subject. The visible bodies themselves create an interface that articulates a new collective identity.

Turning to the power relations between anonymous subjects, we can see how the constellation of human bodies, their emotive connections and social hierarchies, affect which form anonymity takes. These relations do not simply emerge out of nothing in a democratic space. Rather, they partly mirror and partly suspend and reconfigure external relations. Their respective social locations afford different power resources to protesters and riot police, affluent and poor party funders, and heterosexual and homosexual graffiti scribblers. These pre-established hierarchies can be disrupted or amplified by anonymity. The anonymity of the hood reverses its meaning when it is employed by activists to protest against racism in comparison to its use in executions. While the anonymity afforded by the hood enhances the position of protesters, it dehumanizes and degrades the condemned criminal (Kinney 2016). Similarly, the veil can amplify patriarchal structures disciplining its wearer, while also empowering its wearer to confront state repression (Zakaria 2017). To understand specific cases of anonymous political engagement, the pre-existing and the newly emerging power structures, thus, need to be taken into account.

Finally, the configuration of identity knowledge forms another crucial contextual condition of anonymous engagement. First, it matters which identity knowledge is conveyed by the identifiers used (pseudonyms, social security numbers, initials, etc.) and which identity markers (gender, age, ethnicity, etc.) of the legally identified and physically embodied persona are revealed. Second, it matters who is anonymous within a democratic space and who is not. The confrontation between unmasked protesters who are legally prohibited from covering their faces and masked riot police is an obvious example. A more subtle case are online pseudonyms, which anonymize user-to-user interaction but reveal identities to website operators. Third, it matters whether or not anonymous participants have previous knowledge of each other and have pre-established social relations. In workplace participation via anonymous online feedback tools, for example, participants might be formally unidentified but as the anonymity set is small, their identity might be easily deduced via social cues such as recognizable wording or content (Hayne, Pollard and Rice 2003). In short, the form anonymity takes is affected by the constellation of who knows what about whom. Together, the materiality of the communicative infrastructure, the power relations between participants, and the configuration of identity knowledge explain which form anonymity takes.

Conclusion

When considering the antithetical character of anonymity as identity negation *and* creation, and the resulting three sets of contradictory freedoms, the stark contrast between privacy and anonymity becomes evident. Neither inclusion, exclusion, subversion, submission, honesty, nor deception have much, if anything, in common with privacy. This is because they all relate to a crucial aspect of anonymity besides concealment. They all hint at the inherently *communicative* character of anonymity. This is also illustrated by the four modes of anonymous engagement: voting, campaign funding, political writing, and masked protesting are all modes of communication in the public sphere. Thus, anonymity does not entail being let alone. On the contrary, anonymity gives the democratic subject presence in the space of appearance. The public sphere—the opposite of privacy—is the precondition for anonymity (see Barendt 2016: 13).

That said, this does not mean that privacy and anonymity do not share any features in common. They clearly overlap in their functions of shielding the democratic subject from interference by others—be they state actors, economic actors, or peers. However, while privacy withdraws content from public scrutiny and the identity of the subject remains known, anonymity shields identity *while communicating content* in the public sphere. Anonymity thus conveys one crucial feature of privacy, concealment, into the public sphere (see Ponesse 2014; Moore 2018). It reconfigures the boundaries between private and public space and facilitates a *private* form of engagement in the *public* discursive arena. In her elaboration of the defiant act of public veil wearing by Muslim women, Zakaria (2017: 71–2) claims: 'Veils thus are ... an extension of the private space of the harem where [the women] are protected, into the public realm.' By negating some aspects of the legally identified and physically embodied persona, anonymity transcends publicity and privacy, transforming private sentiments into political claims and transmitting them into the public sphere, thereby facilitating *absence as presence*.

As such, we need a new understanding of presence—one in which visibility of the physically embodied persona does not function as the only criterion. When common modes of identity performance are interrupted through anonymity, subjects appear differently. Anonymous presence is expressed through voice, sound, written words, images that represent the body, improper names, and blank spaces. Presence is perceptible through many ways that partly include and partly go beyond the visibility of the body. It takes multiple forms and in doing so it reconfigures the identity assemblage of the subject. It brings often hidden aspects of the self to the fore when anonymous subjects are free to express themselves honestly or when they playfully engage with the many things that constitute their identities. The multiple self is reconfigured through the decentralizing effects of anonymity. What we usually engage in when we present ourselves publicly is an effort of integration that keeps our identity assemblage coherent. In performing our established persona, we enforce and harden the boundaries of identity space that confine the fugitive self. Anonymity's inherently liberating effects make these boundaries more porous:

> An adequate concept of anonymity, therefore, will need to take account of the ways in which anonymization dissociates or disintegrates what is naturally integrated. Because anonymity is a way of segregating an otherwise integrated self—of

packaging selves piecemeal for the world—anonymity involves a loss of visible integrity, and as such creates ambiguous identities.

(Ponesse 2014: 316)

Rather than speaking of natural coherence, as suggested by Ponesse, I think that integration is an artificial act, a forceful act resulting from the disciplinary power that Rancière (1999) describes as the police. In post-anarchist terms, it is an act of self-domination or voluntary servitude (Newman 2010c). The act of forcing the multiple self into a unity is described by Butler (1990) as masquerade, as discussed in the previous chapter. The everyday performance of the self consists of an effort of picking up and constantly reproducing a mask that is handed to us through citation and recitation. Interestingly, the etymology of the term 'person' leads to the Latin *personare* 'to sound through', which is derived from the use of wooden masks in dramatic performances in the Roman Empire (Napier 1986). The original persona as mask or 'false face' inverts our current understanding of the identifiable person as real while the mask is understood as fake. However, when applying the original meaning of the word 'person' to its current use, the identifiable person appears not as the true self, but as public performance, as masquerade. Anonymity is not masquerade, but the disintegration of masquerade. This is achieved through the disidentifactory practices of rejecting the mask, rejecting the hail of dominant discourses (Muñoz 1999) and thus interrupting the identification through the police (Rancière 1999).

Such a rejection can never be entirely successful, since the subject can never break out of discourses. But the interruption of continuous identification through practices of anonymity opens up new spaces for exploring and reassembling the multiple self, for playing with the many things that constitute us. Anonymity does not end identification; it merely interrupts it. It creates a space, a gap between periods of continuous identification. After the interruption, identification takes hold and puts the subject back into its place in the normalized order of things.

This chapter has shown how anonymity can function as a practice of disidentification and can contribute to a politics of becoming by reconfiguring presence in the space of appearance. As illustrated in the discussion of the history of anonymity, this phenomenon has grown in importance throughout history from anonymous publishing to anonymous online communication. The emerging digital age has rapidly accelerated this process. While a hundred years ago anonymity was mostly the privilege of those with access to publishing text, already the invention of the telephone made anonymity more accessible. With the advent of the internet, anonymity has become an inherent aspect of everyday communication. '[T]o fully understand the nature of online anonymity, it is necessary to adopt a position that views anonymity not in absolute terms but as an inherently fluid and transitional condition that characterizes to a certain extent any kind of social inter-action online' (Sardá et al. 2019: 559). Online tools both mediate communication and simultaneously interrupt identification. A decentring of identity assemblages through anonymity becomes an integral part of our selves. The next chapter will explore which new democratic subjectivities emerge through anonymous online communication, how this affects the politics of presence, and what potential it harbours for democratic spaces to enable the subject to change.

6

Becoming Cyborg

New (Inter)faces

> The radio is one-sided when it should be two-. It is purely an apparatus
> for distribution, for mere sharing out. So here is a positive suggestion:
> change this apparatus over from distribution to communication. The
> radio would be the finest possible communication apparatus in public
> life, a vast network of pipes.
>
> Bertolt Brecht 1932

Technological progress has always inspired imaginations of democratic futures.
Bertolt Brecht's vision of a decentralized multi-user network of communication
via radio frequencies developed in the 1930s bears striking resemblances to today's
digital communication network known as the internet. Brecht's radio democracy
was followed by conceptions of teledemocracy that imagined telephone and later
teletext voting following televized political debates (Arterton 1987). New electronic communication tools also inspired discussions about participatory democracy which developed ideas of electronic townhall meetings (Barber 1998). With
the spread of popular access to the internet in the 1990s, such imaginings found
new inspiration. The poststructuralist-inspired discussions about cyberdemocracy envisioned a new digital public sphere (Vedel 2006). Anonymity was at the
heart of these debates, which assumed that anonymous online communication
would enable the exploration of alternative selves.

Cyberdemocracy viewed the subject as being transformed in the context of a
new spatial configuration captured by the term 'cyberspace', which was seen as
a sphere separate from 'real life'. Here the subject would dwell as a disembodied
self, perceptible only by virtue of the words it uttered. The disembodied subject
appealed not only to deliberative democrats as cyberspace promised to realize a
public sphere free from domination (Ward 1997; Bohman 2004), but also to postmodern theorists (Poster 1997), unwittingly replicating the modern dichotomies
of online and offline, body and mind, reality and illusion:

> When on-line, one does not occupy a fixed physical form. That is, in cyberspace
> there is no such thing as a body, at least not in the sense that we inhabit a body.
> All that exists are fleeting electronic images loosely associated with a self-selected

The Politics of Becoming. Hans Asenbaum, Oxford University Press. © Hans Asenbaum (2023).
DOI: 10.1093/oso/9780192858870.003.0006

screen name (another fleeting electronic image). In this sense, cyberselves are literally disembodied. The self is freed from any physical form and thus challenges the traditionally perceived relationship between body and self.

(Waskul and Douglass 1997: 388)

While the disembodiment thesis has been rigorously criticized from feminist, post-colonialist, and materialist perspectives and is today commonly acknowledged as outdated (Kennedy 2006; Robinson 2007; Beyer 2012), the notion of cyberspace as a realm of equality and freedom overcoming corporeal constraints proves tenacious. In the recent *Politicizing Digital Space*, Trevor Smith (2017) characterizes digital networks as a realm of disembodied universal reason:

> The simple act of going online and entering into a pseudonymous space automatically strips away identities, as your body and social background are invisible to the other commenters as a source of prejudice … Online interactions within a website dedicated to political discussion are the ultimate form of Cartesian subjectivity, as what we think and share with others is what defines us to the others, not the sight of our bodies. (47)

Smith employs Arendt's concept of the space of appearance to argue that in digital space all that counts is the content of speech and action, while bodies and their inscribed identities are left behind. According to Smith, digital space entails 'separating political participation from presence' (54). This separation of the embodied subject from its political articulation is necessary because '[b]ecoming a political subject means elevating oneself out of the particulars of identity and into the realm of universal concern' (43).

In this chapter, I will contest the disembodiment thesis. I will make the argument that a politics of becoming through online anonymity does not preclude embodied presence. Rather than overcoming a politics of presence by leaving the body behind, the chapter will show how digital modes of communication reconfigure presence. Performing the self through the technological tools that both mediate and interrupt identity illustrates how presence is always a mode of becoming. Rather than understanding the democratic subject in digital space as a universal being existing merely through discursive expression, the chapter will explore the materialities both of digital space and of the subjectivities emerging on its grounds. The self in the digital age, I will argue, emerges as cyborg as our established identity assemblages are interrupted by the screens of digital devices, which offer an interface for new self-representations.

Paying attention to the double role of interrupting yet mediating identity that digital devices fulfil allows us to understand that anonymity is an inherent condition to any kind of online communication. Whether engaging in a chatroom under a pseudonym or curating images on our Facebook profiles, digital communication

devices always interrupt established identity performances: 'one should acknowledge that online anonymity is a phenomenon that characterizes to a certain extent
any kind of social interaction online. Whenever users connect to the internet,
degrees of anonymity and non-anonymity are established that contribute to shape
their experience online, its implications, and effects' (Sardá et al. 2019: 562).
Online anonymity, then, always frees the fugitive self to a certain degree and
affords temporary digital corporealities.

From the beginnings of the popular use of the internet to this day, the imagination of online communication was dominated by metaphors of space and
movement through space. When subjects *go* online, they *surf* through a network
of *websites* and *homepages* employing browsers such as *Safari*. As *space cowboys*
and *cybernauts* they push the *electronic frontier* further. They travel on the *information superhighway* to *visit* various *chatrooms* and *forums*. Their navigations are
limited by *firewalls* and *paywalls*. On their *search* for information they *follow* others, become trapped in *echo chambers* or *leak* information from secret spaces to
the public sphere. And, of course, all this happens in *cyberspace*.

But what the 'space' in cyberspace stands for—and thus what constitutes the
spatiality of cyberspace—has changed over time. Today, a radical counter thesis
has developed that opposes the notion of cyberspace as a separate realm following
unique logics. Current theories argue that through the Internet of Things, which
positions the human subject amid a network of various smart devices and common
things equipped with smart technology including refrigerators, cars, clothing, and
thermostats, new spaces emerge. These spaces overcome the distinction between
analogue and digital, so that the two collapse into one (e.g. Isin and Ruppert 2015).
While I find a lot of value in this position, it also leaves us with a problem. If
digital space and analogue space are conflated, we lack an adequate conceptual
framework in which to talk about two things that, intuitively, appear to be very
different. Does it not make a difference whether I start up a conversation with a
stranger in a supermarket or on social media? Rather than collapsing the digital
and the physical, we need to understand how the two relate to each other and how
they interact.

Here, once again, Butler's work is insightful. Looking at the role of smartphones
and social media in street protest, Butler challenges the disembodiment thesis.
Rather than seeing physical corporeality and the materiality of spaces as separate
from a digital world, Butler observes how the digital and the analogue relate to
each other, resulting in new subjectivities and new spatial configurations:

> And if this conjuncture of street and media constitutes a very contemporary ver-
> sion of the public sphere, then bodies on the line have to be thought of as both
> there and here, now and then, transported and stationary, with very different
> political consequences following from those two modalities of space and time.
>
> (Butler 2015: 94)

Here, Butler shows how the analogue and the digital are simultaneously distinct and closely related. In this chapter, I will generate a theory of digital space that neither understands the digital and the physical as separate spheres nor seeks to entirely collapse the distinction between the two. Rather, I will explain them as spatial assemblages of material objects, sentient bodies, and performative expressions. The notion of assemblage developed in Chapter 2 provides a productive way to understand how the digital and the analogue relate to each other, while maintaining distinct concepts to describe them. The resulting theory of digital space will provide new answers to the question of what it means to appear and what role the body plays in digital spaces. Drawing on current debates in corporeal cyberfeminism, critical race studies, and digital new materialism, I will reread difference democratic thought and generate an understanding of a digital politics of presence.

In doing so, I will explore the question whether digital spaces can function as spaces of becoming. Elizabeth Grosz points to the transformative potential of the reconfigurations of digital and physical materiality. They disrupt conventional perceptions and open up spaces of becoming for new subjectivities to emerge:

> The virtuality of the space of computing, and of inscription more generally, is transforming at least in part how we understand what it is to be in space ... it threatens to disrupt or reconfigure the very nature of information, communication, and the types of social interaction and movement they require.
>
> (Grosz 2001: 87)

These reconfigurations of space uncover potential for 'transformations, the usage of spaces outside their conventional functions, the possibility of being otherwise—that is, of becoming' (90).

To explore this transformative potential, I will first revisit the poststructuralist cyberdemocracy discourse of the 1990s, which imagined the self as disembodied. I will then consider the criticism articulated against the disembodiment thesis in critical race studies, which condemns the invisibility of difference. To find conceptions that overcome the disembodiment thesis, I will engage with early cyberfeminist and current corporeal cyberfeminist debates, which offer notions of the digital subject as both embodied and transformative. The next section will draw on the concepts of the cyborg (Haraway 1991 [1985]) and evocative objects (Turkle 1984) that will help to explain how the digital and the physical relate to each other. This will enable the generation of a new theory of digital space explained as assemblage of material, sentient, and discursive things. I will then outline a new digital politics of presence by exploring identity articulations in several examples of digital online engagement.

Revisiting E-topia: Of Disembodied Subjects in Cyberspace

[Being online] means existing in pure language ... in cyberspace, one
dwells in language. and through language.
                    Internet user cited in Markham 1998: 204

In the 1990s, the notion of cyberdemocracy came to prominence, which theorized new means of digital communication from a poststructuralist perspective. The emergence of the cyberdemocracy discourse can be understood in the context of two preconditions. First, it was spurred by the development of the world wide web in 1989 and the spread of internet access in the Global North. Second, this socio-technological development was paralleled by increasing academic interest in poststructuralist thought. With Judith Butler's theory of performativity updating and popularizing the work of French philosophers including Michel Foucault and Jacques Derrida in the US, poststructuralism acquired an almost hegemonic position in social theory. Theories of the construction of reality through language appeared to be realized in the early popular use of the internet that was dominated by pure textuality. What appeared as new worlds of online interaction became so mesmerizing that scholars paid little attention to their material infrastructures. Virtual reality in cyberdemocracy was often compared to hallucinating from drug use or travelling to another universe.

The core concept of cyberdemocracy is cyberspace, a realm constituted by pure discursivity. As a sphere of freedom and equality, cyberspace is perceived as discontinuing—as interrupting—'real life'. Cyberspace is

> ... another life-world, a parallel universe, offering the intoxicating prospect of
> actually fulfilling—with a technology very nearly achieved—a dream thousands
> of years old: the dream of transcending the physical world, fully alive, at will,
> to dwell in some Beyond—to be empowered or enlightened there, alone or with
> others, and to return.
>
>   (Benedikt 1991: 131)

As spatial interruption, cyberspace is understood as dispensing with the limitations of the analogue sphere and generating a utopian space: 'Cyberspace is a habitat of the imagination, a habitat for the imagination. Cyberspace is the place where conscious dreaming meets subconscious dreaming, a landscape of rational magic, of mystical reason' (Novak 1991: 266).

Cyberspace appears to work according to entirely different rules. It undermines all logics of common space and throws reality into disorder (Lipton 1996: 336). In an (auto)ethnographic study, Annette Markham (1998: 23) recalls her experience of going online, which felt 'like entering a strange new world where the very metaphysics defied my comprehension of how worlds should work.' This transcendental space of electronic networks is founded on two related core elements: the collapse of both distance and materiality. While in analogue space distance stands in relation to movement and in particular speed of movement, in cyberspace all distance is overcome. The world appears to shrink in the palm of one's hand. Interlocutors are perceived as immanently present, while they are physically located far away, which results in a reconfiguration of social relations. As an early internet user (cited in Turkle 1995: 198) explains:

> It was a lot easier to talk to people [about my problems] ... because they're not there. I mean, they are there but they're not there. I mean, you could sit there and you could tell them about your problems and you don't have to worry about running into them on the street the next day.

Collapsing distance and eradicating travel time signals 'the end of space through cyberspace' (Nunes 1997: 172). A new kind of space is perceived as 'a "nonspace", a hyperdimensional realm that we enter through technology' (Barnes 1996: 195).

The second and related feature that characterizes cyberspace as a 'nonspace' is its perceived lack of materiality. A space entirely constructed of zeros and ones, of digits and bytes, of digital simulation, cyberspace is detached from physicality (Markham 1998: 86). This point is also crucial for understanding the cyberdemocratic notion of subjectivity. As the digital replaces the physical, cyberdemocracy is defined by the invisible subject. Anonymity strips subjects of their bodies tainted with identities that are subject to discrimination. Cyberspace promises to liberate the human spirit from its fleshy cage. The notion of disembodiment in cyberspace originates in the very text that coined the term 'cyberspace'. In the cyberpunk novel *Neuromancer* William Gibson (2016 [1984]: 6) writes about 'the bodiless exaltation of cyberspace', 'contempt for the flesh', and how the hero of the story was denied access to cyberspace and 'fell into the prison of his own flesh'. The notion of disembodiment created in this dystopian science fiction novel resonated with the personal experiences of many early 'cybernauts': 'When I spend a lot of time in disembodied spaces, I forget my body. Often, I don't remember it until the physical pain is extreme, and then I resent my body's intrusion on my life online' (Markham 1998: 59). They often felt like stripping off the body when entering the world of text: 'By logging onto my computer, I ... exist separately from my body in "places" formed by the exchange of messages' (Markham 1998: 17). By enabling users to 'leave their bodies behind', Cyberspace reconfigured not just space, but also the identities expressed in this 'nonspace', as online 'where I am and who I am are up for grabs' (Lipton 1996: 342). This kind of identity play 'offers the possibility of forgetting about the real body' (344).

Exploring the Multiple Self through Online Anonymity

Anonymity features prominently in the central works that define the cyberdemocratic discourse. *The Network Nation* by Starr Roxanne Hiltz and Murray Turoff, published as early as 1978, constitutes one of the founding texts of cyberdemocracy. The book provides detailed empirical work on computer conferencing, comparable to current synchronous online chats. As in these early forms of digital communication interlocutors were unidentified by default, this study provides one of the earliest cases of online anonymity. Its findings resonate with the concept of anonymity developed in the previous chapter. Online anonymity does not simply entail the negation of established identity; rather: 'A pen name is like a mask or a costume; it helps people to play a role' (95–6). The study examines how anonymity enables participants to 'feel more free to express disagreement' (27), to use different pen names for deliberate deception, to 'suggest potentially unpopular ideas' (27), and to express aggression towards others. Most importantly, however, anonymity contributes to inclusion:

> General appearance, such as height, weight, and other culturally determined aspects of 'attractiveness' and the clothes, makeup, jewelry, and other props used by persons to present themselves to others, provide an important filtering context for face-to-face communication. So do the visibly apparent cues that are provided by sex, age, and race and by visually apparent physical handicaps ... [Through online anonymity, however,] it is the content of the communication that can be focused on, without any irrelevant status cues distorting the reception of the information ...
>
> (Hiltz and Turoff 1978: 78, 91)

These early observations of online anonymity strongly resonate with the 'e-topias' of the 1990s,[1] of which Howard Rheingold's *The Virtual Community* (1993) is probably the most influential and characteristic. The focus of the book is Rheingold's personal experiences of the WELL (Whole Earth 'Lectronic Link), one of the early virtual communities with discussion forums on different topics. Anonymity is a core feature of this kind of textual interaction:

> Mask and self-disclosures are part of the grammar of cyberspace, the way quick cuts and intense images are part of the grammar of television. The grammar of CMC [Computer-Mediated Communication] media involves a syntax of identity play: new identities, false identities, multiple identities, exploratory identities, are available in different manifestations of the medium. (147)

---

[1] I borrow this term from William Mitchell (1999), who is himself not a cyberdemocrat but more a cyborgian-inspired theorist.

While Rheingold welcomes the fluidity of identity boundaries, he conceptualizes digital identity performances that diverge from analogue identity as deception. To illustrate this, Rheingold tells a story that is cited repeatedly in many cyberdemocratic texts. An online character called Joan in some accounts (Rheingold 1993: 164; Turkle 1995: 228; Poster 1997: 222) and Julie Graham in others (Stone 1991; 82; Wajcman 2004: 68), claiming to be a psychologist based in New York who had been paralysed and muted in a car accident, had won the trust of several women in online communities, who shared intimate details. When it later turned out that Joan/Julie was really Alex, a psychiatrist who was curious about women's private lives, many users felt exploited and betrayed.

In *Life on the Screen* Sherry Turkle (1995) tells the same story and observes how internet users 'use the anonymity of cyberspace to project alternate personae' (209). These online identities are not perceived as fake as such, but rather as a form of living out a true aspect of the self, which is hidden in common public interaction. Thus, 'donning a mask, adopting a persona, is a step towards reaching a deeper truth about the real' (219). Through digital communication the lines between analogue reality and digital reality blur. In an interview, a teenage girl complains about her friends disappearing behind computer screens: 'Now they just want to talk online. It used to be that things weren't so artificial' (237). While the interviewee perceives telephone conversations as real—as they are conveyed through an old, naturalized medium—online communication appears as fake. These shifts in the perception of reality do not indicate that the virtual is just as real as analogue reality. Rather, online subjectivity is situated in a liminal space between the real and the artificial: 'In the real-time communities of cyberspace, we are dwellers on the threshold between the real and the virtual, unsure of our footing, inventing ourselves as we go along' (10).

Turkle provides an extensive ethnographic investigation of MUDs (Multi-User Dungeons/Domains)—online spaces for synchronous textual role play, where users collectively create an interactive story. In group and one-on-one chatrooms, they construct online personae and objects and navigate through textual sceneries. As in analogue role play or improvisational theatre, participants can experiment with sides of their personality which are usually excluded from the continuous identity performances in everyday interaction. Some users even claim that their online identities feel more real than their analogue identities: 'I feel very different online. I am a lot more outgoing, less inhibited. I would say I feel more like myself' (179). And another user explains: 'I am not one thing, I am many things. Each part gets to be more fully expressed in MUDs than in the real world. So even though I play more than one self on MUDs, I feel more like "myself" when I'm MUD-ding' (185). Online role play functions as a therapeutic activity, in which hidden and underdeveloped qualities can be practiced and eventually carried over into analogue interaction. MUDs work as a 'transitional space' for 'reaching greater freedom' (263).

In MUDs identities are multiple and ephemeral so that users do not have to commit to one of them. This also includes the common practice of gender change, as users define the sex of their characters as female, male, or neuter. As Turkle tries to perform male characters online, she feels freer, more confident, and relieved of certain social pressures. Another female interviewee reports that when communicating through male characters, she feels that her firm and strict attitude is appreciated and not perceived as 'bitchy'. A male user, on the other hand, reports feeling relieved of the demands of competitiveness and that he could engage in more cooperative interaction without being perceived as too soft or effeminate. Thus, online gender swapping can relieve users from gender stereotypes which can be experienced as liberating by users of all sexes (see Bruckman 1996).

Turkle's notion of the decentred, multiple self is deeply rooted in postmodern thought. The rhizomatic structure of the internet itself embodies the fragmentation of the online self. Turkle illustrates this by the curious digital object called a 'window':

> Windows provide a way for a computer to place you in several contexts at the same time ... [W]indows have become a powerful metaphor for thinking about the self as a multiple, distributed system ... The life practice of windows is that of a decentred self that exists in many worlds and plays many roles at the same time.
>
> (Turkle 1995: 13–4)

The postmodern character of the internet is also reflected in the hypertext structure of the world wide web, through which users navigate. This replaces the modern linear logic of teleological thinking with a rhizomatic logic of infinitely multiple directionalities. Hypertext increases the reader's freedom and breaks up established hierarchies: 'Electronic readers ... can genuflect before the text or spit on its altar, add to a text or subtract from it, rearrange it, revise it, suffuse it with commentary. The boundary between creator and critic (another current vexation) simply vanishes' (Lanham 1993: 6). While modern writing practices created a stark asymmetry between the writer with sole power over the text and the reader as its passive recipient, hypertext flattens these hierarchies. Not only can the reader alter the text, the reader can also decide the order in which text passages are read. Thus, readers freely navigate through the text according to their preferences. This fundamentally changes the approach to understanding text. While textual interpretation methods such as hermeneutics assume that by careful interpretation the correct, essential meaning can be detected, in hypertext no one reads the same version of a text as the orders of text passages are nearly endless—as are its subjective interpretations (Landow 1992).

The rhizomatic nature of hypertext also plays a central role in what is arguably the most elaborate attempt at developing a poststructuralist theory of new communication technologies presented in the work of media theorist Mark Poster (1990; 1995; 1999). Poster contends that the deep transformations of communication cause profound reconfigurations of the subject. The modern subject of the Enlightenment period is constituted by a stable relationship between senders and receivers of communication, who are fixed entities positioned in time and space through words that function as a clear representation of intelligible reality. Senders call upon readers as subjects through their sole authority—thus author—via the word. This configuration is drastically changed through digital communication: while the spatial distance between senders and receivers remains, the temporal difference is eliminated. The rhizomatic structure of hypertext alters the representational character of the word. Text takes on a performative character, continuously resituating both senders and receivers in a process of mutual interpellation. Thus, 'the subject can only be understood as partially stable, as repeatedly reconfiguring at different points of time and space, as non-self-identical and therefore as always partly Other' (Poster 1995: 59). Anonymity is at the heart of this reconfiguration:

On the Internet individuals construct their identities, doing so in relation to ongoing dialogue, not as an act of pure consciousness ... [This] does connote a 'democratization' of subject constitution because the acts of course are not limited to one-way address and not constrained by the gender and ethnic traces inscribed in face-to-face communications.

(Poster 1997: 222)

The mere fact that gender and other identity categories have to be actively chosen and can be completely rejected by creating neuter characters provides space for resistance to analogue identity hierarchies:

Internet communities function as places of difference from and resistance to modern society. In a sense, they serve the function of a Habermasian public sphere, however reconfigured, without intentionally or even actually being one. They are places not of the presence of validity-claims or the actuality of critical reason, but of the inscription of new assemblages of self-constitution.

(Poster 1997: 224)

The postmodern discussions of democratic subjectivity in digital communication generate invaluable insights for democratic thought. While these debates are often perceived as naïve in hindsight, it is important to understand that the early internet was indeed a more democratic place: not in terms of access, but in terms of its participatory characteristics (Walker Rettberg 2014: 12–3). Most importantly, cyberdemocrats highlight how anonymity facilitates the exploration of the multiple self. It expands the freedom of the democratic subject to change and opens the perspective on digital communication as part of a politics of becoming. The creation of alternative online personae can be seen as a rejection of hegemonic identity interpellations, a temporary interruption of identification. Yet, their understanding of cyberspace as a sealed-off realm that is separate from analogue space, one that can serve to leave the body behind, is problematic. For example, Turkle (1995: 9) claims that by employing digital communications '[w]e are able to step through the looking glass'. Employing the metaphor of wonderland characterizes virtual reality as unreal, as a dream from which one can awake. Elaborating her thesis of the multiple self, Turkle cites an interviewee: 'Why grant such superior status to the self that has the body when the selves that don't have bodies are able to have different kinds of experiences?' (14) So, is cyberspace really disembodied? Does the space of appearance described by cyberdemocrats only allow content to appear? To suggest otherwise, I will explore the work of the critics of cyberdemocracy and their alternative conceptions.

Diversity Reconfigured: Of Race in Cyberspace

From the early 2000s, cyberdemocratic thought faced a critical response which draws attention to racialized bodies both online and offline. In the textual online communication of the 1990s that inspired the cyberdemocracy discourse, race had become entirely invisible, much more so than gender. Whereas in MUDs gender is a required category in a user's character description and is also evident in most pseudonyms in online chats, race is absent. Moreover, many users in anonymous online spaces ask their interlocutors for their 'asl': age, sex, and location. The requested information excludes race, which is perceived as an inappropriate or otherwise uncomfortable question. Any expression of race is often perceived as aggressive and controversial. The mere textuality of early online communication provided users with the opportunity to finally forget about an issue commonly perceived as a sensitive and divisive (Kolko 2000). This results in 'default whiteness'. Users whose physical skin colour is not white are under pressure to negate their racial identity and try to 'pass' as white. The ideal of equality through disembodiment appears to have conformist effects. While whites express themselves freely, people with other skin colours are limited in their self-expression (Nakamura 2002). It is also crucial to bear in mind that the internet is not a neutral medium. It is designed predominantly by a specific group of people, namely white, middle-class men from the Global North. Default whiteness is a design choice (Kolko 2000: 213).

If online anonymity appears problematic because of identity negation that erases non-white identities, then the other core element of anonymity, identity creation through the construction of racially heterogeneous selves, could contribute to enhancing diversity. Alas, the practice of identity creation online takes the form of 'identity tourism'. According to critical race scholars, changing the sex, race, or other attributes of online identities only serves to reproduce existing stereotypes:

> Chat-space participants who take on identities as samurai and geisha constitute the darker side of postmodern identity, since the 'fluid selves' they create (and often so lauded by postmodern theorists) are done so in the most regressive and stereotyped of ways. These kinds of racial identity play stand as critique of the notion of the digital citizen as an ideal cogito whose subjectivity is liberated by cyberspace. On the contrary, only too often does one person's 'liberation' constitute another's recontainment within the realm of racialized discourse.
>
> (Nakamura 2002: xv)

Users constructing alternative racial identities rely on their limited knowledge and stereotyped conceptions of other cultures. Moreover, these constructions need to conform to the simplistic modes of online expression. Identity tourism does not represent a shift in situatedness as experience of oppression, but rather a recreational endeavour experiencing the self as an exoticized Other. This kind of digital 'blackfacing' deters participation of racial minorities and their expression of authentic racial identity (Nakamura 2002).

To counter the problem of default whiteness and stereotyping, critical race scholars advocate an active online presence of racially marginalized groups. They call for claiming spaces as a way of expressing difference through the digital embodiment of race. The figure of the decentred, fluid, and ephemeral self in cyberdemocratic thought is opposed by the representation of racial diversity in order to build resilient communities akin to difference democratic counterpublics (Kolko and Reid 1998). Unlike whites, who use their privileged position to explore their inner multiplicity, many people with other skin colours living in white-majority contexts already experience their identities as unpleasantly fragmented and disorientated and are longing for consistent identification (Nakamura 2002).

While these debates in critical race studies aptly criticize conceptions of cyberdemocratic post-racial selves, they also partly support the core ideals of cyberdemocracy: 'A diversification of the roles that are permitted and played can enable a thought-provoking detachment of race from the body and questioning of the essentialness of race as a category. Performing alternative versions of the self and race jams the ideology-machine' (Nakamura 2002: 49). Nevertheless, this debate points to a crucial problem with the cyberdemocratic notion of disembodiment. The negation of established identities can obscure marginalization and reinforce the hegemonic identity constructions in our heads. At this point, we are back to the dilemma of difference. The mere continuation of analogue identities online allows for a politics of presence through the representation of marginalized groups, but limits the freedom of the subject to explore its multiple self. What is needed is a concept of a digital space of appearance, where embodied identities are perceptible yet free to change.

Cyberfeminism: The Subversive Alliance of Women and Robots

Debates around the term 'cyberfeminism' provide some answers to our predicament. Cyberfeminism in many ways builds on cyberdemocratic thought and imagines digital spaces that allow for identity play through online anonymity. They understand anonymity as levelling power relations between men and women (Blair 1998) and describe the use of online avatars to perform post-gender identities (Danet 1998). At the same time, however, cyberfeminists position themselves in critical distance to the cyberdemocracy discourse:

> The utopian promise so often associated with the new technologies demands our
> sharpest critical attention, for it is foolish to believe that major social, economic,
> and political issues can be addressed by throwing technology at them. As radical
> net critics have repeatedly pointed out, cyberspace is not an arena inherently free
> of the old feminist struggle against a patriarchal capitalist system. The new media
> are embedded in a framework of pan-capitalist social relations and economic,
> political, and cultural environments that are still deeply sexist and racist.
>
> (Fernandez and Wilding 2002: 23–4)

This critique is enabled by the materialist perspective cyberfeminists apply, which draws attention to the continuity of inequalities. They criticize the postmodern disembodied subject, which navigates through cyberspace 'as body-free environment, a place of escape from the corporeal embodiment of gender and race' (Balsamo 1996: 123). This does not preclude an exploration of identity transformation. In cyberfeminist writing the politics of presence and a politics of becoming appear to go hand in hand. The subject takes a corporeal and identified form in the space of appearance, but at the same time engages in self-transformation.

Cyberfeminism as a movement extends beyond academia and brings together discussions from three sources: feminist Science and Technology Studies (STS), digital artistic spaces such as the Old Boys Network (www.obn.org) and Sub-Rosa (cyberfeminism.net), and digital spaces for women's empowerment such as peer groups conveying technological knowledge and skills. In their Cyberfeminist

Manifesto, a foundational text of the movement, the art collective VNS Matrix (1991) write:

> we are the virus of the new world disorder
> rupturing the symbolic from within
> saboteurs of big daddy mainframe
> the clitoris is a direct line to the matrix
> VNS MATRIX

Here the transformation of society is linked to the material body. This combination of transformation and corporeality is also at the heart of Sadie Plant's *Zeros + Ones* (1997). The book starts with the lines: 'Those were the days when we were all at sea. It seems like yesterday to me. Species, sex, race, class: in those days none of this meant anything at all' (3). The idealisation of identity contingency goes along with a biologist view. Embodiment and transformation do not preclude each other. Plant observes a disorder of the established binary identity codes caused by new possibilities of anonymous communication. Bigendered thinking is reflected in the computational logic of zeros and ones. While in traditional Western thought, the phallic 1 is associated with presence, power, and masculinity, women are associated with the 0 as absence, weakness, and passivity. Men are everything and women nothing, an image corroborated by the division of global wealth and political power. The computer disrupts this logic, however, and turns the established binary upside down. In original computer punch cards, the 0 constitutes the something and the 1 the nothing, so that the world is '[n]o longer a world of ones and not-ones, or something and nothing, thing and gap, but rather not-holes and holes, not-nothing and nothing, gap and not-gap' (57).

Instead of focusing on what is happening on the screen, Plant describes the history of computing through a materialist/corporeal perspective, relocating the focus to the forgotten contributions of women, such as Ada Lovelace whose work in the 1840s foresaw the potentials of computing beyond mere calculation. Primarily, though, women undertook repetitive work to fulfil the plans developed by men. When weaving was automated through punch cards, women moved to the industrial assembly lines. Today it is women in the Global South, mainly in Asia, who assemble computers for their use in the Global North. Plant describes an intimate relationship between women and machines, both abused as tools of men. She invokes the many popular fictional narratives of robots, often designed as women and thus connoted with sexual objectification, who rebel against their human, male creators. The alliance between women and robots results in a social revolution that takes an evolutionary form. With the change from industrial to information societies, muscular strength loses its relevance. Contemporary precarious work relations rather demand flexibility, multi-tasking, emotional intelligence, and cooperative teamwork. According to Plant, women are better equipped for current work relations through their historical positioning as weavers and will soon outplay inflexible, stubborn, and competitive men.

Plant's book undoubtedly contributes a lot to cyberdemocratic thought, drawing attention to women's subordinate role in both the Global North and South, their forgotten contributions to the development of technology, and the possibilities of new gender constellations online. Nevertheless, the book has been rightfully criticized for its techno-determinism and essentialism (Wajcman 2004: 73). Similar to some debates in difference democracy, it affirms established gender stereotypes in positive terms.

Despite these essentializing tendencies, cyberfeminism provides a promising outlook on how to combine an attention to corporeality with self-transformation. Rather than associating the body with presence and disembodiment with becoming, cyberfeminism points towards a mode of *embodied becoming*. It provides two core arguments to counter the disembodiment thesis. First, cyberfeminists advocate privileging physical matter as the source and foundation of the digital: 'No matter how virtual the subject may become, there is always a body attached. It may be off somewhere else—and that "somewhere else" may be a privileged point of view—but consciousness remains firmly rooted in the physical' (Stone 1991: 111). Hence, now is the time to 'put back into the picture the flesh that continues to be erased in contemporary discussions about cybernetic subjects' (Hayles 1999: 5). Second, the *digital* body itself needs to be understood as matter. Upon entering cyberspace, the subject is divided into a biological and a digital body (Reichle 2004: 253). The digital body acquires materiality as a tool for self-exploration. It is an 'object-to-think-with' (Turkle 1996: 121).

Cyberfeminism acknowledges physical embodiment allowing for the expression of difference and yet it is open to self-transformation: 'If we think of the body not as a product, but rather as a process—and embodiment as effect—we can begin to ask questions about how the body is staged differently in different realities' (Balsamo 1996: 131). However, the bifurcation of the democratic subject into a physical and a digital configuration appears only as a partly satisfactory solution. To further develop cyberfeminist thought, two aspects are in need of development. First, the splitting of the subject into a digital and an organic unit appears to replicate the crude binarism of the body/mind split so extensively criticized. Subjects in the digital age are more complex and diverse configurations. Second, what is needed is an explanation of how these physical and digital aspects of the self relate to one another.

In the remainder of this chapter, I will develop a new theory of digital space and the subject by drawing on the notion of assemblage. To this end, I will first go back to the roots of corporeal cyberfeminism and examine the notions of the cyborg (Haraway 1991 [1985]) and evocative objects (Turkle 1984). Building on these concepts, I will then draw on the spatial theory of democracy developed in Chapter 2 to advance a new understanding of digital space. This will, finally, put me in the position to ask what a digital politics of presence that allows for both embodiment and transformation looks like.

A Democratic Theory of Digital Space

'How did the trope of immateriality colonize our imagination to the point where we came to believe computing exists beyond the material world?' (Casemajor 2015: 4). This question is at the centre of current debates on digital democracy. Most theorists position themselves at a critical distance from the cyberdemocracy discourse and the concept of cyberspace as a disembodied realm separate from the physical world. Engin Isin and Evelyn Ruppert (2015: 41), for example, emphatically argue that digital space and physical space 'are no two different spaces'. They draw on Paolo Gerbaudo (2012) and Christian Fuchs (2014) to argue for the conflation of digital and physical space. However, they do not provide an alternative. They fail to explain what it means that there is no separation between the digital and the physical. In my view, the reason for this failure is that the separation actually makes sense, at least to a certain degree. It is as unproductive to speak of cyberspace as an entirely separate realm that follows different logics to physical space as it is to deny any distinction between digital and physical space. Rather than completely conflating or completely divorcing digital and physical space, we need to think about how they relate to each other, how they connect, and, as I will argue, how they assemble.

Donna Haraway's trope of the cyborg provides a point of departure for understanding how the physical relates to the digital in novel configurations of space and the self (Haraway 1991 [1985]). In contrast with the disembodied beings in cyberdemocracy that exist merely through the words they utter, the cyborg emerges as a configuration of human-machine, organism-technology, mind-software. Its human body of flesh and blood is augmented through computer technology. This amalgam appears as a liberating subject in a world confined by hierarchical identity formations, in which '[g]ender, race, or class consciousness is an achievement forced on us by the terrible historical experience of the contradictory social realities of patriarchy, colonialism, and capitalism' (155).

The cyborg as monstrous agent breaks out of this dichotomous thinking by overcoming the boundaries between animal/human, human/machine, and physical/non-physical. It does not, however, reconfigure those binaries into a new unity, a higher synthesis as in Hegelian-Marxist theory, but rather leaves the riddle unresolved. The irony of the cyborg is constituted by plurality, dissolving unity into permanent contradiction. Haraway encourages us to give up the struggle for simple dichotomous thinking and instead to indulge in the pleasures of the cyborg—the pleasures of incoherence, friction, and disorientation. This disorientation has important implications for cyborgian space. As cyborgs experience 'pleasure in the confusion of boundaries', existing configurations of space and the self are disrupted. Indulging in spatial disorientation, cyborgs leave behind binary gender codes and traditional models of sexuality and family. This also affects the constitution of politics and of democratic spaces. The cyborgian reconfiguration of the boundaries of private and public echoes Pateman's *Disorder of Women* (1989) calling for a democratization of the private sphere: 'No longer structured by the polarity of the public and the private, the cyborg defines a technological polis based partly on a revolution of social relations in oikos, the household' (Haraway 1991 [1985]: 151). This disorder results in 'partial, contradictory, permanently unclosed constructions of personal and collective selves' (157).

The cyborg, then, goes beyond cyberfeminism by suggesting endless multiplicity instead of a simple bifurcation of a physical here and a digital there. The figure of the cyborg itself is, however, mainly left in the dark in Haraway's text. When cyborgs are part human part machine, however, looking at how humans relate to computers can make this figure more comprehensible. While today computers disappear as smartphones in our pockets or as smartwatches on our wrists and thus often escape our attention, the early generation of household computers prompted curiosity. At the time when Haraway developed her cyborg theory, Sherry Turkle wrote about computers as 'evocative objects'. Whereas in overviews of cyberdemocratic thought Turkle's *Life on the Screen* (1995)—discussed earlier— is frequently cited, her book from eleven years earlier, *The Second Self* (1984), goes largely unnoticed—and even less attention is given to its cyborgian conceptions. Turkle does not use the term 'cyborg' in her 1984 book. In her later reprise on evocative objects, however, she explicitly describes the relationships between humans and computers as cyborgian configurations (Turkle 2007: 325).

Computers appear both as objects used by humans, and at the same time as agentic subjects, which call upon their users in different ways. In their double role as evocative objects, computers influence their users' identities. They enter into processes of becoming: 'We search for a link between who we are and what we have made, between who we are and what we might create, between who we are and what, through our intimacy with our own creations, we might become' (Turkle 1984: 2). Humans can employ computers as tools to create their own individual worlds. As soon as they enter these worlds, they are affected by them. Humans become the object of the computer's creation as 'computers enter into the development of personality, of identity, and even of sexuality' (6). Not only do we humanize computers as 'friends' that 'are stupid' at times or need to 'rest for a while', but humans also start to perceive themselves in technological terms as they might not 'function well' or something forgotten is perceived as being 'erased from the hard drive'.

Turkle's point is not to mystify computers and understand them as alive. Rather, she develops a deep understanding of how we *perceive* computers as vital objects. Through careful observations of how children engage with computers, she provides an account of their conception of vitality. At a very young age, children follow a simple classificatory scheme of motion: what moves is alive—a bird, a cloud, a rolling stone. Later they understand that not all things that move are alive; they move because outside forces set them in motion. In the eyes of children, however, computers upset this system. They move by themselves. They appear as autonomous actors that are intelligent. They can talk, ask questions, and they have answers. They think! Depending on their age, children are often not sure whether computers are alive. At a certain point, they develop a new classification scheme to determine vitality: Their classification shifts from motion to emotion. As adults, while we rationally know that computers are not alive, there is still a certain part of us—the child in us, if you will—that believes in the vitality of computers. We humanize them because we have an emotional connection with them. In this way, computers 'upset the distinction between things and people ... The computer too seems to have a psychology—it is a thing that is not quite a thing' (33, 54).

The double function as inanimate object and vital subject gives computers a special role in the constitution of the self. They function as mirrors for the self. The story of Narcissus can explain the use of computers, although, according to Turkle, it has been misinterpreted in the past. Narcissus did not fall in love with himself out of vanity, but seeing his reflection in the water he perceived himself as someone else, thus falling in love with the self as other. Computers function as mirrors to see the self as reconfigured other. It objectifies the self, resulting in a representational object vis-à-vis the self. Yet, the purpose of this objectified other/self is not vain self-love. It rather serves the anxious search for the self, as reassurance of our own existence. Unlike regular mirrors, which are inanimate objects, computers are agentic. As evocative objects they do not create objective representations of their subjects. Rather, they call upon and co-construct the human subject. Computers bring established processes of self-constitution into disorder, resulting in cyborgian configurations:

> Because they stand on the line between mind and not-mind, between life and not-life, computers excite reflection about the nature of mind and the nature of life. They provoke us to think about who we are ... The effect is subversive. It calls into question our ways of thinking about ourselves: most dramatically if mind is machine, who is the actor? Where is responsibility, spirit, soul? *There is a new disorder* ... Where we once were rational animals, now we are feeling computers, emotional machines. But we have no way to really put these terms together. The hard-to-live-with, self-contradictory notion of the emotional machine captures the fact that what we live now is a new and deeply felt tension.
>
> (Turkle 1984: 320–1, 326, emphasis added)

In Chapter 2 I outlined a theory of the democratic subject as assemblage. At this point, the notions of the cyborg and evocative objects enable us to further

deepen this concept. If the subject is thought of as an assemblage of its physical body parts, skin pigments, sexual organs, and body chemistry interacting
with culturally-coded objects, such as clothing, makeup, and jewellery, and with
discursive concepts that describe gender, race, religion, and political affiliation,
then processes of cyborgization can be understood as evocative objects and digital self-representations entering these assemblages. The subject is an 'amalgam,
a collection of heterogeneous components, a material-informational entity whose
boundaries undergo continuous construction and reconstruction' (Hayles 1999:
3). Understanding the subject as a diverse assemblage opens up potential for a politics of becoming as 'persons can be reasonably thought of in terms of disassembly
and reassembly' (Haraway 1991 [1985]: 162).

I thus propose to understand the democratic subject in the digital age as constituted as an assemblage of human body parts, material artefacts, discursive
concepts, and digital objects. Within such assemblages, smart devices fulfil a special role as evocative objects. They are, in the human perception, more lively
than other things. They actively call upon us and thus co-construct our identities. The notion of the assemblage complicates the cyberfeminist binary. Instead
of dividing the body into a physical and a material component, assemblage takes
into consideration the manifold elements including discursive interpellations and
material performances that together constitute the subject. It also explains how
these various parts relate to each other. They assemble through human cognition
as discussed in Chapter 2. By relating discursive concepts, material artefacts, and
digital representations to each other, humans assemble these various parts into a
perceived unity. The notion of assembling, then, draws attention not only to the
fragility of this apparent whole but also to the potential of dis- and reassembling.

Here, again, it becomes clear how the notions of subject and space follow
the same logic. They both assemble through human perception. Their respective modes of assembling overlap, which is furthered through the digital, so that
identity assemblages and space assemblages form intersecting networks: 'Increasingly, we are living at the points where electronic information flows, mobile bodies,
and physical places intersect ... These points are becoming the occasions for a
characteristic new architecture of the twenty-first century' (Mitchell 2003: 4). If
assembling subjects and assembling space work according to the same principles,
the cyborgian theories above have a lot to contribute to developing a theory of
digital space.

How Digital Spaces Assemble

Today, cyborgs are not science fiction. Rather, cyborgs are very real in the here
and now. Interhuman relations are mediated through the smartphones in our
pockets, the smartwatches on our wrists, headsets, earpieces, tablets, laptops, and

touch screens. These many things that provide connectivity do so through wireless networks and cloud computing, which define a new cyborgian space in which we constantly move, even when not using digital devices. The Internet of Things further extends the connectivity of evocative objects that constantly hail us from different angles. We are connected with the thermostats, light bulbs, and refrigerators in our smart homes. The sensors in our shoes connect to the internet, as do the sensors applied to our pets and babies. We should not, however, understand such assemblages as entirely breaking down the boundaries between human and machine; rather, humans shape and are shaped by these machines. As noted earlier, this interwoven nature of digital societies has led current thinkers to dispute the distinction between digital and analogue space. I have argued that this is as unhelpful as completely divorcing the two as the cyberdemocracy discourse does. I follow Forestal (2017: 160) in claiming that 'the role of space in democratic politics highlights the continuities between the physical and digital environments, even as it clarifies differences between the two'. So, what does a theory of digital space look like that does not conflate the physical and the digital but at the same time overcomes their stark separation?

To answer this question, I will employ the spatial theory of democracy developed in Chapter 2 and explain digital space as an assemblage containing material objects, sentient bodies, and performative expressions. So, if digital space consists of the same three dimensions as analogue space, how is it different? Why do we need a theory of digital space at all? In other words, are digital and analogue space the same thing, as the current debate suggests (Isin and Ruppert 2015)? I will argue that in digital space, material objects, sentient bodies, and performative expressions assemble in profoundly different constellations. The main feature that distinguishes digital from analogue space is an interruption within each of the three dimensions. Analogue democratic spaces are characterized by a material place in which participants meet face-to-face. It is in this common location that social relations between sentient bodies form and performative expressions are both uttered and perceived. Material, sentient, and performative space are deeply intertwined. These spaces of appearance are constituted by the copresence of physical bodies. Digital spaces, in contrast, interrupt the common material space and dislocate subjects across the globe. They interrupt the sentient dimension when subjects experience community in isolation. And they interrupt performative expression when online communication is interpreted within diverse contexts.

The key to understanding digital space is to acknowledge the diverse material contexts in which subjects are located. The digital does rest on physical space, but it is not primarily the technological infrastructure of the hardware which current media theorists are so eager to point to. Instead, scholars of democracy need to attend to the physical places in which participants are located. Digital space, then, is constituted as a decentred kind of material space, much like I described anonymous democratic spaces in the previous chapter. When imagining digital space, instead of thinking about what happens on the screen and dreaming about an immersive digital beyond, I plead for thinking about the concrete physical sites where participants are located. Digital space is an assemblage of diverse material locations, a mosaic of living rooms, offices, parks, cafés, gyms, libraries, public squares, and bedrooms.

This constitution of digital space is enabled by the things that both mediate and interrupt interaction. The screens of electronic devices intercept analogue space but at the same time mediate communication. As discussed in the previous chapter, anonymity always depends on the interruption of spatial assemblages by diverse objects such as masks, bathroom walls, sheets of paper, and computer screens. These things interrupt identity while at the same time providing an interface for the creation of new personae. Digital communication always entails a moment of anonymity and is hence characterized by the same modes of interruption and mediation. Digital communication devices always negate some aspects of identity and call for their reconstruction. This interruption/mediation changes things. It harbours a potential for disidentification that reconfigures, to a certain extent, how we perceive and present ourselves. But this does not entail the constitution of an entire new reality—new identities, new spaces—as proposed by cyberdemocrats. Rather than a new world of pure discursivity and disembodiment, digital space is comprised of many continuities—continuities of inequalities, discrimination, and social hierarchy. These continuities also depend on the fact that we are not autonomous in these processes of self-constitution. Since the digital objects that enter our identity assemblages are evocative, they co-constitute us. These processes of cocreation are heavily influenced by the economic interests of tech companies. Yet there rests a subversive potential in digitally-mediated interruption, the potential to reject identity interpellations and engage in playful explorations. Continuities are always partially reconfigured through interruption. They can never be perfectly translated.

The interruption between materiality, sentience, and the performativity that constitutes digital space goes along with several shifts and reconfigurations on all three levels of spatiality.

The materiality of digital space. Beyond the topography of satellites, cables, routers, servers, monitors, and keyboards, the materiality of digital space consists of the electronic light pulses and microwaves that travel through this wired landscape. Often the information age is thought of as immaterial because what is displayed on a screen appears as just an illusion. Yet, in reality, bits and bytes are electronic light pulses mediated through cables, transmitted to computers, where they interact with phosphors on screens or activate circuits on sound cards (Saco 2002; Cohen 2012). Hence, digital space is 'made up of both physical and mediated components' (Kavada and Dimitriou 2017: 86).

Conceptualizing digital space in this way, we can begin to understand communication online as a physical network of electronic pulses generated by our fingertips on keyboards and touch screens. Each tap sends an electronic signal that makes its way through a wide network and ends up on someone else's screen. While democratic subjects in digital spaces might be located in their homes, at work or in public parks, they connect these physical locations through electronic pulses. As discussed in Chapter 2, the arrangement of physical things that constitutes the materiality of democratic spaces affects human interaction. Decentring material space, then, means that each participant in digital spaces is affected by different physical surroundings that are mostly unknown to other participants. Together these individual physical locations constitute a new kind of fragmented, decentred, yet connected space.

The material dimension of digital space, however, does not end here. It extends far into what we perceive as 'regular' physical space which we do not associate with digitality. The everyday spaces we live in and move through are progressively more permeated by electronic hardware and hence become increasingly cyborgian in nature. The boundaries between private and public are reconfigured through the infusion of material space with digital technology. Public spaces are increasingly subject to video surveillance from private spaces, generating a private-to-public channel. The information flow goes the other way through video conferencing enabling private spaces to be broadcast to the public (Mitchell 2003: 28). Social movements, for example, can enlarge their claimed spaces through live streaming (Kavada and Treré 2019). This 'ability of electronic media to remove, or at least rearrange, boundaries between public and private space' (Papacharissi 2010: 68) has significant consequences for the perception of the material spaces in which democratic subjects are located during digital engagement. As noted in the previous chapter, because citizens now engage in politics online, their private homes are reconfigured as public spaces: 'This relocation suggests that we re-examine the spatiality of citizenship. Within this private sphere, the citizen is alone, but not lonely or isolated' (Papacharissi 2010: 132). This trend is amplified by pandemic lockdown politics, which make the home the central location of democratic engagement (Parry, Asenbaum, and Ercan 2021). The reconfiguration and partial dissolution of the boundaries between public and private physical spaces is partly due to the elements of anonymity inherent to digital space. As online communication is facilitated by things that mediate and interrupt communication, the subject can more easily express private things in the public sphere.

Finally, the materiality of digital space extends even further. Beyond the material network and the light pulsus running through it, beyond our everyday spaces with their increasing cyborgian nature, the internet also extends into our natural environment. Online communication causes very real, material effects on the global ecosystem. The vast amount of physical data storage needed generates CO_2 emissions that ultimately cause ice caps to melt and ocean levels to rise (Gabrys 2014). The material dimension of digital space, then, is not only global in scale, but also extends into spheres commonly not associated with online communication.

The sentience of digital space. While the cyberdemocracy discourse in many ways simply assumed that cyberspace was indeed a space, without further questioning its spatiality, today's discourse on digital democracy is more aware of the need to provide a convincing explanation. The answer to the question about the spatiality of cyberspace is not only found in investigating its material aspects but also by pointing to the social relations between sentient bodies: 'networked information technologies do not call into being a new, virtual space that is separate from real space. Instead they have catalyzed the emergence of a new kind of *social space*' (Cohen 2012: 33, emphasis added). It is the emotional quality of interaction online that constitutes spatial relations between interlocutors. The physically displaced bodies are reconstituted as digital bodies which together engender a new kind of habitat: 'virtual worlds are social spaces, and I would argue that it is this sense of spatiality that contributes to their sense of being real "places of human culture"' (Lau 2010: 372).

As elaborated in Chapter 2, sentient space is constituted by corporeal relations. It comes into existence where bodies interact and vanishes with them (Arendt 1958). While in online communication subjects do not come together physically, digital space is nevertheless constituted by their interaction. Digital space as 'a unique kind of social space' (Saco 2002: 27) is constituted by the networking activities of its users which relate their digital bodies and different digital objects in a spatial network. Of course, social interaction differs in several respects from analogue interaction: the main difference being that it comprises a 'sociality without a face' (29). One might object that since the rise of Facebook the facelessness of online interaction is disputable. Social media generally engender continuous identity performances that mirror the offline persona. Attempts at authentic self-representation, however, always contain elements of self-transformation, which can be explained via Butler's concept of citationality discussed in Chapter 4. Even if the subject tries to replicate its body as authentic self on the electronic interface, it is bound to fail as citational representations always differ (J. Butler 2004). Online communication is realized through interfaces that always to a certain extent interrupt established identity performances. The sentient dimension of digital space is defined by a moment of anonymity and a potential for disidentification as subjects curate their identities online.

The performativity of digital space. Digital space has long moved beyond the mere discursivity of cyberspace. It is based on performative expressions through selfies, videos, GIFs, memes, audio recordings, and emojis. This does not mean that discursivity as one aspect of performative expression has lost its significance online. Despite the increased visuality of social media such as Instagram, Flickr, or Snapchat, in digital spaces textuality remains the dominant form of communication. Digital space comes into being as 'a relational space of digital acts' (Isin and Ruppert 2015: 39). It exists by clicking, liking, following, sharing, poking, tweeting, messaging, searching, filtering, hacking, tracking, camming, and, of course, social networking. If we imagine all these digital acts as electronic light pulses making their way from our fingertips through the vast cable and satellite networks of the internet, we can begin to imagine how the materiality and the performativity of digital space are interrelated.

When comparing performative expression in analogue democratic spaces with digital engagement, what stands out is the reification and durability of content in the latter. While in analogue engagement, the spoken word and bodily expression are perceptible in one particular moment in time and are thus highly ephemeral, expressions become reified in text, video, or audio recordings online. They become a digital object. Online, content can be read or listened to repeatedly; it can be copied. It is displayed on digital interfaces and remains stored on servers. Content online is searchable and accessible to greater and sometimes unintended publics. Understanding performative space as a cognitive structure of meaning through which the subject navigates as elaborated in Chapter 2, the hypertextual structure of the world wide web appears as an accurate realization of this image. In this regard, cyberdemocratic thought is still insightful today (Landow 1992; Poster 1995). This networked nature of performative space is characteristic of hashtag activism, in which political content assembles around hashtags on social media, such as #MeToo (Mendes, Ringrose, and Keller 2018) and #BlackLivesMatter (Mislán and Dache-Gerbino 2018).

In summary, we need to understand digital space neither as a separate realm disconnected from analogue space, nor as entirely of a piece with analogue space, but rather as an intricate assemblage in which material objects, sentient bodies, and performative expressions interact. While digital space is intimately intertwined with analogue space, they nevertheless differ profoundly. Digital spaces are characterized by an interruption and decentralization of material space, by the networked nature of sentient space, and by the durable textuality, visuality, and audibility of performative space.

A Digital Politics of Presence

The theory of digital space and the subject as cyborgian assemblage provides new insight into the dilemma of difference. As discussed in Chapter 3, the politics of presence advanced in debates about difference democracy suggests a strategy of physically embodied identity performances of marginalized groups as a way of promoting inclusion. While this successfully advances equality as it draws attention to marginalization and particular standpoints, it also limits the freedom of the democratic subject to define, explore, and transform its own identity. It limits the freedom of the subject to change. In Chapters 4 and 5, I proposed understanding the politics of presence as part of a politics of becoming and suggested anonymity as a potential means to realize moments of disidentification. The rich accounts of identity change through online anonymity in debates about cyberdemocracy lend support to this thesis. While cyberdemocracy appears compatible with a politics of becoming, it seems to be at odds with a politics of presence. Its notion of disembodiment, which renders difference imperceptible, threatens to cover up inequalities. The disembodiment argument is still prevalent in current debates, for example in Smith's account of digital space, wherein he suggests 'untying political speech from bodies' and goes on to argue:

> What really matters for the political realm in terms of appearing and visibility is the ability to make one's opinions heard and for collective actions to have a lasting impact. *The presence of the body is not necessary for any of this*, as what distinguishes us from others politically is not our bodies or faces, but our words and deeds.
>
> (Smith 2017: 28, emphasis added)

I find the conception of digital space as a realm of disembodied, universal reason problematic. It rests on an understanding of anonymity as the mere negation of identity. Understood thus, spaces of appearance online only make content visible, but negate bodies and identities. As I have argued in the previous chapter, however, anonymity entails as much identity creation as identity negation. Digital images, text, pseudonyms, emojis, and avatars reconfigure bodies and identities. The disembodiment position is not just problematic politically insofar as it further undermines the status of those who are already disadvantaged by encouraging images of default whiteness and default masculinity; it also overlooks the fact that the body is always there. Disembodiment means ignoring the body rather than actually leaving it behind. We are thus in need of a formulation of a digital politics of presence that allows for the embodied articulation of diverse identities and still harbours the potential for the subject to change.

To generate such a renewal of the politics of presence in the digital age, a novel understanding of presence is needed. In the previous chapter, I argued that anonymity reconfigures presence by channelling the absent from the private into the public sphere. This reconfiguration of presence through moments of disidentification, then, becomes an inherent part of everyday communication in the digital age. Understanding presence as a performative act of becoming, we can see how the interruption and mediation through digital devices allows us to reassemble our selves. Online presence is constituted as a curated assemblage of digital images, words, and sounds that reveal otherwise hidden aspects. Identity is constantly reshuffling, bringing different things to the fore at different times.

The concept of presence is invoked repeatedly both in the early debate on cyberdemocracy, speaking of 'a fantastic presence' (Nunes 1997: 170), and in the current literature on digital democracy, speaking of 'telepresence' (Senft 2018: 55), for example. These debates show that presence does not necessarily entail the sight of the physical body. Without sharing one physical location, through online communication subjects can still '*create* embodied presence' (Markham 1998: 17). Mediated through these digital bodies people 'feel a *sense of presence* when they are online' (24). It is 'making the subject "here" without being here' (Nunes 1997: 168). What emerges is a new concept of presence, one that does not depend on a shared physical place and the visibility of the body, a presence that assembles words, images, sounds, flesh, machines, and digital body representations through a new mode of becoming.

It is not just presence as the core concept of difference democracy, but the entire debate on difference democracy that can be reread through the digital. The three strategies of inclusion promoted by difference democracy outlined in Chapter 3— presence, emotion, and contestation—are reflected in many critical and especially feminist accounts of digital democracy today. Digital democracy is characterized by the emergence of digital counterpublics of marginalized groups who contest domination (Travers 2003; Dahlberg 2007). Accounts of digital democracy also focus on emotions (Dahlgren 2009; Castells 2012; Asenbaum 2018) and shed light on affective publics online (Papacharissi 2015). In what follows, however, I will focus on a new politics of presence and examine how marginalized groups articulate their identities in digital spaces of appearance.

Digital Spaces of Appearance

The cyberfeminist debates in many ways echo the difference democratic concept of a politics of presence. They draw attention to online bodies and corporeal difference in digital engagement. What is crucial in understanding this new politics of presence is the fact that presence does not necessarily entail physical copresence. This is corroborated by the original debate of difference democracy, in which presence was always thought of as a mode of *representation* of identity across time and space (Phillips 1995: 30; Young 1997a: 352; 2000: 124). The representative of an identity group in difference democracy is mirrored by the classed, raced, and queered bodies of digital avatars and online images. In both the original and the digital politics of presence, the representation of the marginalized body functions as an affective thing that reconfigures spaces towards equality.

Here, I will provide several empirical examples that illustrate how bodies appear online. I start with three examples of how classed, raced, and queered bodies claim digital space. The discussion thereafter will draw on further examples to illustrate how cyborgian identity reconfigurations facilitate a digital politics of presence.

The classed bodies of the 99 percent. In August 2011, just a few weeks before the first major protest erupted in New York's Zuccotti Park, an Occupy activist named Chris created a Tumblr blog titled 'We are the 99 percent'. On this blog, he invited people to tell their personal stories of hardship caused by austerity politics through selfies: 'Let us know who you are. Take a picture of yourself holding a sign that describes your situation ... Below that, write "I am the 99 percent"' (We are the 99 percent blog 2011). Within weeks, the blog was flooded with around 100 selfies per day of people telling their stories. These images walk a thin line between self-exposure and anonymity. Individual self-portraits of people holding up handwritten signs that cover their faces either completely, in part, or not at all both reveal and cover physical embodiment. Some are signed with first names or pseudonyms, but most carry no name at all (McDonald 2015: 976).

An obese man, probably in his thirties, with his naked shoulders, arms, and chest exposed, holds up a sign close to his face that reads, 'I play World of Warcraft naked 40 hours a week. I eat mostly McDonald's. I am probably unemployable. I am the 99 percent' (We are the 99 percent blog 2011). Another naked man with a noticeable scar on his chest holds up a sign telling his story of cancer, precarious work, and difficulties in getting health insurance. Another picture shows a pregnant belly with only the lower part of a female face. Her sign reads, 'At 21 years old I am ... about to become mother to a baby whose illness has gotten us booted off gov't health insurance ... Scared for our future. I am the 99 percent' (We are the 99 percent blog 2011).

The raced bodies of anti-racist raiders. Habbo Hotel is a social media site providing a virtual hotel setting in which users create human avatars for social interaction and role play. In 2006, users of Habbo Hotel repeatedly faced difficulties navigating the virtual outdoor hotel areas. The entrance to the pool was blocked by African-American avatars with big afros in black suits, who shouted 'Pool's closed due to AIDS'. The repeated raids of Habbo Hotel were the work of an online swarm that had formed in response to alleged discrimination against Black avatars by moderators and the overrepresentation of white avatars. As moderators started to block Black avatars and automatically impede their registration to regain control, the online protesters charged them with racism (Asenbaum 2018). These 'online-sit ins', mimicking peaceful protest tactics of the US civil rights movement of the 1960s, were repeated on Habbo Hotel and other sites. Manuals were circulated online that instructed protesters on how to design the uniform Black avatar and avoid deletion by moderators. In a follow-up action on World of Warcraft, Black avatars were marched to a virtual slave market to be sold (McDonald 2015). Memes inspired by the raids, such as the slogan 'Pool's closed', spread via social media. The memetic protest action even materialized in analogue space as white people dressed in black suits with afro wigs formed a swastika out of their bodies in front of the headquarters of Habbo Hotel's mother company, Sulake, in Finland.

The queered bodies of social media users. On 13 June 2016, Facebook, Twitter, and Instagram were flooded with rainbow flags. Social media users changed their profile pictures to the rainbow flags of the LGBTIAQ movement or shared the flag in their newsfeeds. It was one day after the mass shooting inside a gay nightclub in Orlando, USA, in which forty-nine were killed and fifty-eight wounded by a terrorist claiming to be affiliated with the Islamic State. By altering their digitally embodied appearance, social media users performed support for the victims of the attack, made a political statement against homophobia, and advocated values of a pluralist and open society (see Jenkins et al. 2019). The practice of replacing one's profile picture, which usually depicts one's own face, with the rainbow flag served to negate the user's identity and replace it with an improper name—a collective call for freedom and diversity.

The use of the rainbow flag on social media is not restricted to this individual case. Every year in the early summer months, many social media users apply a filter to their regular profile pictures so that their faces appear behind a transparent rainbow colour scheme (see Gerbaudo 2015). Annual Pride demonstrations and celebrations recall the Stonewall riots in New York in 1969, in which queer people publicly claimed their equal rights. Today, many who define themselves as heterosexual use the rainbow filter. By queering their image, they do not proclaim a homosexual identity, but they claim the possibility of living queer desires in a diverse society. They perform a politically progressive identity that rejects heteronormativity.

In summary, pictures of pregnant bodies concealing the face, the use of Black avatars by white activists, and the alteration of profile pictures through rainbow filters all illustrate that digital engagement does not entail leaving the body behind. Rather, it facilitates the expression of diversity through embodied presence. Yet, the mediation and interruption provided by computer interfaces enables and even necessitates a reconstruction of embodiment, a rearticulation of identity that generates some leeway for the discontinuity of identity. While the selected examples focus on cases with a high degree of anonymity, other examples that explicitly focus on continuing analogue identity performances online also lend support to this argument. The #MeToo campaign, for example, consists of victims of sexual harassment and rape disclosing their identities through social media (Mendes, Ringrose, and Keller 2018). In another case of hashtag activism, sex workers shared pictures of themselves in their everyday lives to counter the prejudice directed towards them under #FacesOfProstitution (Middleweek 2019). In both of these cases, anonymity is not an evident element. Yet, the interruption of established modes of identity performances through interfaces necessitates a reconstruction of identity. At the beginning of this process, the screen is always blank. Hence the subject has some freedom to reconceptualize the self, to select specific pictures or to relay certain stories. Through social media 'we represent different versions of ourselves in each profile picture we choose' (Walker Rettberg 2014: 42).

Transforming Physical Bodies through the Digital

The continuity of identity addressed in the examples of hashtag activism is the central focus of current debates in cyberfeminism. They observe the extension of analogue to online identity performances. While it might appear as if this has little to contribute to an understanding of self-transformation, they nevertheless add crucial insights. Digitally enabled self-transformation does not only happen on the screen, as cyberdemocratic discourses suggest, they also bleed into analogue space. This happens in two ways. First, online body images change how we *perceive* analogue bodies; they alter how we see ourselves and others offline. We are looking at analogue bodies through a digitized perspective and hence digitize offline corporeality. Second, online body images are used as a tool for the physical transformation of analogue bodies. The following examples are less explicitly cases of democratic engagement, although they do illustrate a new participatory culture. They nevertheless have important political implications. The transformation of offline bodies affects the formation of democratic subjectivity in political interaction.

Current cyberfeminist debates illustrate how analogue bodies are transformed through the digital. On pro-anorexia websites, mostly young girls suffering from anorexia exchange diet and self-starving tips and share digital images of skinny bodies as 'thinspiration' (Gies 2008). In a similar vein, websites of transgender communities give advice on physical body transformations, from makeup tips to hormone therapy and surgery experiences. 'Instead of seeing cyberspace as a place in which to experience the absence of the body ... these girls and self-identified women use digital technologies in ways that simultaneously bring the body "online" (through digital photos uploaded to the web) and take the digital "offline" (through information gleaned online to transform their embodied selves)' (Daniels 2009: 117). Anorexic girls and trans people strive to transform their *physical* bodies *through the digital*. Other websites serve communities of obese men to positively affirm their body image and reinterpret mainstream beauty ideals (Monaghan 2005). While here the analogue body is not physically changed, its perception is profoundly altered. Again, the subject of these digital/analogue transformations is not entirely autonomous. It depends on technological apparatuses that function as evocative objects affording and restricting possibilities for performing the self (Brophy 2010; Cohen 2012). The analogue body is not a stable unit, but a material process constituted by performance through body language, clothes, and makeup. The digital body follows the same logic. It relies on materiality. Digital embodiment is generated through the performative act of going online and reconstituting the self as an assemblage of digital objects (Brophy 2010).

Such digital/analogue self-transformations are also evident in the recent emergence of the so-called quantified self. Here the idea of the transformation of the physical body and even of personalities with the help of digital tools is taken to the next level. Those who seek self-transformation use various websites and smartphone applications to quantify their bodies and activities. Through smartphones and other wearable devices such as wrist bands, clothing clips, necklaces, rings, and even sensors in disposable patches, self-quantifiers measure their calorie intake, physical activity, blood chemistry, blood pressure, body temperature, heart rate, and sleeping patterns (Walker Rettberg 2014).

> The long-term vision of QS [quantified self] activity is that of a systemic moni-toring approach where an individual's continuous personal information climate provides real-time performance optimization suggestions ... The individual body becomes a more knowable, calculable, and administrable object through QS activity, and individuals have an increasingly intimate relationship with data as it mediates the experience of reality.
>
> (Swan 2013: 85)

Around the practice of self-quantification, a movement formed that promotes this life style. In regular meetings self-quantifiers share experiences and encourage each other in their respective projects of self-improvement (V. Lee 2014). Because of these participatory aspects of the movement and the personal control over one's own data, some see self-quantification as democratic practice: 'One impor-tant outcome of big data QS is the empowerment of the individual through an intuitive understanding and ongoing interaction with their data. Data is democ-ratized from scientific practices and made universal and meaningful for use by all individuals' (Swan 2013: 95). Others, however, warn of self-quantification as a neoliberal strategy in which discipline is internalized and appears as pleasur-able (Whitson 2013). An important aspect of self-quantification is the gamification of every aspect of life. Self-quantification apps provide points, ratings, and peer acknowledgement. These are the same mechanisms that make social media attrac-tive for many who enjoy the attention and competitive elements of quantified likes, friends, and followers. Increasing these numbers becomes a game that profoundly affects relationships and identities.

Self-quantification results in assemblages of data that represent specific aspects of the self and, in combination with other data from social media and smart-phone apps, produce a 'data double'—a digital replica or (failing) citation of the self (Walker Rettberg 2014). This 'self is one that is spatially expanded, with a broad suite of exosenses' (Swan 2013: 95). In many ways, this data double resem-bles the self-reflection in computers as mirrors described by Turkle (1984: 156–7). Her anxious Narcissus, who looks at his own reflection not out of vanity but out of anxiety about the existence of the self, corresponds to today's trends of self-quantification: 'Apps which allow us to see our own data allow us to see ourselves. We look at our data doubles as we gaze into a mirror as teenagers wondering who we are and who we might be' (Walker Rettberg 2014: 87).

Can Anonymity Enable Diversity?

The observations of self-quantification and continuous identity performances on social media point to a diminishing role of anonymity online when compared to the default textuality of the 1990s. Beyond my contention that all of these continuous identity performances entail elements of anonymity through the disruptive power of interfaces, there are still ample digital spaces in which anonymity plays a central role today (Asenbaum 2017). For example, the findings in Tom Boellstorff's (2008) study on identity performance through visual avatars in the online game Second Life bear remarkable similarities to those of Turkle (1995) published twenty-three years earlier. Although the medium of online role play had changed profoundly from text-only to communication through digitally embodied avatars, the observations are consistent overall.

In Second Life individual participants create multiple avatars of various sexes, races, and species. Users experiment with aspects of their selves not usually expressed offline. These performances are often perceived as revealing true aspects of the self. This can be illustrated by the story of the digital avatar Pavia who explains:

> I'm a man in real life, but about three weeks ago I learned that I'm transsexual ... Here in Second Life I created something new in myself that I never realized was there before. At first it was just role playing, but then I grew to love Pavia. I kept infusing myself into her, but then something unexpected started to happen: Pavia started coming out in the real world. I became her, she became me.
>
> (cited in Boellstorff 2008: 138)

These forms of anonymous identity play are also relevant in political contexts today. Social media and online games such as Second Life are often appropriated as claimed spaces when they are used against their original commercial intentions. The annual 16 Days of Activism Against Gender-Based Violence, for instance, have spread to Second Life. Here feminist activists set up virtual discussion events, meetings, and exhibitions around the topic of gendered violence. Participants design female avatars with black eyes, bruises, and bleeding wounds as a way of raising awareness (Motter 2011). In another example, an LGBTAIQ community established itself in the virtual role play fantasy game World of Warcraft. Apart from political discussions on LGBTAIQ issues, the community also organized virtual Pride parades. The fact that the 5000 users of the community created 15,000 characters, including the practice of gender swapping, is indicative of playful identity exploration. Global in scope, this community also included participants from countries where homosexual practices are banned (McKenna et al. 2011).

Besides claiming commercial space on social media, anonymous online activists also create their own spaces as alternative media. The New York art collective Guerrilla Girls, for example, extends its analogue interventions in the disguise of gorilla masks through digital images and videos of gorilla performances online. In particular, the breakaway group Guerrilla Girls Broadband have created a subversive online presence. On their website, users can join by virtually dressing up as gorillas. Core members of Guerrilla Girls Broadband themselves take on the identities of female artists who have not gained the recognition they deserve in the male-dominated art business. A 'cartography of choice' maps abortion clinics and emails can be sent to 'bad bosses' anonymously to address sexual harassment, unequal pay, or other work-related grievances (Stein 2011). Precarious work relations were also central to the digital claimed spaces of the Euro Mayday Netparades in 2004 and 2005. The annual Euro Mayday Parade draws attention to the current precariousness of work, which especially affects women. On the website of the Mayday Netparade, users could create their individual protest avatars and join a digital street demonstration. Women, who are often underrepresented in the imagery of traditional Labour Day parades, took centre stage online as 'the parade's visual icons of protests positively underlined diversity and differences as an asset of the collective struggle' (Mattoni and Doerr 2007: 132).

Identity exploration in claimed spaces on the internet does not require an entire virtual world with fully animated avatars like in the cases discussed so far. Rather, social media provide tools for the everyday practice of identity play as part of political engagement. On sites such as Facebook and Twitter, users frequently change their social media profile pictures for flags, logos, or portraits of others. In the uprising in Egypt in 2011, for example, thousands of social media users changed their profile picture for the image of Khaled Said, a twenty-eight-year-old blogger killed by police in Alexandria (Gerbaudo 2015). These profile pictures then become part of the personal assemblage that defines the self. For social media users, employing profile pictures that depict someone else or stand for a political cause is 'a move that simultaneously anonymises them a little and shows how profile pictures can function as metonyms: this is a part of me' (Walker Rettberg 2014: 41).

Conclusion

So after all of this, how is the space of appearance reconfigured in the digital age? How can subjects appear when they are not physically present? The poststructuralist-inspired cyberdemocracy debate of the 1990s conceptualizes cyberspace as a separate realm from analogue space that follows its own logics. Here subjects appear only through their words as disembodied beings—a notion that is still advocated today (T. Smith 2017). Along with several critics, I have argued that this position overlooks the central role that bodies and materiality play in these digital spaces. The subject, even if anonymous, is always embodied and materializes its identity in multiple ways. In contrast with the cyberdemocracy debate, which explains cyberspace as divorced from physical space, the current literature conflates the two. The distinction between the digital and the physical collapses. I find neither of these positions productive. Overcoming the distinction between digital and physical space leaves us without sufficient concepts to differentiate between them. Rather than collapsing physical and digital space, we need an understanding of how they relate to each other. This will also explain how subjects appear in digital spaces.

To this end, the chapter explained digital space as an assemblage in which material objects, sentient bodies, and performative expressions interact. The material spaces in which participants are located and connected through a network of cables and satellites interact with the sentient bodies of participants and their performative expressions online. Yet, digital space is distinct insofar as the interfaces that mediate communication always also interrupt identity. The transfer from offline to online entails an interruption, an opening that facilitates innovation, exploration, and play. The digital representation of the subject fails to perfectly copy the offline self. Even Members of Parliament, for example, who strive to maintain continuous online self-representations, present themselves differently on different websites (Koop and Marland 2012).

This interruption that compels the subject to reconstruct its identity contains a moment of anonymity. The potential for disidentification, even if we are mostly unaware of it, is inherent to the act of going online. It resides in the selection of profile pictures on social media that represent a certain version of the self, in curating selfies, creating avatars, choosing the skin colour of emojis, and in the creation of pseudonyms. This performative repertoire affords new possibilities for the fugitive self to express its multiplicity.

All these digital self-representations—selfies, avatars, emojis, profile pictures, digital ribbons, colour filters, pseudonyms, videos, and textual expressions—enter into the identity assemblages that define us. The interaction of these digital self-representations with our physical bodies, clothing, and hairstyle mediated through the technological devices in our pockets, on our wrists, necks, feet, and ears, reconfigure the subject as cyborg. The questions we need to ask are not about the separateness or convergence of the digital and physical, but rather about how all of these things that constitute the self assemble. In cyborgian assemblages, technological devices are never neutral, but have political implications. They are created with a purpose. And as evocative objects they call on us in certain ways. More than other things, they actively enter processes of subject constitution.

These concepts of digital space and cyborgian subjects as assemblages explain how the space of appearance functions in the digital age. The body is not absent from digital engagement. On the contrary, the physical body is always there; without it, the perception of the digital would not be possible (Cohen 2012; Butler 2015: 94). The physical body interacts with digital body images. It is replicated in the selfies of the 99 percent who digitize their bodies in protest against austerity. New bodies are created as stereotypical Black avatars to protest racism. Bodies are altered through rainbow colour filters to promote open societies. The bodies of female avatars are depicted as bruised to protest sexual violence. Images of human ribs covered only by skin are shared through digital networks to inspire self-starvation. Fat bodies are shown to counter established beauty standards. Transgendered bodies are digitized to encourage those who wish to transition.

These examples lead the way to a new digital politics of presence by providing novel answers to the dilemma of difference. Digital spaces often serve the representation of bodies with marginalized identities as advocated by the politics of presence. Cyberfeminist counterpublics as claimed spaces online provide the context for peer support, reaffirming and expressing identity in public discourses. Digital spaces can also be employed for radical re-embodiment as in the case of the Habbo Hotel raid. The performance of Black digital bodies by majority white users can be seen as part of a politics of presence as it articulates diversity and challenges domination. Whether identities online are performed in a continuous or a discontinuous manner, it is crucial that the reconfiguration of identity online always entails a moment of anonymity and a potential for disidentification. The interruption of identity results in new identities, even if they come in the shape of old ones. The recreation of the self online always entails a choice—of images, of avatars, of pseudonyms. This enhances our agency over the performance of the self and can be part of a politics of presence, in which identity articulation becomes an intentional performance of marginalization.

7

Unleashing the Democratic Microverse

Towards Systemic Transformations

We are currently experiencing new freedoms in defining our identities. Nonbinary and fluid gender definitions are entering the mainstream. The heterosexual matrix appears deeply disrupted. The #MeToo movement reflects and contributes to a paradigm shift towards equality of the sexes. The Black Lives Matter movement, as the largest movement in US history, challenges structural racism and in doing so contests racial stereotyping. The decolonization of theory and practice has become one of the leading mantras in the social sciences and humanities. The emancipation of the self and the deconstruction of identity-based hierarchies are opening the way towards more democratic futures.

At the same time, however, it appears as if the world around us is about to collapse. Our everyday lives, the daily routines that we had taken for granted, are being shaken by the COVID-19 pandemic. Our living spaces are being drastically redefined by lockdown policies. The pandemic strikes against the backdrop of an ever-accelerating advancement of neoliberal policies around the world, decomposing welfare state regimes and dismantling workers' rights. The climate emergency, meanwhile, only begins to fully unravel. The material impact of these three parallel emergencies—the pandemic, neoliberalism, and the climate crisis—is causing disproportionate devastation in the Global South, and is only slowly dawning on many in the Global North.

So what is the role of the politics of becoming advanced in this book in a world characterized by material devastation? In the face of current destruction and destabilization, the material aspects of a good life, which have been temporarily overshadowed by post-material values (Norris and Inglehart 2019), resurface. This concluding chapter reflects on the place of the politics of becoming within a broader emancipatory strategy that calls for a profound redistribution of resources. It situates the personal freedom to self-identify in a movement towards democratic transformations. The key argument I am advancing is that not only are the self and identity constantly becoming, but so are the societal configurations of which they are a part. Personal and systemic transformation are inherently linked. Building on Nancy Fraser's argument, I intend to move beyond playing off identity and recognition against materiality and distribution: 'Only by joining a robustly

The Politics of Becoming. Hans Asenbaum, Oxford University Press. © Hans Asenbaum (2023).
DOI: 10.1093/oso/9780192858870.003.0007

egalitarian politics of distribution to a substantively inclusive, class-sensitive politics of recognition can we build a counterhegemonic bloc leading us beyond the current crisis to a better world' (Fraser 2019: 61).

To make sense of the interdependency of personal and systemic transformation, I propose the concept of a 'democratic microverse', which draws attention to the prefigurative powers of democratic spaces. These spaces afford a temporal projection, making potential democratic futures real in the here and now. Democratic spaces are always a future-making exercise—one that does not simply produce futures through their output (e.g. decision making) but one that produces futures by disturbing the established power distribution of the present and in doing so demonstrates that democracy could be otherwise (Asenbaum and Hanusch 2021). This prefiguration makes real a democratic microverse—a miniature version of what democracy could look like. It starts from within the democratic subject and projects its hopes and democratic aspirations to a societal and potentially planetary level. In saying that the democratic revolt starts within each of us, I do not mean to individualize the responsibility for democratic transformation. To democratize self and society, we need a democratic movement and a community that treats each of us with love and respect. Through a Black trans feminist vision we can see that:

> we might become anything at all, something wildly other than what we are, and in order to give in to that we need to be encountered by a world that really, actually truly holds and loves us by never, ever presuming to know what shape we will take, what we will want, before we show up.
>
> (Bey 2022: 6)

To develop the notion of a democratic microverse, I draw on two central concepts advanced in this book: assemblage and interruption. I claim that if we think about society, and reality more broadly, in terms of assemblage as a mosaic of objects, subjects, and moments, then we can begin to think about how to reassemble society anew. Assemblage thinking allows us to include nonhumans, inanimate objects, and natural forces in the project of radicalizing democracy. It enables us to transcend the binary thinking of identity recognition vs material redistribution. The notion of interruption is central to this endeavour. It signals a pause for rethinking and remaking, a structural intervention that leads to a sustainable form of change. Interruption is a tool for breaking up established patterns of domination and unleashing the transformative potential of democratic innovation (Asenbaum 2021a). I follow Graham Smith (2021: 112), who argues that moving towards sustainable, democratic futures may require 'a more disruptive political strategy—one that brings into question the dominant position of established democratic institutions'.

Rather than the end of a book, I think of this chapter as the start of a conversation—a conversation about personal and systemic transformation. Academic specialization often results in overlooking the big picture. Questions of structural inequalities, environmental destruction, and systemic change, however, are more pressing than ever.

To take a step back and look at the big picture, my concluding reflections to this book will proceed in four steps. I will first recap the politics of becoming developed throughout this book. Second, I will turn to debates about recognition vs redistribution and explore basic income as a redistributive mechanism that may enable democratic self-transformation. Third, I will engage with debates about deliberative and democratic systems. I identify the emancipatory potential of the systems debate, which allows to think about inclusive and equal participation beyond small-scale forums. At the same time, however, systems thinking also tends to project democratic ideals onto real-world polities that are deeply unequal. To unlock the emancipatory potential of systems thinking, in the fourth step I will employ assemblage theory and the concept of interruption to put forward a transformative vision of democracy. I will propose the concept of a democratic microverse as a starting point for systemic change towards socially and ecologically just democratic futures.

The Politics of Becoming: A Recap

The politics of becoming offers a novel strategy to counter the discrimination of marginalized groups within democratic spaces such as citizens' assemblies, parliamentary debates, and social movement meetings. Everyday modes of discrimination are carried over into democratic spaces as participants are judged by their looks, accents, and culturally-coded mannerisms. Such prejudice results in power asymmetries, which compromise the democratic core ideal of equality. What is more, prejudice also confines freedom of expression for everyone, whether they belong to marginalized or non-marginalized communities. Categorization according to visual identity markers of gender, race, class, sexuality, bodily ability, and age prevents participants from exploring their inner multiplicity and expressing themselves in an unrestricted manner, which compromises the democratic core ideal of freedom.

To counter discrimination, feminist debates associated with the term 'difference democracy' suggest a politics of presence (Phillips 1995). Marginalized subjects need to draw attention to their gendered, sexualized, and racialized bodies in the space of appearance in order to advance their equality. However, this identity politics—often realized through quota regulations—entails the dilemma of difference: it promotes equality through the visual presence of marginalized identities, but in doing so it also entails the reification and confinement of identities (Young

1989). While subjects might, indeed, be regarded as more equal, they are also less free to express the multiple aspects of their selves.

To find ways out of the dilemma of difference, in this book I have offered a reformulation of the politics of presence as part of a broader strategy of a politics of becoming that combines the embodied expression of diversity with the freedom of self-transformation. The politics of becoming affords new freedoms to the fugitive self, which is always on the run, trying to escape identity reifications through hegemonic identity interpellations. It rests on practices of disidentification that entail the rejection of dominant identity ascriptions and interrupt established modes of identification (Muñoz 1999; Rancière 1999). This interruption of the coherent performance of an officially identified persona reconfigures the space of appearance by enlarging the subject's freedom to explore different sides of the multiple self. This kind of disidentification always goes along with subjectivization. It entails not only the rejection of identity interpellations but also the creation of new identities (Mouffe 2013: 28) through improper names (Deseriis 2015), thus allowing for temporary self-transformation. The democratic subject becomes subject to change.

The literature on disidentification suggests that such an interruption of identity can be achieved through critical engagement with hegemonic discourses that produce hierarchical identities. It proposes modes of deconstruction as a means of critically interrogating discourses, and thus loosens the grip of identity categories (Mouffe 1995b; Muñoz 1999). It also suggests the resignification of the concepts that describe identity so as to recast their meanings in positive terms (Butler 2004; Lloyd 2007)—a strategy also advocated by difference democrats (Young 1990). The politics of becoming includes, but also goes beyond, such intellectual endeavours and explores more practical means of disidentification. It suggests that disidentification can be realized by employing anonymity as a radical democratic practice. Anonymity and disidentification are by no means the same. Rather, anonymity harbours the potential for disidentification. It can function as a tool that interrupts hegemonic identity interpellations by negating some aspects of the physically embodied and legally identified persona. But anonymity consists of more than mere concealment, as is commonly supposed. Anonymity entails producing new identities and exploring sides of the multiple self that are otherwise hidden. It affords the articulation of private sentiments in the public sphere. Anonymity makes the absent present.

To make sense of such identity reconfigurations through anonymity, I have suggested understanding identity as a spatial assemblage of things. Things such as blood flows, skin pigments, (sex) organs, clothing, accessories, hairstyles, makeup, and discursive concepts of race, gender, sexuality, class, age, occupation, and religion circulate in assemblages that define the self. This new materialist-inspired perspective argues that rather than constructing identities, as suggested in poststructuralist debates, subjects *assemble* (Bennett 2010). Anonymity interrupts these assemblages through things such as masks, veils, voting booths, pen and paper, walls and spray cans, computer screens, pseudonyms, avatars, and blank spaces. This interruption allows subjects to reassemble. It facilitates a temporary reconfiguration of the identity assemblage in which the subject can experience different sides of the multiple self. After the anonymizing things are ejected from the assemblage—after the masks are taken off and the voting booths are left—bodies return to their positions assigned by the established order. Normalcy prevails, but the experience of the interruption lasts.

In the digital age, anonymity becomes an inherent part of everyday communication as subjects (re)articulate their identities on digital interfaces. The subject is reconfigured as a cyborg (Haraway 1991 [1985]) as smartphones, electronic wrist bands, clothing clips, necklaces, rings, and sensors in disposable patches are applied to the physical body and thus enter the assemblage of the self. These physical objects applied to the human body carry a moment of anonymity that is built into them. They both mediate and interrupt identity. Through this interruption, subjects are compelled to reassemble their identities online. They can perform their selves in a more continuous manner on social media platforms such as Facebook where they circulate visual self-representations. In democratic spaces generated through hashtag activism such as the #MeToo campaign, they reify their digital identities, mirroring analogue ones. However, these digital objects that enter into identity assemblages are not mere replications of the offline identity. Rather, they involve acts of curation and expand the sphere of personal agency over self-representations. Other digital spaces call for more discontinuous identity performances and invite users to construct different avatars or pseudonyms, to employ emojis, colour filters, flags, political symbols, images of others such as partners, relatives, or political figures, or to construct the self through mere textuality.

In both digital and analogue spaces, which in the digital age are reconfigured as cyborgian spaces, it is the particular spatial configurations that invite such varied identity performances. The architecture of particular website interfaces affects the identity configurations assembled on them (Kavada 2012; Beyer 2014a; Forestal 2017), as does the physical architecture of parliaments and public squares (Parkinson 2012). These spaces themselves, however, are constructed by humans and through human agency. Space and identity, then, are part of a dialectical process of mutual constitution. Assemblages of identity and space are in constant flux; through their mutual affectivity, they continuously assemble and reassemble each other.

Assembling identity through modes of disidentification afforded by anonymity explains the politics of presence in novel ways. Such disidentifactory articulations of the self are neither disembodied, private, nor necessarily invisible. They are public performances that re-embody the subject through digital, textual, or physical identity reifications that are perceptible in multiple ways through images, sounds, and words. This rearticulation of identity, making the absent present, generates new prospects for the politics of presence. When subjects reify their bodies as stereotypical Black avatars to block an online space in protest against racism, when they assemble as bruised, digital bodies to protest against sexual abuse, and when they depict their obese, pregnant, or ill bodies in selfies to challenge austerity policies, they take part in the politics of presence. When the activists of Pussy Riot employ colourful balaclavas to articulate femininity, strength, and diversity, when Guerrilla Girls wear gorilla masks to challenge the entrenched patriarchal structures of the art world, when queer teenagers negotiate their identities through the use of graffiti on bathroom walls, and when people wear hoods to perform their marginalized race/class identity in protest against racially motivated police brutality, they take part in the politics of presence.

Certainly, not every example discussed in this book can be seen as part of a politics of presence. While the white, grinning Guy Fawkes mask of Anonymous and the pseudonyms employed by Hamilton and Madison in the debate about the American Constitution do facilitate an exploration of the multiple self, they do not perform marginalized identities. For this reason, I have developed a broader concept of a politics of becoming of which the politics of presence is one strategy. All practices within the politics of becoming employ moments of disidentification to rearrange identity assemblages and explore the multiple self. The politics of presence, in particular, focuses on identity reifications that articulate diversity and embody the marginalized in the public sphere. This even includes the intentionally continuous performances of the #MeToo campaign or the self-representations of Members of Parliament on various websites and social media (Asenbaum 2020). These continuous identity expressions always articulate a subject-in-process (Lloyd 2005) and perform future selves (Connolly 1996). Participants in SlutWalks, Black Lives Matter protests, and Pride marches express a certain version of their selves. Each citation of the self slightly diverges from the previous (Butler 2004). This is because the coherent performance of the self is always an act of masquerade, an effort to hold together what drifts apart. The self, however, remains forever fugitive.

The politics of becoming, then, does not promote one particular type of space that facilitates one particular kind of identity performance. Rather, the politics of becoming, as part of a progressive strategy for deep societal transformation, calls for a wide variety of democratic spaces: spaces that allow for discontinuous identity performances by constructing alternative selves and spaces that rearticulate established identities. The digital spaces of marginalized groups that form counterpublics for peer support and challenging inequality are as central to the politics of becoming as spaces that facilitate discontinuous digital embodiments and identity play. Some spaces might employ mere textuality, while others make use of avatars, and others still invite people to meet in the flesh. It is the plurality of such diverse democratic spaces that characterizes the politics of becoming.

Beyond Recognition vs Redistribution

The politics of becoming responds to questions of identity and discrimination. It contributes to an agenda Nancy Fraser calls 'the politics of recognition'. Disidentification, I have argued, allows for new identity articulations—alternative claims for recognition. The politics of becoming, however, says little about structural economic inequality. So far, it does not provide structural solutions that enable systemic transformations. The politics of redistribution championed by many critical thinkers appears hardly affected by novel identity configurations and the newly won freedom of self-expression. In revisiting her work on recognition and redistribution, Fraser argues that today's societies have made great strides towards the recognition of diverse identities. This progress, however, comes at the expense of the politics of redistribution. In other words, while the call of the marginalized for equality has been met by an enhancement of their standing, economic resources are increasingly concentrated. Concessions in recognition, then, appear as tokens for the exacerbation of economic inequality (Fraser 2019).

To advance systemic transformations, we need to move beyond political strategies that divorce recognition and redistribution. It is not difficult to see how the two are linked, as social status (recognition) correlates with the ownership of economic resources (distribution). This connection also affects the politics of becoming. Exploring the multiple self often requires economic resources. Consider the concrete approaches to multiplying and reconstructing the self suggested in this book. Online communication needs access to the internet. Building new cyborgian selves requires costly smart devices. Digital divides and digital inequalities constitute significant barriers to participation on both a global and a national scale (Robinson et al. 2015). Exclusion from online participation along gender, race, class, age, bodily ability, and geographic divides leaves these new possibilities of engagement beyond the reach of many. Exploring the inner multiplicity through artistic engagement, psychotherapy, and discourse analysis all require financial resources.

The availability of these resources has often been framed as social and economic rights. Carole Pateman, in contrast, argues that access to economic resources for self-realization is a *democratic* right. Pateman makes the case for unconditional basic income set at a level that enables a modest but decent life. 'My argument', she claims, 'is that a basic income should be seen, like the suffrage, as a democratic right, or a political birthright' (Pateman 2006: 86). The systemic impact of basic income is not to be underestimated. It would make people less dependent on exploitative work relations and afford 'the freedom not to be employed' (86). This is why 'basic income [is] an element in a democratic social transformation' (87). My point is not to blindly support basic income irrespective of its appeal for neoliberal strategies to dismantle the welfare state or conservative aspirations to confine women to their homes. My point is rather to consider which democratic spaces could be opened up for self-transformation through a more equal distribution of resources. Self-transformation and systemic transformation go hand in hand.

(Deliberative) Democratic Systems: Emancipation or Conservation?

An emancipatory strategy encompassing both recognition and redistribution calls for attention to the *systemic* nature of democratic interaction. What is needed, then, is a theory of how various democratic spaces connect. The systemic turn in democratic scholarship has made considerable advancements in this regard. Deliberative systems are conceptualized as networks of communicative interaction throughout society (Mansbridge 1999a; Mansbridge et al. 2012). Deliberative system theorists point to the spatial nature of democratic engagement as they explore deliberation 'across a comprehensive system incorporating a range of differentiated but interconnected spaces' (Kuyper 2016: 311). Just like democratic space (discussed in Chapter 2), the deliberative system is defined by the delimitation of an inside and an outside: 'The boundaries of a deliberative system should enable us to distinguish what is internal and what is external to it. These boundaries might be conceptualized solely in spatial terms, such that we think of a deliberative system as a distinct set of sites and linkages between them' (Smith 2016: 154). While various approaches within the deliberative system debate can be differentiated (Owen and Smith 2015), they commonly focus on scaling up deliberation through the transmission from public space (including invited and claimed spaces) to the empowered space of state institutions (closed spaces) (Dryzek 2009).

The debate about deliberative systems has recently been diversified much in the sense called for by the multi-perspectival understanding of radical democracy advanced in this book with participatory, pragmatist, and agonistic systems thinking adding new insights (Asenbaum 2022b). Michael Saward challenges 'deliberation's dominant hold on the imagination of democratic theorists' and asks, 'if a systemic view is what matters to our thinking about democracy, why is it not the democratic system, rather than the deliberative system, that is the focus?' (Saward 2021: 22). Contributions from a participatory perspective have particularly enriched this debate. Inspired by Pateman's (2012) argument that participatory democracy needs to connect several participatory sites within an institutional structure—such as the participatory budgeting processes in Porto Alegre—several scholars are exploring the systemic connections in large-scale democratic innovations (Dean, Boswell, and Smith 2019; Parry, Asenbaum, and Ercan 2021). Beyond the connectivity between various democratic innovations, the debate about participatory systems also highlights the interaction between social movements and state institutions and hybrid online/offline modes of engagement (Bussu 2019).

There is an emancipatory potential inherent to systems thinking. Connecting various democratic spaces enables us to envision alternative democratic futures that challenge the established distribution of power (Curato, Hammond, and Min 2019). At the same time, however, there lies a danger in systems thinking that is often overlooked—a danger that profoundly hampers its emancipatory potential. When we look at the connections between our everyday talk, activist engagements, democratic innovations, media discourses, and formal governance structures, and we observe these connections as democratic process, hence charging them with the democratic values we cherish, we tend to see democracy where it is not. We project our democratic ideals onto a system that is deeply flawed, ridden with corruption and pervaded by structural inequalities, colonial legacies, racism, misogyny, and homophobia.

In *Deliberation Naturalized*, Ana Tanasoca argues that deliberation is already at work everywhere we look. To grasp deliberative systems in this manner, Tanasoca's realist account of deliberative democracy builds on a 'more capacious' concept of democratic deliberation of which 'some criteria must be relaxed' (Tanasoca 2020: 6). Instead of unfolding the emancipatory potential of systems thinking, the normative ambitions of such accounts are modest. Systems thinking may serve to conserve or even exacerbate the status quo characterized by structural inequalities. In some instances, Ricardo Mendonça argues, 'the system warrants and nurtures a vicious cycle of political exclusion, while claiming to maintain the appearance of inclusion' (Mendonça 2016: 175).

From the Democratic Microverse to Alternative Futures

So how can the emancipatory potential of systems thinking in democratic theory be unlocked? The concepts of assemblage and interruption developed throughout this book can make a valuable contribution. New materialist theories, in which assemblage thinking is situated, afford an opportunity to refocus on materiality and structural inequality (Coole and Frost 2010: 25). Thinking about systems as assemblages draws our attention to the many things—human and nonhuman— that come together in ever-novel and unforeseen configurations. Rather than a static and hierarchical system, assemblages are constantly evolving, changing, becoming. The term 'assemblage' does not only denote the constellation of various things, but also the very process by which such a formation is brought about. Assemblage is both a state and a becoming, which indicates its agentic and vital nature (Bennett 2010; DeLanda 2016).

If both the self and democratic spaces are composed of multiple things of different qualities that through various forces adhere to each other, then systems are too. Through its flat ontology that includes humans and nonhumans equally, assemblage theory opens up new prospects for thinking about democracy in more inclusive terms. It opens the view on a democracy constituted by the interaction of human bodies (Machin 2022), verbal and nonverbal performances (Ercan, Asenbaum, and Mendonça 2022), nonhuman animals (Meijer 2019), material objects (Honig 2017), natural events (Javier and Dryzek 2020), digital technology (Asenbaum 2021b), future generations (Smith 2021), and planetary boundaries (Dryzek and Pickering 2019).

In the same manner as identity assemblages can be interrupted and rearranged, so can systems. In the case of identity, I have proposed that the anonymity afforded through objects such as masks, veils, computer screens, and digital avatars can cause an interruption. This potentially leads to a moment of disidentification—a distance from the coherent, public persona—that temporarily rearranges the identity assemblage and thus allows for living the multiple self. How does this idea apply to governance systems?

In the introduction to this book, I argued that democratic spaces themselves function as an interruption of the established order of things. They disturb the representative institutional logic of liberal democracy by opening spaces that work differently. Here, I deepen this idea. My core argument is that by reordering things, these spaces function as a 'democratic microverse' that prefigures alternative democratic futures in the here and now. They are moments where possible democratic configurations break into the present. In assembling democratic spaces, we live alternative futures today (Asenbaum and Hanusch 2021).

Let's take a step back and unpack this argument. Andrea Felicetti critiques systems thinking for conceptualizing democracy in terms of clear connections and hierarchies between formal institutions: 'the very idea of a system might not alone suffice to account for the complexities involved in our democracies. The notion of assemblage offers a valuable alternative to that of a system in theorizing about democratic societies' (Felicetti 2021: 1599). Assemblage, then, accounts for more than formal institutions and clear structures. It pays attention to emergence, complexity, informality, spontaneity, and unforeseen change. Alongside Felicetti I argue that assemblage theory has much to offer for the democratic systems debate. One of the contributions highlighted by Felicetti is the attention paid by assemblage thinking not only to connection but also to disconnection—what I have conceptualized as interruption: 'Referring to the idea of assemblage might strengthen our ability to reflect on how disruption concurs to shape democratic politics' (Felicetti 2021: 1598).

Deliberative systems theory is preoccupied with connectivity—it aims at mending a broken system (Hendriks, Ercan, and Boswell 2020). Invited and claimed democratic spaces, in this context, are often seen as the remedy that may 'cure' or 'save' the democratic system (Geissel and Newton 2012; della Porta 2020). Disconnection is understood as the democratic failure to establish and maintain functioning communication channels between the citizenry and governments. Assemblage thinking, in contrast, enables us to see the democratic value of disconnection. Interruption breaks up established modes of governance, however temporarily, and opens up possibilities for reassembling democracy differently. As I have noted in the introduction, interruption is by no means always democratic. Interruption unfolds its democratic potential when it breaks up hierarchies and enables the temporary experience of freedom and equality (Rancière 1999).

Interrupting the established configuration of things brings out an important aspect that is neglected in democratic theory, which is the value of disorder, spontaneity, and serendipity. Just as the democratic systems debate focuses on clear structures and connectivity, the literature on democratic innovations focuses on design. Intentionally planned democratic spaces attempt to pre-structure—and to a certain extent pre-determine—human interaction. The perspective of design thinking in democratic theory makes imperceptible, however, the democratic value of spontaneity, unforeseen encounters, and coincidence. This is what Frederic Hanusch and I call *democratic serendipity* (Asenbaum and Hanusch 2021). Democratic serendipity unfolds its potential through a creative, open, and joyful exploration as a part of democratic interaction. This open engagement with novelty breaks up established patterns and reassembles the known in unknown ways (Asenbaum 2022c). This resonates with what Rahel Süß calls 'democratic provocation'. Süß argues that instead of conflict resolution as the aim of established democratic spaces, 'we can conceptualize democratic action first and foremost as a provocative force, one that opens spaces for critique' (Süß 2021: 12). Instead of repairing a broken system, we can then move towards more substantial democratic transformations as 'provocation is defined as a democratic practice that aims to keep the future open' (Süß 2021: 13).

We need new democratic spaces that are not so much focused on design and pre-structuring democratic engagement, but on affording democratic serendipity. Instead of a pure focus on rational deliberation, new democratic spaces may entail playfulness and creativity, for example as democratic playgrounds and democratic ateliers (Asenbaum and Hanusch 2021). They function as democratic openings by drawing on verbal and nonverbal interaction which express that which is beyond words (Mendonça, Ercan, and Asenbaum 2020). These spaces prefigure alternative futures. Any participatory formation constitutes a *democratic microverse*—a miniature constellation of what the future may hold. In assembling material objects, sentient bodies, and performative expressions in a certain way, democratic spaces enact and materialize visions of democracy. They connect the identity constellations of participants, their democratic hopes and aspirations, to a potential democratic society that the future might hold.

If we think of democratic spaces as small-scale pre-figurations of potential democratic futures—or as real utopias (Wright 2010)—then we can also think beyond the divide between systems and democratic innovations that today dominates the debate. Rather than arguing whether we need to perfect democratic spaces or scale up engagement to democratic systems, we can think about reconfiguring the system *through* alternative democratic practices. These practices are not confined to a given democratic space but are always interwoven with society. The bodies, performances, and ideas of democratic subjects circulate through societies mediated through digital and other communication devices and through everyday talk with family, friends, and wider networks (Asenbaum 2022b).

To unfold the full potential of democratic serendipity, we also need to reflect on the role of designers. In writing about democracy, we—the community of democracy scholars and practitioners—often make the designers of democratic spaces invisible. By saying things like 'we need to build inclusive democratic spaces', we address a subject whose identity is taken for granted and therewith obscured. We withdraw ourselves from the space of appearance and impede public accountability, as Young criticizes (Young 1990: 96–107). Critical attention to who designs democratic spaces reveals that it is mostly privileged actors—politicians, bureaucrats, academics, and practitioners—who have the power to convene democratic interaction. The attention to claimed spaces advanced in this book partly alleviates this problem. But we (yes, I mean us, the scholarly and practitioners community designing democratic innovations) need to go further. We need to muster the courage to let go of control. We need to cocreate democratic spaces with participants. We need to invite those outside academia into our research activity—not as objects of study, but as research participants, who cocreate knowledge (Ackerly et al. 2021; Asenbaum 2022a; 2022d).

The politics of becoming, then, is part of a transformative strategy towards socially and ecologically just democratic futures. It starts from the temporary interruption and rearticulation of identity, goes on to reassemble democratic space, and finally reconfigures the democratic system. The democratic microverse starts within us and potentially extends to the planetary level. Democracy is more than structured design and clearly delineated systems. It is a constantly evolving assemblage made of infinite assemblages. Interruption of the established order may be scary and it comes with risks. We do not know what follows the break. But interruption does not need to start on the systemic level. Rather, as this book has argued, it starts on the micro level within the democratic subject. The personal experience of alterity, the experience that things can be otherwise, is only the starting point. It has the potential for systemic change. To work towards socially and ecologically just democratic futures, we need to recognize the democratic microverse within us—the potential for interrupting who we believe ourselves to be, who we have been taught to be, and muster the courage to be otherwise—just for a moment, a moment carrying the seed for systemic transformation.

References

Ackerly, Brooke, Luis Cabrera, Fonna Forman, Genevieve Fuji Johnson, Chris Tenove, and Antje Wiener. 2021. 'Unearthing Grounded Normative Theory: Practices and Commitments of Empirical Research in Political Theory'. *Critical Review of International Social and Political Philosophy* (advance online publication): 1–27. https://doi.org/10.1080/13698230.2021.1894020.

Adorno, Theodor. 1973. *Negative Dialectics*. New York: Continuum.

Aiyar, Yamini. 2010. 'Invited Spaces, Invited Participation: Effects of Greater Participation on Accountability in Service Delivery'. *India Review* 9 (2): 204–29. https://doi.org/10.1080/14736489.2010.483370.

Akdeniz, Yaman. 2002. 'Anonymity, Democracy, and Cyberspace'. *Social Research* 69: 223–37.

Andersen, Vibeke Normann, and Kasper Hansen. 2007. 'How Deliberation Makes Better Citizens: The Danish Deliberative Poll on the Euro'. *European Journal of Political Research* 46 (4): 531–56. https://doi.org/10.1111/j.1475-6765.2007.00699.x.

Arendt, Hannah. 1958. *The Human Condition*. Chicago: University of Chicago Press.

Arendt, Hannah. 1981. *Vita activa oder Vom tätigen Leben*. 3rd ed. München: Piper.

Arterton, Frederick. 1987. *Teledemocracy: Can Technology Protect Democracy?* Newbury Park: Sage.

Asenbaum, Hans. 2012. 'Imagined Alternatives: A History of Ideas in Russia's Perestroika'. *Socialist History* 42: 1–23.

Asenbaum, Hans. 2013. *Demokratie Im Umbruch: Alternative Gesellschaftsentwürfe Der Russischen Perestroikabewegung [Democracy in Times of Change: Alternative Societal Concepts of the Russian Perestroika Movement]*. Vienna: New Academic Press.

Asenbaum, Hans. 2016. 'Facilitating Inclusion: Austrian Wisdom Councils as Democratic Innovation between Consensus and Diversity'. *Journal of Public Deliberation* 12 (2): 1–11.

Asenbaum, Hans. 2017. 'Revisiting E-Topia: Theoretical Approaches and Empirical Findings on Online Anonymity'. 3. Working Paper Series of the Centre for Deliberative Democracy & Global Governance. Canberra.

Asenbaum, Hans. 2018. 'Cyborg Activism: Exploring the Reconfigurations of Democratic Subjectivity in Anonymous'. *New Media & Society* 20 (4): 1543–63. https://doi.org/10.1177/1461444817699994.

Asenbaum, Hans. 2020. 'Making a Difference: Toward a Feminist Democratic Theory in the Digital Age'. *Politics & Gender* 16 (1): 230–57. https://doi.org/10.1017/S1743923X18001010.

Asenbaum, Hans. 2021a. 'Rethinking Democratic Innovations: A Look through the Kaleidoscope of Democratic Theory'. *Political Studies Review* 20 (4): 1–11. https://doi.org/10.1177/14789299211052890.

Asenbaum, Hans. 2021b. 'Rethinking Digital Democracy: From the Disembodied Discursive Self to New Materialist Corporealities'. *Communication Theory* 31 (3): 360–79. https://doi.org/10.1093/ct/qtz033.

Asenbaum, H. 2022a. 'A Democratic Ethos for Democracy Research'. In PhD Confessions: From Democracy Scholars, Students, and Supporters, edited by Lea Heyne and Christian Ewert, 41–6. Norderstedt: BoD.

Asenbaum, Hans. 2022b. 'Beyond Deliberative Systems: Pluralizing the Debate'. Democratic Theory 9 (1): 87–98.

Asenbaum, Hans. 2022c. 'Democratic Assemblage'. In What Makes an Assembly? Stories, Experiments, and Inquiries, edited by Anne Davidian and Laurent Jeanpierre, 249–60. Antwerp: Evens Foundation and Sternberg Press.

Asenbaum, Hans. 2022d. 'Doing Democratic Theory Democratically'. International Journal of Qualitative Methods, 21: 1–12. https://doi.org/https://doi.org/10.1177/16094069221105072

Asenbaum, Hans, and Frederic Hanusch. 2021. '(De)Futuring Democracy: Labs, Ateliers, and Playgrounds as Democratic Innovation'. Futures 134: 1–11. https://doi.org/10.1016/j.futures.2021.102836.

Avritzer, Leonardo. 2009. Participatory Institutions in Democratic Brazil. Washington: Woodrow Wilson Center Press.

Bächtiger, André, Markus Sörndli, Marco Steenbergen, and Jürgen Steiner. 2005. 'The Deliberative Dimensions of Legislatures'. Acta Politica 40 (2): 225–38. https://doi.org/10.1057/palgrave.ap.5500103.

Bäck, Hanna, and Marc Debus. 2018. 'When Do Women Speak? A Comparative Analysis of the Role of Gender in Legislative Debates'. Political Studies, 1–21. https://doi.org/10.1177/0032321718789358.

Bakhtin, Mikhail. 1968. Rabelais and His World. Cambridge, MA: MIT Press.

Balsamo, Anne. 1996. Technologies of the Gendered Body. Durham/London: Duke University Press.

Barad, Karen. 2008. 'Posthumanist Performativity: Toward an Understanding of How Matter Comes to Matter'. In Material Feminisms, edited by Stacy Alaimo and Susan Hekman, 120–54. Bloomington/Indianapolis: Indiana University Press.

Barber, Benjamin. 1998. 'Three Scenarios for the Future of Technology and Strong Democracy'. Political Science Quarterly 113 (4): 573–89.

Barber, Benjamin. 2003. Strong Democracy: Participatory Politics for a New Age. Berkeley: University of California Press.

Barendt, Eric. 2016. Anonymous Speech: Literature, Law and Politics. Oxford: Hart Publishing.

Barnes, Sue. 1996. 'Cyberspace: Creating Paradoxes for the Ecology of the Self'. In Communication and Cyberspace: Social Interaction in an Electronic Environment, edited by Lance Strate, Ron Jacobson, and Stephanie Gibson, 193–216. Cresskill: Hampton Press.

Bartlett, Jamie. 2015. The Dark Net. London: Windmill Books.

Bastos, Marco, and Dan Mercea. 2017. 'The Brexit Botnet and User-Generated Hyperpartisan News'. Social Science Computer Review, 1–18. https://doi.org/10.1177/0894439317734157.

Baxter, Hillary. 2015. 'Masquerade, Pride, Drag, Love and Marriage'. In Masquerade: Essays on Tradition and Innovation Worldwide, edited by Deborah Bell, 103–12. Jefferson: McFarland & Company.

Beasley-Murray, Jon. 2011. Posthegemony: Political Theory and Latin America. Minneapolis: University of Minnesota Press.

Beauvais, Edana. 2019. 'The Gender Gap in Political Discussion Group Attendance'. Politics and Gender, 1–24. https://doi.org/10.1017/S1743923X18000892.

Benedikt, Michael. 1991. 'Cyberspace: Some Proposals'. In *Cyberspace: First Steps*, edited by Michael Benedikt, 119–224. Cambridge: MIT Press.

Bennett, Jane. 2010. *Vibrant Matter: A Political Ecology of Things*. Durham/London: Duke University Press.

Bennett, W. Lance, and Alexandra Segerberg. 2012. 'The Logic of Connective Action'. *Information, Communication & Society* 15 (5): 739–68. https://doi.org/10.1080/1369118X.2012.670661.

Berlin, Isaiah. 1969. *Four Essays on Liberty*, 118–72. Oxford: Oxford University Press.

Bessi, Alessandro, and Emilio Ferrara. 2016. 'Social Bots Distort the 2016 U.S. Presidential Election Online Discussion'. *First Monday* 21: 1–14.

Bey, M. (2022). *Black Trans Feminism*. Croydon: Duke University Press.

Beyer, Jessica. 2012. 'Women's (Dis)Embodied Engagement with Male-Dominated Online Communities'. In *Cyberfeminism 2.0*, edited by Radhika Gajjala and Yeon Ju Oh, 153–70. New York: Peter Lang Publishing.

Beyer, Jessica. 2014a. *Expect Us: Online Communities and Political Mobilization*. Oxford: Oxford University Press.

Beyer, Jessica. 2014b. 'The Emergence of a Freedom of Information Movement: Anonymous, WikiLeaks, the Pirate Party, and Iceland'. *Journal of Computer-Mediated Communication* 19 (2): 141–54. https://doi.org/10.1111/jcc4.12050.

Blair, Charlene. 1998. 'Netsex: Empowerment through Discourse'. In *Cyberghetto or Cybertopia? Race, Class, and Gender on the Internet*, edited by Bosah Ebo, 205–18. Westport: Praeger.

Blau, Adrian. 2004. 'Against Positive and Negative Freedom'. *Political Theory* 32 (4): 547–53. https://doi.org/10.1177/0090591704265520.

Blee, Kathleen, and Amy McDowell. 2013. 'The Duality of Spectacle and Secrecy: A Case Study of Fraternalism in the 1920s US Ku Klux Klan'. *Ethnic and Racial Studies* 36 (2): 249–65. https://doi.org/10.1080/01419870.2012.676197.

Blum, Christian, and Christina Isabel Zuber. 2016. 'Liquid Democracy: Potentials, Problems, and Perspectives'. *Journal of Political Philosophy* 24 (2): 162–82. https://doi.org/10.1111/jopp.12065.

Boellstorff, Tom. 2008. *Coming of Age in Second Life: An Anthropologist Explores the Virtually Human*. Princeton: Princeton University Press.

Bohman, James. 2004. 'Expanding Dialogue: The Internet, the Public Sphere and Prospects for Transnational Democracy'. *Sociological Review* 52 (1): 131–55.

Boyd, Richard, and Laura Field. 2016. 'Blind Injustice: Theorizing Anonymity and Accountability in Modern Democracies'. *Polity* 48 (3): 332–58. https://doi.org/10.1057/pol.2016.11.

Brecht, Bertold. 1932. *Brecht on Theatre*. New York: Hill and Wang.

Brock, Karen, Andrea Cornwall, and John Gaventa. 2001. 'Power, Knowledge and Political Spaces in the Framing of Poverty Policy'. 143. Working Papers of the Institute of Development Studies. Brighton. https://opendocs.ids.ac.uk/opendocs/bitstream/handle/123456789/3908/Wp143.pdf.

Brophy, Jessica. 2010. 'Developing a Corporeal Cyberfeminism: Beyond Cyberutopia'. *New Media & Society* 12 (6): 929–45. https://doi.org/10.1177/1461444809350901.

Brown, Michael. 1997. *Replacing Citizenship: AIDS Activism & Radical Democracy*. New York/London: The Guildford Press.

Bruce, Caitlin. 2015. 'The Balaclava as Affect Generator: Free Pussy Riot Protests and Transnational Iconicity'. *Communication and Critical/Cultural Studies* 12 (1): 42–62. https://doi.org/10.1080/14791420.2014.989246.

Bruckman, Amy. 1996. 'Gender Swapping on the Internet'. In *High Noon on the Electronic Frontier: Conceptual Issues in Cyberspace*, edited by Peter Ludlow, 317–26. Cambridge, MA: MIT Press.

Bruner, M. Lane. 2005. 'Carnivalesque Protest and the Humorless State'. *Text and Performance Quarterly* 25 (2): 136–55. https://doi.org/10.1080/10462930500122773.

Buchstein, Hubertus. 1997. 'Bytes That Bite: The Internet and Deliberative Democracy'. *Constellations* 4 (2): 248–63.

Bussu, Sonia. 2019. 'Collaborative Governance: Between Invited and Invented Spaces'. In *Handbook of Democratic Innovations and Governance*, edited by Stephen Elstub and Oliver Escobar, 60–76. Cheltenham Glos: Edward Elgar.

Butler, Ella. 2006. 'The Anthropology of Anonymity: Toilet Graffiti at the University of Melbourne'. 30. Research Paper Series of the University of Melbourne. School of Anthropology, Geography and Environmental Studies. Melbourne.

Butler, Judith. 1990. *Gender Trouble: Feminism and the Subversion of Identity*. New York/London: Routledge.

Butler, Judith. 1993. *Bodies That Matter: On the Discursive Limits of 'Sex'*. New York: Routledge.

Butler, Judith. 2004. *Undoing Gender*. London/New York: Routledge.

Butler, Judith. 2015. *Notes toward a Performative Theory of Assembly*. Cambridge, MA/London: Harvard University Press.

Cambre, Maria-Carolina. 2014. 'Becoming Anonymous: A Politics of Masking'. In *Educational, Psychological, and Behavioral Considerations in Niche Online Communities*, edited by Vivek Venkatesh, Jason Wallin, Juan Carlos Castro, and Jason Edward Lewis, 297–321. Hershey: Information Science Reference.

Cardell, Kylie, and Emma Maguire. 2015. 'Hoax Politics: Blogging, Betrayal, and the Intimate Public of A Gay Girl in Damascus'. *Biography* 38 (2): 205–21.

Casemajor, Nathalie. 2015. 'Digital Materialisms: Frameworks for Digital Media Studies'. *Westminster Papers in Culture and Communication* 10 (1): 4–17. https://doi.org/10.16997/wpcc.209.

Castells, Manuel. 2012. *Networks of Outrage and Hope: Social Movements in the Internet Age*. Cambridge: Polity Press.

Chambers, Simone. 1996. *Reasonable Democracy: Jürgen Habermas and the Politics of Discourse*. Ithaca, NY: Cornell University Press.

Clough, Patricia. 2010. 'The Affective Turn: Political Economy, Biomedia, and the Body'. In *The Affect Theory Reader*, edited by Melissa Gregg and Gregory Seigworth, 206–25. Durham/London: Duke University Press.

Coffé, Hilde, and Catherine Bolzendahl. 2010. 'Same Game, Different Rules? Gender Differences in Political Participation'. *Sex Roles* 62 (5–6): 318–33. https://doi.org/10.1007/s11199-009-9729-y.

Cohen, Julie. 2012. *Configuring the Networked Self: Law, Code, and the Play of Everyday Practice*. New Haven/London: Yale University Press.

Coleman, Gabriella. 2012. 'Our Weirdness Is Free'. *May* 9: 83–111.

Coleman, Gabriella. 2014. *Hacker, Hoaxer, Whistleblower, Spy: The Many Faces of Anonymous*. London: Verso.

Coleman, Gabriella. 2019. 'How Has the Fight for Anonymity and Privacy Advanced Since Snowden's Whistle-Blowing?' *Media, Culture and Society* 41 (4): 565–71. https://doi.org/10.1177/0163443719843867.

Connolly, William. 1991. *Identity/Difference: Democratic Negotiations of Political Paradox*. Ithaca/London: Cornell University Press.

Connolly, William. 1995. *The Ethos of Pluralization*. Minneapolis/London: University of Minnesota Press.

Connolly, William. 1996. 'Suffering, Justice, and the Politics of Becoming'. *Culture, Medicine and Psychiatry* 20 (3): 251–77.

Connolly, William. 2013. 'The "New Materialism" and the Fragility of Things'. *Millennium: Journal of International Studies* 41 (3): 399–412. https://doi.org/10.1177/0305829813486849.

Coole, Diana, and Samantha Frost, eds. 2010. *New Materialisms: Ontology, Agency, and Politics*. Durham/London: Duke University Press.

Cornwall, Andrea. 2002. 'Making Spaces, Changing Places: Situating Participation in Development'. 170. IDS Working Papers. Brighton.

Cornwall, Andrea. 2004a. 'New Democratic Spaces? The Politics and Dynamics of Institutionalised Participation'. *IDS Bulletin* 35 (2): 1–10.

Cornwall, Andrea. 2004b. 'Spaces for Transformation? Reflections on Issues of Power and Difference in Participation in Development'. In *Participation: From Tyranny to Transformation?*, edited by Samuel Hickey and Giles Mohan, 75–91. London/New York: Zed Books.

Cornwall, Andrea, and Vera Schattan Coelho, eds. 2007. *Spaces for Change? The Politics of Citizen Participation in New Democratic Arenas*. London & New York: Zed Books.

Cornwall, Andrea, and Alex Shankland. 2013. 'Cultures of Politics, Spaces of Power: Contextualizing Brazilian Experiences of Participation'. *Journal of Political Power* 6 (2): 309–33. https://doi.org/10.1080/2158379X.2013.811859.

Creighton, James. 2005. *The Public Participation Handbook: Making Better Decisions through Citizen Involvement*. San Francisco, CA: Jossey-Bass.

Curato, Nicole. 2019. *Democracy in a Time of Misery: From Spectacular Tragedies to Deliberative Action*. Oxford: Oxford University Press.

Curato, Nicole. 2021. 'Interruptive Protests in Dysfunctional Deliberative Systems'. *Politics* 41 (3): 388–403. https://doi.org/10.1177/0263395720960297.

Curato, Nicole, David Farrell, Brigitte Geissel, Kimmo Grönlund, Patricia Mockler, Jean-Benoit Pilet, Alan Renwick, Jonathan Rose, Maija Setälä, and Jane Suiter. 2021. *Deliberative Mini-Publics: Core Design Features*. Bristol: Bristol University Press.

Curato, Nicole, Marit Hammond, and John Min. 2019. *Power in Deliberative Democracy: Norms, Forums, Systems*. Cham: Palgrave Macmillan.

Dacombe, Rod. 2018. *Rethinking Civic Participation in Democratic Theory and Practice*. London: Palgrave Macmillan.

Dahl, Robert. 1986. *A Preface to Economic Democracy*. Berkeley: University of California Press.

Dahlberg, Lincoln. 2005. 'The Habermasian Public Sphere: Taking Difference Seriously?'. *Theory and Society* 34 (2): 111–36.

Dahlberg, Lincoln. 2007. 'The Internet and Discursive Exclusion: From Deliberative to Agonistic Public Sphere Theory'. In *Radical Democracy and the Internet: Interrogating Theory and Parctice*, edited by Lincoln Dahlberg and Eugenia Siapera, 128–47. Houndmills: Palgrave Macmillan.

Dahlberg, Lincoln, and Eugenia Siapera. 2007. 'Tracing Radical Democracy and the Internet'. In *Radical Democracy and the Internet: Interrogating Theory and Practice*, edited by Lincoln Dahlberg and Eugenia Siapera, 1–16. Houndmills: Palgrave Macmillan.

Dahlgren, Peter. 2009. *Media and Political Engagement: Citizens, Communication and Democracy*. Cambridge: Cambridge University Press.

Danet, Brenda. 1998. 'Text as Mask: Gender, Play, and Performance on the Internet'. In *Cybersociety 2.0: Revisiting Computer-Mediated Communication and Community*, edited by Steven Jones, 129–58. Thousand Oaks: Sage.

Daniels, Jessie. 2009. 'Rethinking Cyberfeminism(s): Race, Gender, and Embodiment'. *Women's Studies Quarterly* 37 (1&2): 101–24.

Daskalaki, Maria. 2018. 'Alternative Organizing in Times of Crisis: Resistance Assemblages and Socio-Spatial Solidarity'. *European Urban and Regional Studies* 25 (2): 155–70. https://doi.org/10.1177/0969776416683001.

Dean, Rikki, John Boswell, and Graham Smith. 2019. 'Designing Democratic Innovations as Deliberative Systems: The Ambitious Case of NHS Citizen'. *Political Studies* 68 (3): 1–21. https://doi.org/10.1177/0032321719866002.

Dean, Rikki, Jean Paul Gagnon, and Hans Asenbaum. 2019. 'What Is Democratic Theory?' *Democratic Theory* 6 (2): v–xx. https://doi.org/10.3167/dt.2019.060201.

Dean, Rikki, Jonathan Rinne, and Brigitte Geissel. 2019. 'Systematizing Democratic Systems Approaches: Deven Conceptual Building Blocks'. *Democratic Theory* 6 (2): 41–57. https://doi.org/10.3167/dt.2019.060205.

de Lagasnerie, Geoffroy. 2017. *The Art of Revolution: Snowden, Assange, Manning*. Stanford: Stanford University Press.

DeLanda, Manuel. 2016. *Assemblage Theory*. Edinburgh: Edinburgh University Press.

Deleixhe, Martin. 2018. 'Conflicts in Common(s)? Radical Democracy and the Governance of the Commons'. *Thesis Eleven* 144 (1): 59–79. https://doi.org/10.1177/0725513618756089.

della Porta, Donatella. 2009. *Democracy in Social Movements*. Houndmills: Palgrave Macmillan.

della Porta, Donatella. 2020. *How Social Movements Can Save Democracy: Democratic Innovations from Below*. Cambridge: Polity Press.

della Porta, Donatella, and Dieter Rucht. 2013. *Meeting Democracy: Power and Deliberation in Global Justice Movements*. Cambridge: Cambridge University Press.

Deseriis, Marco. 2015. *Improper Names: Collective Pseudonyms from the Luddites to Anonymous*. Minneapolis: University of Minnesota Press.

Diaz, Claudia, Stefaan Seys, Joris Claessens, and Bart Preneel. 2003. 'Towards Measuring Anonymity'. In *Privacy Enhancing Technologies*, edited by Roger Dingledine and Paul Syverson, 54–68. Berlin: Springer.

Dikeç, Mustafa. 2015. *Space, Politics and Aesthetics*. Edinburgh: Edinburgh University Press.

Dobusch, Leonhard, and Dennis Schoeneborn. 2015. 'Fluidity, Identity, and Organizationality: The Communicative Constitution of Anonymous'. *Journal of Management Studies*, 1–31. https://doi.org/10.1111/joms.12139.

Dovey, Kim. 1999. *Framing Places: Mediating Power in Built Form*. London/New York: Routledge. https://doi.org/10.1177/030981680207700114.

Dovi, Suzanne. 2009. 'In Praise of Exclusion'. *The Journal of Politics* 71 (3): 1172–86. https://doi.org/10.1017/S0022381609090951.

Downs, Anthony. 1957. *An Economic Theory of Democracy*. New York: Harper & Row.

Dryzek, John. 2000. *Deliberative Democracy and Beyond: Liberals, Critics, Contestation*. Oxford: Oxford University Press.

Dryzek, John. 2009. 'Democratization as Deliberative Capacity Building'. *Comparative Political Studies* 42 (11): 1379–402. https://doi.org/10.1177/0010414009332129.

Dryzek, John, and Simon Niemeyer. 2008. 'Discursive Representation'. *American Political Science Review* 102 (04): 481. https://doi.org/10.1017/S0003055408080325.

Dryzek, John, and Jonathan Pickering. 2019. *The Politics of the Anthropocene*. Oxford: Oxford University Press.

Dzur, Albert. 2019. *Democracy Inside: Participatory Innovation in Unlikely Places*. Oxford: Oxford University Press.

Elster, Jon, ed. 1986. *The Multiple Self*. Cambridge: Cambridge University Press.

Elstub, Stephen, Selen Ercan, and Ricardo Fabrino Mendonça. 2016. 'The Fourth Generation of Deliberative Democracy'. *Critical Policy Studies* 10 (2): 139–51. https://doi.org/10.1080/19460171.2016.1175956.

Ercan, Selen, Hans Asenbaum, and Ricardo Fabrino Mendonça. 2023. 'Performing Democracy: Non-verbal Protest through a Democratic Lens'. *Performance Research* 27 (3-4): 25–36.

Ercan, Selen, Carolyn Hendriks, and John Dryzek. 2018. 'Public Deliberation in an Era of Communicative Plenty'. *Policy & Politics* 47 (1, January): 1–17. https://doi.org/10.1332/030557318X15200933925405.

Eve, Martin. 2016. *Password*. New Haven/London: Bloomsbury.

Felicetti, Andrea. 2021. 'Learning from Democratic Practices: New Perspectives in Institutional Design'. *Journal of Politics* 83 (4): 1589–601. https://doi.org/10.1086/711623.

Ferguson, Michaele. 2007. 'Sharing without Knowing: Collective Identity in Feminist and Democratic Theory'. *Hypatia: A Journal of Feminist Philosophy* 22 (4): 30–45. https://doi.org/10.2979/HYP.2007.22.4.30.

Fernandez, Maria, and Faith Wilding. 2002. 'Situating Cyberfeminism'. In *Domain Errors! Cyberfeminist Practices*, edited by Maria Fernandez, Faith Wilding, and Michelle Wright, 17–28. New York: Autonomedia and SubRosa.

Ferry, Anne. 2002. '"Anonymity": The Literary History of a Word'. *New Literary History* 33 (2): 193–214.

Font, Joan, Graham Smith, Carol Galais, and Pau Alarcon. 2017. 'Cherry-Picking Participation: Explaining the Fate of Proposals from Participatory Processes'. *European Journal of Political Research* 57 (3): 1–22. https://doi.org/10.1111/1475-6765.12248.

Forestal, Jennifer. 2017. 'The Architecture of Political Spaces: Trolls, Digital Media, and Deweyan Democracy'. *American Political Science Review* 111 (1): 149–61. https://doi.org/10.1017/S0003055416000666.

Forestal, Jennifer, and Menaka Philips. 2020. 'The Masked Demos: Associational Anonymity and Democratic Practice'. *Contemporary Political Theory* 19 (4): 573–95. https://doi.org/10.1057/s41296-019-00368-2.

Foucault, Michel. 1979. *Discipline and Punish: The Birth of the Prison*. Harmondsworth: Penguin.

Fox, Richard, and Jennifer Lawless. 2014. 'Uncovering the Origins of the Gender Gap in Political Ambition'. *American Political Science Review* 108 (3): 499–519. https://doi.org/10.1017/s0003055414000227.

Fraser, Nancy. 1990. 'Rethinking the Public Sphere: A Contribution to the Critique of Actually Existing Democracy'. *Social Text* 25/26: 56–80.

Fraser, Nancy. 1995. 'What's Critical about Critical Theory?' In *Feminists Read Habermas: Gendering the Subject of Discourse*, edited by Johanna Meehan, 21–55. New York: Routledge.

Fraser, Nancy. 1996. 'Equality, Difference, and Radical Democracy: The United States Feminist Debate Revisited'. In *Radical Democracy: Identity, Citizenship, and the State*, edited by David Trend, 197–208. New York: Routledge.

Fraser, Nancy. 1997. *Justice Interruptus: Critical Reflections on the 'Postsocialist' Condition*. New York: Routledge.

Fraser, Nancy. 2019. *The Old Is Dying and the New Cannot Be Born: From Progressive Neoliberalism to Trump and Beyond*. London: Verso.

Freire, Paulo. 2005. *Pedagogy of the Oppressed*. 30th Anniv. New York: The Continuum International Publishing Group.

Fromm, Erich. 1941. *Escape from Freedom*. New York: Farrar & Rinehart.

Fuchs, Christian. 2014. *Digital Labour and Karl Marx*. New York: Routledge.

Fung, Archon. 2003. 'Recipes for Public Spheres: Eight Institutional Design Choices and Their Consequences'. *The Journal of Political Philosophy* 11 (3): 338–67. https://doi.org/10.1111/1467-9760.00181.

Fung, Archon, and Erik Olin Wright. 2001. 'Deepening Democracy: Institutional Innovations in Empowered Participatory Governance'. *Politics & Society* 29 (1): 5–41. https://doi.org/10.1521/siso.2006.70.4.566.

Gabrys, Jennifer. 2014. 'Powering the Digital: From Energy Ecologies to Electronic Environmentalism'. In *Media and the Ecological Crisis*, edited by Richard Maxwell, Jon Raundalen, and Nina Lager Vestberg, 3–18. New York/London: Routledge.

Gardner, James. 2011. 'Anonymity and Democratic Citizenship'. *William & Mary Bill of Rights Journal* 19 (4): 927.

Gaventa, John. 2006. 'Finding the Spaces for Change: A Power Analysis'. *IDS Bulletin* 37 (6): 23–33.

Geissel, Brigitte, and Kenneth Newton, eds. 2012. *Evaluating Democratic Innovations: Curing the Democratic Malaise?* New York: Routledge.

Gerbaudo, Paolo. 2012. *Tweets and the Streets: Social Media and Contemporary Activism*. New York: Pluto Press. https://doi.org/10.1017/CBO9781107415324.004.

Gerbaudo, Paolo. 2015. 'Protest Avatars as Memetic Signifiers: Political Profile Pictures and the Construction of Collective Identity on Social Media in the 2011 Protest Wave'. *Information, Communication & Society* 18 (8): 916–29. https://doi.org/10.1080/1369118X.2015.1043316.

Gerbaudo, Paolo. 2017. *The Mask and the Flag: Populism, Citizenism, and Global Protest*. Oxford: Oxford University Press.

Gerber, Marlène. 2015. 'Equal Partners in Dialogue? Participation Equality in a Transnational Deliberative Poll (Europolis)'. *Political Studies* 63 (1): 110–30. https://doi.org/10.1111/1467-9248.12183.

Gergen, Kenneth. 2000. *The Saturated Self: Dilemmas of Identity in Contemporary Life*. 2nd ed. New York: Basic Books.

Gershenson, Olga, and Barbara Penner, eds. 2009. *Ladies and Gents: Public Toilets and Gender*. Philadelphia: Temple University Press.

Gibson, William. 2016. *Neuromancer*. London: Gollancz.

Gies, Lieve. 2008. 'How Material Are Cyberbodies? Broadband Internet and Embodied Subjectivity'. *Crime Media Culture* 4 (3): 311–30. https://doi.org/10.1177/1741659008096369.

Goffman, Erving. 1956. *The Presentation of Self in Everyday Life*. New York: Doubleday.

Goodsell, Charles. 1988. 'The Architecture of Parliaments: Legislative Houses and Political Culture'. *British Journal of Political Science* 18 (3): 287–302.

Gould, Carol. 1988. *Rethinking Democracy: Freedom and Social Cooperation in Politics, Economy, and Society*. New York: Cambridge University Press.

Gould, Carol. 1993. 'Feminism and Democratic Community Revisited'. In *Democratic Community: NOMOS XXXV*, edited by John Chapman and Ian Shapiro, 396–413. New York: New York University Press

Gould, Carol. 1996. 'Diversity and Democracy: Representing Difference'. In *Democracy and Difference: Contesting the Boundaries of the Political*, edited by Seyla Benhabib, 171–86. Princeton: Princeton University Press.

Griffin, Robert. 1999. 'Anonymity and Authorship'. *New Literary History* 30 (4): 877–95.

Groeneveld, Elizabeth. 2015. 'Are We All Pussy Riot? On Narratives of Feminist Return and the Limits of Transnational Solidarity'. *Feminist Theory* 16 (3): 1–19. https://doi.org/10. 1177/1464700115604134.

Grosz, Elizabeth. 2001. *Architecture from the Outside: Essays on Virtual and Reals Space*. Cambridge, MA: MIT Press.

Habermas, Jürgen. 1992. *The Structural Transformation of the Public Sphere: An Inquiry into a Category of Bourgeois Society*. 1st paperb. Cambridge: Polity Press.

Habermas, Jürgen. 1996. *Between Facts and Norms: Contributions to a Discourse Theory of Law and Democracy*. Cambridge, MA: MIT Press.

Hall, Cheryl. 2007. 'Recognizing the Passion in Deliberation'. *Hypatia: A Journal of Feminist Philosophy* 22 (4): 81–95.

Halpin, Harry. 2012. 'The Philosophy of Anonymous: Ontological Politics without Identity'. *Radical Philosophy* 176: 19–28.

Hammond, Marit. 2021. 'Democratic Innovations After the Post-Democratic Turn: Between Activation and Empowerment'. *Critical Policy Studies* 15 (2): 174–91. https:// doi.org/10.1080/19460171.2020.1733629.

Haraway, Donna. 1991. *Simians, Cyborgs and Women: The Reinvention of Nature*, 149–81. London: Free Association Books.

Hardin, Garrett. 1968. 'The Tragedy of the Commons'. *Science* 162 (3859): 1243–48.

Hardt, Michael, and Antonio Negri. 2004. *Multitude: War and Democracy in the Age of Empire*. New York: Penguin Press.

Hardt, Micheal and Antonio Negri. 2012. *Declaration*. New York: Argo Navis.

Hardt, Micheal and Antonio Negri. 2017. *Assembly*. Oxford: Oxford University Press.

Hayles, Katherine. 1999. *How We Became Posthuman: Virtual Bodies in Cybernetics, Literature, and Informatics*. Chicago: University of Chicago Press.

Hayne, Stephen, Carol Pollard, and Ronald Rice. 2003. 'Identification of Comment Authorship in Anonymous Group Support Systems'. *Journal of Management Information Systems* 20 (1): 301–29.

Held, David. 1987. *Models of Democracy*. Cambridge: Polity Press.

Held, David. 2006. *Models of Democracy*. 3rd ed. Stanford: Stanford University Press.

Hénaff, Marcel, and Tracy Strong. 2001. 'The Conditions of Public Space: Vision, Speech, and Theatricality'. In *Public Space and Demoracy*, edited by Marcel Hénaff and Tracy Strong, 1–32. Minneapolis/London: University of Minnesota Press.

Hendriks, Carolyn, Selen Ercan, and John Boswell. 2020. *Mending Democracy: Democratic Repair in Disconnected Times*. Oxford: Oxford University Press.

Hiltz, Starr Roxanne, and Murray Turoff. 1978. *The Network Nation: Human Communication via Computer*. Cambridge: MIT Press.

Hirst, Paul. 1994. *Associative Democracy: New Forms of Economic and Social Governance*. Cambridge: Polity Press.

Hobbes, Thomas. 1968. *Leviathan*. Baltimore: Penguin Books.

Holman, Christopher, Martin Breaugh, Rachel Magnusson, Paul Mazzochi, and Devin Penner. 2015. 'Radical Democracy and Twentieth-Century French Thought'. In *Thinking Radical Democracy: The Return of Politics in Post-War France*, edited by Christopher Holman, Martin Breaugh, Rachel Magnusson, Paul Mazzochi, and Devin Penner, 3–30. Toronto: University of Toronto Press.

Honig, Bonnie. 1994. 'Difference, Dilemmas, and the Politics of Home'. *Social Research* 6 (3): 563–97.

Honig, Bonnie. 2013. *Antigone, Interrupted*. Cambridge: Cambridge University Press.

Honig, Bonnie. 2017. *Public Things: Democracy in Despair*. New York: Fordham University Press.

Hunter, Christopher. 2002. 'Political Privacy and Online-Politics: How E-Campaigning Threatens Voter Privacy'. *First Monday* 7 (2).

Isin, Engin, and Evelyn Ruppert. 2015. *Being Digital Citizens*. London: Rowman & Littlefield Publishers.

Javier, Romero, and John Dryzek. 2021. 'Grounding Ecological Democracy: Semiotics and the Communicative Networks of Nature'. *Environmental Values* 30 (4): 407–29.

Jenkins, Elizabeth, Zulfia Zaher, Stephanie Tikkanen, and Jessica Ford. 2019. 'Creative Identity (Re)Construction, Creative Community Building, and Creative Resistance: A Qualitative Analysis of Queer Ingroup Members' Tweets After the Orlando Shooting'. *Computers in Human Behavior* 101: 14–21. https://doi.org/10.1016/j.chb.2019.07.004.

Jonker, Hugo, and Wolter Pieters. 2010. 'Anonymity in Voting Revisited'. In *Towards Trustworthy Elections: New Directions in Electronic Voting*, edited by David Chaum et al., 216–30. Berlin: IAVOSS/Springer-Verlag.

Kaika, Maria, and Lazaros Karaliotas. 2016. 'The Spatialization of Democratic Politics: Insights from Indignant Squares'. *European Urban and Regional Studies* 23 (4): 556–70. https://doi.org/10.1177/0969776414528928.

Karpowitz, Christopher, and Jane Mansbridge. 2005. 'Disagreement and Consensus: The Need for Dynamic Updating in Public Deliberation'. *Journal of Public Deliberation* 1 (1): 348–64.

Karpowitz, Christopher, and Tali Mendelberg. 2014. *The Silent Sex: Gender, Deliberation, and Institutions*. Princeton: Princeton University Press.

Karpowitz, Christopher, Tali Mendelberg, and Lee Shaker. 2012. 'Gender Inequality in Deliberative Participation'. *American Political Science Review* 106 (3): 533–47. https://doi.org/10.1017/S0003055412000329.

Kavada, Anastasia. 2012. 'Engagement, Bonding, and Identity Across Multiple Platforms: Avaaz on Facebook, YouTube, and MySpace'. *MedieKultur* 52: 28–48.

Kavada, Anastasia, and Orsalia Dimitriou. 2017. 'Protest Spaces Online and Offline: The Indignant Movement in Syntagma Square'. In *Protest Camps in International Context: Spaces, Infrastructures and Media of Resistance*, edited by Gavin Brown, Anna Feigenbaum, Fabian Frenzel, and Patrick McCurdy, 71–90. Bristol: Policy Press.

Kavada, Anastasia, and Emiliano Treré. 2019. 'Live Democracy and Its Tensions: Making Sense of Livestreaming in the 15M and Occupy'. *Information Communication and Society*, 1–18. https://doi.org/10.1080/1369118X.2019.1637448.

Kennedy, H. 2006. 'Beyond Anonymity, or Future Directions for Internet Identity Research'. *New Media & Society* 8 (6): 859–76. https://doi.org/10.1177/1461444806069641.

Kinney, Alison. 2016. *Hood*. New York: Bloomsbury.

Kioupkiolis, Alexandros. 2017. 'Common Democracy: Political Representation beyond Representative Democracy'. *Democratic Theory* 4 (1): 35–58. https://doi.org/10.3167/dt.2017.040103.

Kohn, Margaret. 2000. 'Language, Power, and Persuasion: Toward a Critique of Deliberative Democracy'. *Constellations* 7 (3): 408–29. https://doi.org/10.1111/1467-8675.00197.

Kolko, Beth. 2000. 'Erase @race: Going White in the (Inter)Face'. In *Race in Cyberspace*, edited by Beth Kolko, Lisa Nakamura, and Gilbert Rodman, 213–32. New York/London: Routledge.

Kolko, Beth, and Elizabeth Reid. 1998. 'Dissolution and Fragmentation: Problems in On-Line Communities'. In *Cybersociety 2.0: Revisiting Computer-Mediated Communication and Community*, edited by Steven Jones, 212–30. Thousand Oaks, CA: Sage.

Konieczny, Piotr. 2010. 'Adhocratic Governance in the Internet Age: A Case of Wikipedia'. *Journal of Information Technology and Politics* 7 (4): 263–83. https://doi.org/10.1080/19331681.2010.489408.

Koop, Royce, and Alex Marland. 2012. 'Insiders and Outsiders: Presentation of Self on Canadian Parliamentary Websites and Newsletters'. *Policy & Internet* 4 (3): 112–35.

Kopley, Emily. 2016. 'Anon Is Not Dead: Towards a History of Anonymous Authorship in Early-Twentieth-Century Britain'. *Studies in Book Culture* 7 (2): 1–23. https://doi.org/10.7202/1036861ar.

Kullmann, Karl. 2018. 'The Shape of Things: Reimagining Landscape Parliaments in the Anthropocene'. *Forty Five: A Journal of Outside Research* 190: 1–30.

Kuran, Timur. 1993. 'Mitigating the Tyranny of Public Opinion: Anonymous Discourse and the Ethic of Sincerity'. *Constitutional Political Economy* 4 (1): 41–78.

Kuyper, Jonathan. 2016. 'Systemic Representation: Democracy, Deliberation, and Nonelectoral Representatives'. *American Political Science Review* 110 (2): 308–24. https://doi.org/10.1017/S0003055416000095.

Laclau, Ernesto, and Chantal Mouffe. 1985. *Hegemony and Socialist Strategy: Towards a Radical Democratic Politics*. London/New York: Verso.

Landow, George. 1992. *Hypertext: The Convergence of Contemporary Critical Theory and Technology*. Baltimore: The John Hopkins University Press.

Lanham, Richard. 1993. *The Electronic Word: Democracy, Technology, and the Arts*. Chicago/London: University of Chicago Press.

Lau, Kimberly. 2010. 'The Political Lives of Avatars: Play and Democracy in Virtual Worlds'. *Western Folklore* 69 (3/4): 369–94.

Le Bon, Gustav. 2009. *The Crowd: A Study of the Popular Mind*. Auckland: Floating Press.

Lee, Caroline. 2014. *Do-It-Yourself Democracy: The Rise of the Public Engagement Industry*. New York: Oxford University Press.

Lee, Victor. 2014. 'What's Happening in the 'Quantified Self' Movement?' In *ICLS Proceedings*, edited by Joseph Polman, Eleni Kyza, Kevin O'Neill, Iris Tabak, William Penuel, Susan Jurow, Kevin O'Connor, Tiffany Lee, and Laura D'Amico, 1032–6. Boulder: ISLS.

Leitner, John. 2015. 'Anonymity, Privacy, and Expressive Equality: Name Verification and Korean Constitutional Rights in Cyberspace'. *Journal of Korean Law* 14 (June): 167–212.

Lipton, Mark. 1996. 'Forgetting the Body: Cybersex and Identity'. In *Communication and Cyberspace: Social Interaction in an Electronic Environment*, edited by Lance Strate, Ron Jacobson, and Stephanie Gibson, 335–49. Cresskill: Hampton Press.

Little, Adrian, and Moya Lloyd, eds. 2009. *The Politics of Radical Democracy*. Edinburgh: Edinburgh University Press.

Lloyd, Moya. 2005. *Beyond Identity Politics: Feminism, Power, and Politics*. London: Sage.

Lloyd, Moya. 2007. 'Radical Democratic Activism and the Politics of Resignification'. *Constellations* 14 (1): 129–46. https://doi.org/10.1111/j.1467-8675.2007.00426.x.

Lloyd, Moya. 2009. 'Performing Radical Democracy'. In *The Politics of Radical Democracy*, edited by Moya Lloyd and Adrian Little, 33–51. Edinburgh: Edinburgh University Press.

Lopes de Souza, Marcelo, and Barbara Lipietz. 2011. 'The 'Arab Spring' and the City'. *City* 15 (6): 618–24. https://doi.org/10.1080/13604813.2011.632900.

Löw, Martina. 2008. 'The Constitution of Space: The Structuration of Spaces through the Simultaneity of Effect and Perception'. *European Journal of Social Theory* 11 (1): 25–49. https://doi.org/10.1177/1368431007085286.

Lupia, Arthur, and Anne Norton. 2017. 'Inequality Is Always in the Room: Language & Power in Deliberative Democracy'. *Daedalus* 146 (3): 64–76. https://doi.org/10.1162/DAED_a_00447.

MacCallum, Gerald. 1967. 'Negative and Positive Freedom'. *Philosophical Review* 76 (3): 312–34.

Machin, Amanda. 2022. *Bodies of Democracy: Modes of Embodied Politics*. Bielefeld: Transcript.

Macpherson, Crawford Brough. 1977. *The Life and Times of Liberal Democracy*. Oxford: Oxford University Press.

Maddicott, John. 2010. *The Origins of the English Parliament 924–1327*. Oxford: Oxford University Press.

Maeckelbergh, Marianne. 2012. 'Horizontal Democracy Now: From Alterglobalization to Occupation'. *Interface: A Journal for and about Social Movements* 4 (1): 207–34.

Mansbridge, Jane. 1981. 'Living with Conflict—Representation in the Theory of Adversary Democracy'. *Ethics* 91 (3): 466–76. https://doi.org/10.1086/292254.

Mansbridge, Jane. 1983. *Beyond Adversary Democracy*. Chicago: University of Chicago Press.

Mansbridge, Jane. 1990. 'Self-Interest in Political Life'. *Political Theory* 18 (1): 132–53.

Mansbridge, Jane. 1991. 'Democracy, Deliberation and the Experience of Women'. In *Higher Education and the Practice of Democratic Politics: A Political Education Reader*, edited by Bernard Murchland, 122–35. Dayton: Kettering Foundation.

Mansbridge, Jane. 1993. 'Feminism and Democratic Community'. In *Democratic Community: NOMOS XXXV*, edited by John Chapman and Ian Shapiro, 339–95. New York: New York University Press.

Mansbridge, Jane. 1996. 'Using Power/Fighting Power'. In *Democracy and Difference: Contesting the Boundaries of the Political*, edited by Seyla Benhabib, 46–66. Princeton: Princeton University Press.

Mansbridge, Jane. 1998. 'Feminism and Democracy'. In *Feminism and Politics*, edited by Anne Phillips, 141–60. Oxford: Oxford University Press.

Mansbridge, Jane. 1999a. 'Everyday Talk in the Deliberative System'. In *Deliberative Politics: Essays on Democracy and Disagreement*, edited by Stephen Macedo, 211–39. Oxford: Oxford University Press.

Mansbridge, Jane. 1999b. 'Should Blacks Represent Blacks and Women Represent Women? A Contingent "Yes"'. *The Journal of Politics* 61 (3): 628–57.

Mansbridge, Jane. 2003. 'Anti-Statism and Difference Feminism in International Social Movements'. *International Feminist Journal of Politics* 5 (3): 355–60. https://doi.org/10.1080/1461674032000122713.

Mansbridge, Jane. 2005. 'Quota Problems: Combating the Dangers of Essentialism'. *Politics & Gender* 1 (4): 621–53. https://doi.org/10.1017/S1743923X05050191.

Mansbridge, Jane. 2012. 'Conflict and Commonality in Habermas' Structural Transformation of the Public Sphere'. *Political Theory* 40 (6): 789–801.

Mansbridge, Jane. 2015. 'Should Workers Represent Workers?' *Swiss Political Science Review* 21 (2): 261–70. https://doi.org/10.1111/spsr.12160.

Mansbridge, Jane, James Bohman, Simone Chambers, Thomas Christiano, Archon Fung, John Parkinson, Thomas Hopkins, and Mark Warren. 2012. 'A Systemic Approach to Deliberative Democracy'. In *Deliberative Systems: Deliberative Democracy at the Large Scale*, edited by John Parkinson and Jane Mansbridge, 1–26. Cambridge: Cambridge University Press.

Mansbridge, Jane, James Bohman, Simone Chambers, David Estlund, Andreas Follesdal, Archon Fung, Cristina Lafont, Bernard Manin, and José Luis Martí. 2010. 'The Place of Self-Interest and the Role of Power in Deliberative Democracy'. *The Journal of Political Philosophy* 18 (1): 64–100. https://doi.org/10.1111/j.1467-9760.2009.00344.x.

Markham, Annette. 1998. *Life Online: Researching Real Experience in Virtual Space*. Walnut Creek: AltaMira Press.

Marx Ferree, Myra, William Gamson, Jürgen Gerhards, and Dieter Rucht. 2002. 'Four Models of the Public Sphere in Modern Democracies'. *Theory and Society* 31 (3): 289–324. https://doi.org/10.1023/A:1016284431021.

Marx, Gary. 1999. 'What's in a Name? Some Reflections on the Sociology of Anonymity'. *The Information Society* 15 (2): 99–112. https://doi.org/10.1080/019722499128565.

Marx, Karl, and Friedrich Engels. 1998. *The German Ideology*. Amherst: Prometheus Books.

Massey, Doreen. 1995. 'Thinking Radical Democracy Spatially'. *Environment and Planning D: Society and Space* 13 (3): 283–8. https://doi.org/10.1068/d130283.

Matthews, Steve. 2010. 'Anonymity and the Social Self'. *American Philosophical Quarterly* 47 (4): 351–63.

Mattoni, Alice, and Nicole Doerr. 2007. 'Images Within the Precarity Movement in Italy'. *Feminist Review* 87 (1): 130–5.

McAfee, Noelle and Claire Snyder. (2007). 'Feminist Engagements in Democratic Theory'. *Hypatia: A Journal of Feminist Philosophy* 22(4): vii–x.

McCarthy, Matthew. 2015. 'Toward a Free Information Movement'. *Sociological Forum* 30 (2): 439–58. https://doi.org/10.1111/socf.12170.

McCarthy-Cotter, Leanne-Marie, Matthew Flinders, and Tom Healey. 2018. 'Design and Space in Parliament'. In *Exploring Parliament*, edited by Cristina Leston-Bandeira and Louise Thompson, 53–66. Oxford: Oxford University Press.

McDonald, Kevin. 2015. 'From Indymedia to Anonymous: Rethinking Action and Identity in Digital Cultures'. *Information, Communication & Society* 18 (8): 968–82. https://doi.org/10.1080/1369118X.2015.1039561.

McEwan, Cheryl. 2005. 'New Spaces of Citizenship? Rethinking Gendered Participation and Empowerment in South Africa'. *Political Geography* 24 (8): 969–91. https://doi.org/10.1016/j.polgeo.2005.05.001.

McGlashan, Hayley, and Katie Fitzpatrick. 2018. '"I Use Any Pronouns, and I'm Questioning Everything Else": Transgender Youth and the Issue of Gender Pronouns'. *Sex Education* 18 (3): 239–52. https://doi.org/10.1080/14681811.2017.1419949.

McKenna, Brad, Lesley A Gardner, and Michael D Myers. 2011. 'Social Movements in World of Warcraft'. In *Proceedings of the Seventeenth Americas Conference on Information Systems*, 1–8. Detroit.

McManus, Helen. 2008. 'Enduring Agonism: Between Individuality and Plurality'. *Polity* 40 (4): 509–25. https://doi.org/10.1057/pol.2008.12.

Meijer, Eva. 2019. *When Animals Speak: Toward an Interspecies Democracy*. New York: New York University Press.

Mendes, Kaitlynn, Jessica Ringrose, and Jessalynn Keller. 2018. '#MeToo and the Promise and Pitfalls of Challenging Rape Culture through Digital Feminist Activism'. *European Journal of Women's Studies* 25 (2): 236–46. https://doi.org/10.1177/1350506818765318.

Mendonça, Ricardo Fabrino. 2016. 'Mitigating Systemic Dangers: The Role of Connectivity Inducers in a Deliberative System'. *Critical Policy Studies* 10 (2): 171–90. https://doi.org/10.1080/19460171.2016.1165127.

Mendonça, Ricardo Fabrino, Selen A Ercan, and Hans Asenbaum. 2020. 'More than Words: A Multidimensional Approach to Deliberative Democracy'. *Political Studies* 70 (1): 1–20. https://doi.org/10.1177/0032321720950561.

Mercer, John. 2004. 'Commercial Places, Public Spaces: Suffragette Shops and the Public Sphere'. *University of Sussex Journal of Contemporary History* 7.

Middleweek, Belinda. 2019. 'Pussy Power Not Pity Porn: Embodied Protest in the #FacesOfProstitution Twitter Network'. *Sexualities*, 1–19. https://doi.org/10.1177/1363460718818964.

Miller, John, Michèle Irwin, and Kelly Nigh, eds. 2014. *Teaching From the Thinking Heart: The Practice of Holistic Education*. Charlotte: Information Age Publishing.

Mislán, Cristina, and Amalia Dache-Gerbino. 2018. 'The Struggle for "Our Streets": The Digital and Physical Spatial Politics of the Ferguson Movement'. *Social Movement Studies* 17 (6): 676–96. https://doi.org/10.1080/14742837.2018.1533810.

Mitchell, William. 1999. *E-Topia: Urban Life, Jim—But Not as We Know It*. Cambridge, MA/London: MIT Press.

Mitchell, William. 2003. *Me++: The Cyborg Self and the Networked City*. Cambridge, MA/London: MIT Press.

Mitchell, William. 2012. 'Image, Space, Revolution: The Arts of Occupation'. *Critical Inquiry* 39 (1): 8–32. https://doi.org/10.1086/668048.

Monaghan, Lef. 2005. 'Big Handsome Men, Bears and Others: Virtual Constructions of "Fat Male Embodiment"'. *Body & Society* 11 (2): 81–111. https://doi.org/10.1177/1357034X05052463.

Moore, Alfred. 2018. 'Anonymity, Pseudonymity, and Deliberation: Why Not Everything Should Be Connected'. *The Journal of Political Philosophy* 26 (2): 169–92. https://doi.org/10.1111/jopp.12149.

Morris, Adam. 2012. 'Whoever, Whatever: On Anonymity as Resistance to Empire'. *Parallax* 18 (4): 106–20. https://doi.org/10.1080/13534645.2012.714560.

Motter, Jennifer. 2011. 'Feminist Virtual World Activism: 16 Days of Activism against Gender Violence Campaign, Guerrilla Girls BroadBand, and SubRosa'. *Visual Culture & Gender* 6: 108–18.

Mouffe, Chantal. 1992a. 'Citizenship and Political Identity'. *The Identity in Question* 61 (October): 28–32.

Mouffe, Chantal. 1992b. 'Democratic Citizenship and the Political Community'. In *Dimensions of Radical Democracy: Pluralism, Citizenship, Community*, edited by Chantal Mouffe, 225–38. London/New York: Verso.

Mouffe, Chantal. 1993. *The Return of the Political*. New York: Verso.

Mouffe, Chantal. 1994. 'For a Politics of Nomadic Identity'. In *Travelers' Tales: Narratives of Home and Displacement*, edited by Jon Bird, Barry Curtis, Melinda Mash, Tim Putnam, George Robertson, and Lisa Tickner, 105–13. London: Routledge.

Mouffe, Chantal. 1995a. 'Feminism, Citizenship and Radical Democratic Politics'. In *Social Postmodernism: Beyond Identity Politics*, edited by Linda Nicholson and Steven Seidman, 315–31. Cambridge: Cambridge University Press.

Mouffe, Chantal. 1995b. 'Post-Marxism: Democracy and Identity'. *Environment and Planning D: Society and Space* 13 (3): 259–65. https://doi.org/10.1068/d130259.

Mouffe, Chantal. 1999. 'Deliberative Democracy or Agonistic Pluralism?' *Social Research* 66 (3): 745–58. https://doi.org/10.2307/40971349.

Mouffe, Chantal. 2005. *The Democratic Paradox*. London: Verso.

Mouffe, Chantal. 2006. 'Democratic Politics in the Age of Post-Fordism'. *Open* 16: 1–7. http://www.onlineopen.org/article.php?id=47.

Mouffe, Chantal. 2013. *Agonistics: Thinking the World Politically*. London & New York: Verso.

Mouffe, Chantal. 2018. *For a Left Populism*. London: Verso.

Muñoz, José Esteban. 1999. *Disidentifications: Queers of Color and the Performance of Politics*. Minneapolis: University of Minnesota Press.

Nakamura, Lisa. 2002. *Cybertypes: Race, Ethnicity, and Identity on the Internet*. New York/London: Routledge.

Nancy Burns, Kay Schlozman, Ashley Jardina, Shauna Shames, and Sidney Verba. 2018. 'What Happened to the Gender Gap in Political Participation? How Might We Explain It?' In *100 Years of the Nineteenth Amendment: An Appraisal of Women's Political Activism*, edited by Holly McCammon and Lee Ann Banaszak, 69–104. Oxford: Oxford University Press.

Napier, David. 1986. *Mask, Transformation, and Paradox*. Berkeley/London: University of California Press.

Newman, Saul. 2010a. 'The Horizon of Anarchy: Anarchism and Contemporary Radical Thought'. *Theory & Event* 13 (2): 1–12. https://doi.org/10.1353/tae.0.0132.

Newman, Saul. 2010b. *The Politics of Postanarchism*. Edinburgh: Edinburgh University Press.

Newman, Saul. 2010c. 'Voluntary Servitude Reconsidered: Radical Politics and the Problem of Self-Domination'. *Anarchist Developments in Cultural Studies* 1.

Newman, Saul. 2011. 'Postanarchism and Space: Revolutionary Fantasies and Autonomous Zones'. *Planning Theory* 10 (4): 344–65. https://doi.org/10.1177/1473095211413753.

Newman, Saul. 2016. *Postanarchism*. Cambridge: Polity Press.

Newton, Kenneth. 2012. 'Making Better Citizens?' In *Evaluating Democratic Innovations: Curing the Democratic Malaise?*, edited by Brigitte Geissel and Kenneth Newton, 137–62. New York: Routledge.

Nguyen, Mimi Thi. 2015. 'The Hoodie as Sign, Screen, Expectation, and Force'. *Signs* 40 (4): 791–816.

Nissenbaum, Helen. 1997. 'Toward an Approach to Privacy in Public: Challenges of Information Technology'. *Ethics & Behavior* 7 (3): 207–19. https://doi.org/10.1207/s15327019eb0703.

Nissenbaum, Helen. 1999. 'The Meaning of Anonymity in an Information Age'. *The Information Society: An International Journal* 15 (2): 141–4. https://doi.org/10.1080/019722499128592.

Nissenbaum, Helen. 2010. *Privacy in Context: Technology, Policy, and the Integrity of Social Life*. Stanford: Stanford University Press.

Norris, Pippa, and Ronald Inglehart. 2019. *Cultural Backlash: Trump, Brexit, and Authoritarian Populism*. Cambridge: Cambridge University Press.

Norval, Aletta. 2001. 'Radical Democracy'. In *Encyclopedia of Democratic Thought*, edited by Paul Clarke and Joe Foweraker, 725–33. London/New York: Routledge.

Norval, Aletta. 2007. *Aversive Democracy: Inheritance and Originality in the Democratic Tradition*. Cambridge: Cambridge University Press.

Novak, Marcos. 1991. 'Liquid Architectures in Cyberspace'. In *Cyberspace: First Steps*, edited by Michael Benedikt, 225–54. Cambridge: MIT Press.

Nunes, Mark. 1997. 'What Is Cyberspace? The Internet and Virtuality'. In *Virtual Politics: Identities & Community in Cyberspace*, edited by David Holmes, 163–78. London: Sage.

O'Keefe, Theresa. 2014. 'My Body Is My Manifesto! SlutWalk, FEMEN and Femmenist Protest'. *Feminist Review* 107 (1): 1–19. https://doi.org/10.1057/fr.2014.4.

Olwig, Kenneth. 2013. 'Heidegger, Latour and the Reification of Things: The Inversion and Spatial Enclosure of the Substantive Landscape of Things—The Lake District Case'. *Geografiska Annaler, Series B: Human Geography* 95 (3): 251–73. https://doi.org/10. 1111/geob.12024.

Ostrom, Elinore. 1990. *Governing the Commons: The Evolution of Institutions for Collective Action*. Cambridge: Cambridge University Press.

Owen, David, and Graham Smith. 2015. 'Deliberation, Democracy and the Systemic Turn'. *The Journal of Political Philosophy* 23 (2): 213–34.

Pajnik, Mojca. 2006. 'Feminist Reflections on Habermas's Communicative Action: The Need for an Inclusive Political Theory'. *European Journal of Social Theory* 9 (3): 385–404. https://doi.org/10.1177/1368431006065719.

Pang, Laikwan. 2021. 'Mask as Identity? The Political Subject in the 2019 Hong Kong's Social Unrest'. *Cultural Studies* 36 (4): 1–20. https://doi.org/10.1080/09502386.2021. 1882522.

Papacharissi, Zizi. 2010. *A Private Sphere: Democracy in a Digital Age*. Cambridge: Polity Press.

Papacharissi, Zizi. 2011. 'A Networked Self: Identity Performance and Sociability on Social Network Sites'. In *A Networked Self: Identity, Community, and Culture on Social Network Sites*, edited by Zizi Papacharissi, 207–21. New York: Routledge.

Papacharissi, Zizi. 2015. *Affective Publics: Sentiment, Technology, and Politics*. Oxford: Oxford University Press.

Parkinson, John. 2012. *Democracy and Public Space: The Physical Sites of Public Performance*. Oxford: Oxford University Press.

Parry, Lucy, Hans Asenbaum, and Selen Ercan. 2021. 'Democracy in Flux: A Systemic View on the Impact of COVID-19', *Transforming Government: People, Process and Policies* 15 (2): 197–205. https://doi.org/10.1108/TG-09-2020-0269.

Parthasarathy, Ramya, Vijayendra Rao, and Nethra Palaniswamy. 2019. 'Deliberative Democracy in an Unequal World: A Text-As-Data Study of South India's Village Assemblies'. *American Political Science Review* 113 (3): 623–40. https://doi.org/10.1017/ S0003055419000182.

Pateman, Carole. 1970. *Participation and Democratic Theory*. Cambridge: Cambridge University Press.

Pateman, Carole. 1988. *The Sexual Contract*. Stanford: Stanford University Press.

Pateman, Carole. 1989. *The Disorder of Women: Democracy, Feminism, and Political Theory*. Stanford: Stanford University Press.

Pateman, Carole. 2006. 'Democratizing Citizenship: Some Advantages to Basic Income'. In *Redesigning Distribution: Basic Income and Stakeholder Grants as Alternative Cornerstones for a More Egalitarian Capitalism*, edited by Bruce Ackerman, Alstott Anne, and Philippe Van Parij, 83–98. London/New York: Verso. https://doi.org/10.1177/ 0032329203261101.

Pateman, Carole. 2012. 'Participatory Democracy Revisited'. *Perspectives on Politics* 10 (1): 7–19. https://doi.org/10.1017/S1537592711004877.

Pateman, Carole, and Graham Smith. 2019. 'Reflecting on Fifty Years of Democratic Theory: Carole Pateman in Conversation with Graham Smith'. *Democratic Theory* 6 (2): 111–20. https://doi.org/10.3167/dt.2019.060210.

Paxton, Marie. 2020. *Agonistic Democracy: Rethinking Political Institutions in Pluralist Times*. New York: Routledge.

Pfitzmann, Andreas, and Marit Hansen. 2010. 'A Terminology for Talking about Privacy by Data Minimization: Anonymity, Unlinkability, Undetectability, Unobservability,

Pseudonymity, and Identity Management'. http://www.maroki.de/pub/dphistory/2010_Anon_Terminology_v0.34.pdf.

Phillips, Anne. 1991. *Engendering Democracy*. Cambridge: Polity Press.

Phillips, Anne. 1993. *Democracy and Difference*. Cambridge: Polity Press.

Phillips, Anne. 1995. *The Politics of Presence*. Oxford: Oxford University Press.

Phillips, Anne. 1996. 'Dealing with Difference: A Politics of Ideas or a Politics of Presence'. In *Democracy and Difference: Contesting the Boundaries of the Political*, edited by Seyla Benhabib, 139–52. Princeton: Princeton University Press.

Phillips, Anne. 2009. *Multiculturalism Without Culture*. Princeton: Princeton University Press.

Phillips, Anne. 2010. 'What's Wrong with Essentialism?' *Distinktion* 11 (1): 47–60. https://doi.org/10.1080/1600910X.2010.9672755.

Phillips, Anne. 2012. 'Representation and Inclusion'. *Politics and Gender* 8 (4): 512–18. https://doi.org/10.1017/S1743923X12000529.

Phillips, Anne. 2013. *Our Bodies, Whose Property?* Princeton/Oxford: Princeton University Press.

Phillips, Anne. 2015. *The Politics of the Human*. Cambridge: Cambridge University Press.

Phillips, Anne. 2019a. 'Descriptive Representation Revisited'. In *Oxford Handbook of Political Representation in Liberal Democracies*, edited by Robert Rohrschneider and Jacques Thomassen, 175–91. Oxford: Oxford University Press.

Phillips, Anne. 2019b. 'Recognising Difference: Reasons and Risks'. *Japanese Journal of Political Thought*, 1–13.

Pitkin, Hanna. 1967. *The Concept of Representation*. Berkeley/London: University of California Press.

Plant, Sadie. 1997. *Zeros + Ones*. London: 4th Estate Limited.

Polletta, Francesca. 2002. *Freedom Is an Endless Meeting: Democracy in American Social Movements*. Chicago: University of Chicago Press.

Ponesse, Julie. 2014. 'The Ties That Blind: Conceptualizing Anonymity'. *Journal of Social Philosophy* 45 (3): 304–22. https://doi.org/10.1111/josp.12066.

Poster, Mark. 1990. *The Mode of Information: Poststructuralism and Social Contexts*. Cambridge: Polity Press.

Poster, Mark. 1995. *The Second Media Age*. Cambridge: Polity Press.

Poster, Mark. 1997. 'Cyberdemocracy: The Internet and the Public Sphere'. In *Virtual Politics: Identities & Community in Cyberspace*, edited by David Holmes, 201–18. London: Sage.

Poster, Mark. 1999. 'National Identities and Communications Technologies'. *The Information Society* 15 (4): 235–40. https://doi.org/10.1080/019722499128394.

Poulimenakos, Giorgos, and Dimitris Dalakoglou. 2017. 'Hetero-Topias: Squatting and Spatial Materialities of Resistence in Athens at Times of Crisis'. In *Critical Times in Greece: Anthropological Engagements with the Crisis*, edited by Dimitris Dalakoglou and Georgios Agelopoulos, 173–87. London: Routledge.

Puwar, Nirmal. 2004. *Space Invaders: Race, Gender and Bodies Out of Place*. Oxon/New York: Berg.

Puwar, Nirmal. 2010. 'The Archi-Texture of Parliament: Flaneur as Method in Westminster'. *Journal of Legislative Studies* 16 (3): 298–312. https://doi.org/10.1080/13572334.2010.498099.

Rancière, Jacques. 1992. 'Politics, Identification, and Subjectivization'. *The Identity in Question* 61: 58–64.

Rancière, Jacques. 1999. *Disagreement: Politics and Philosophy*. Minneapolis: University of Minnesota Press. https://doi.org/10.1111/j.1467-954X.2011.02009_2.x.

Rancière, Jacques. 2007. 'What Does It Mean to Be Un?' *Continuum* 21 (4): 559–69. https://doi.org/https://doi.org/10.1080/10304310701629961.

Rancière, Jacques. 2014. *Hatred of Democracy*. 3rd ed. London/New York: Verso.

Reicher, Stephen. 1984. 'Social Influence in the Crowd: Attitudinal and Behavioural Effects of De-Individuation in Conditions of High and Low Group Salience'. *British Journal of Social Psychology* 23 (4): 341–50.

Reichle, Ingeborg. 2004. 'Remaking Eden: On the Reproducibility of Images and the Body in the Age of Virtual Reality and Genetic Engineering'. In *Cyberfeminism: Next Protocols*, edited by Ingeborg Reiche and Verena Kuni, 239–58. New York: Autonomedia.

Reiman, Jeffrey. 1976. 'Privacy, Intimacy, and Personhood'. *Philosophy & Public Affairs* 6 (1): 26–44.

Rheingold, Howard. 1993. *Virtual Community: Finding Connection in a Computerized World*. London: Secker & Warburg.

Robinson, Laura. 2007. 'The Cyberself: The Self-Ing Project Goes Online, Symbolic Interaction in the Digital Age'. *New Media and Society* 9 (1): 93–110. https://doi.org/10.1177/1461444807072216.

Robinson, Laura, Shelia Cotten, Hiroshi Ono, Anabel Quan-Haase, Gustavo Mesch, Wenhong Chen, Jeremy Schulz, Timothy Hale, and Michael Stern. 2015. 'Digital Inequalities and Why They Matter'. *Information, Communication & Society* 18 (5): 1–14. https://doi.org/10.1080/1369118X.2015.1012532.

Rodriguez, Armado, and Robin Clair. 1999. 'Graffiti as Communication: Exploring the Discursive Tensions of Anonymous Texts'. *The Southern Communication Journal* 65 (1): 1–15.

Rollo, Toby. 2017. 'Everyday Deeds: Enactive Protest, Exit, and Silence in Deliberative Systems'. *Political Theory* 45 (5): 587–609. https://doi.org/10.1177/0090591716661222.

Roque, Sandra, and Alex Shankland. 2007. 'Participation, Mutation and Political Transition: New Democratic Spaces in Per-Urban Angola'. In *Spaces for Change? The Politics of Citizen Participation in New Democratic Arenas*, edited by Andrea Cornwall and Vera Shattan Coelho, 202–25. London/New York: Zed Books.

Rousseau, Jean-Jacques. 1998. *The Social Contract*. London: Wordsworth Edition.

Ruiz, Pollyanna. 2013. 'Revealing Power: Masked Protest and the Blank Figure'. *Cultural Politics* 9 (3): 263–79. https://doi.org/10.1215/17432197-2346973.

Ryan, Holly Eva, and Matthew Flinders. 2018. 'From Senseless to Sensory Democracy: Insights from Applied and Participatory Theatre'. *Politics* 38 (2): 133–47. https://doi.org/10.1177/0263395717700155.

Saco, Diana. 2002. *Cybering Democracy: Public Space and the Internet*. Minneapolis: University of Minnesota Press.

Sanders, Lynn. 1997. 'Against Deliberation'. *Political Theory* 25 (3): 347–76.

Sanmark, Alexandra. 2013. 'Patterns of Assembly: Norse Thing Sites in Shetland'. *Journal of North Atlantic* 5: 96–110. https://doi.org/10.3721/037.002.sp504.

Sardá, Thais, Simone Natale, Nikos Sotirakopoulos, and Mark Monaghan. 2019. 'Understanding Online Anonymity'. *Media, Culture and Society* 41 (4): 557–64. https://doi.org/10.1177/0163443719842074.

Saward, Michael. 2003. *Democracy*. Cambridge: Polity Press.

Saward, Michael. 2010. *The Representative Claim*. Oxford: Oxford University Press.

Saward, Michael. 2021. *Democratic Design*. Oxford: Oxford University Press.

Schippers, Birgit. 2009. 'Judith Butler, Radical Democracy and Micro-Politics'. In *The Politics of Radical Democracy*, edited by Moya Lloyd and Adrian Little, 73–91. Edinburgh: Edinburgh University Press.

Schmitter, Philippe, and Terry Lynn Karl. 1991. 'What Democracy Is ... and Is Not'. *Journal of Democracy* 2 (3): 75–88. https://doi.org/10.1353/jod.1991.0033.

Schmitz, Rachel. 2016. 'Intersections of Hate: Exploring the Transecting Dimensions of Race, Religion, Gender, and Family in Ku Klux Klan Web Sites'. *Sociological Focus* 49 (3): 200–14. https://doi.org/10.1080/00380237.2016.1135029.

Schumpeter, Joseph. 1947. *Capitalism, Socialism and Democracy*. 2nd ed. New York: Harper.

Scott, Craig. 1998. 'To Reveal or Not to Reveal: A Theoretical Model of Anonymous Communication'. *Communication Theory* 8 (4): 381–407.

Scott, Craig. 1999. 'The Impact of Physical and Discursive Anonymity on Group Members' Multiple Identifications During Computer-Supported Decision Making'. *Western Journal of Communication* 63 (4): 456–87. https://doi.org/10.1080/10570319909374654.

Seeley, Thomas. 2010. *Honeybee Democracy*. Princeton: Princeton University Press.

Senft, Theresa. 2018. *Camgirl: Celebrity & Community in the Age of Social Networks*. New York: Peter Lang Publishing.

Shukaitis, Stevphen. 2005. 'Space. Imagination//Rupture: The Cognitive Architecture of Utopian Political Thought in the Global Justice Movement'. *University of Sussex Journal of Contemporary History* 8: 1–14.

Smith Ekstrand, Victoria, and Cassandra Imfeld Jeyaram. 2011. 'Our Founding Anonymity: Anonymous Speech During the Constitutional Debate'. *American Journalism* 28 (3): 35–60.

Smith, Graham. 2009. *Democratic Innovations: Designing Institutions for Citizen Participation*. Cambridge: Cambridge University Press.

Smith, Graham. 2019. 'Reflections on the Theory and Practice of Democratic Innovations'. In *Handbook of Democratic Innovations and Governance*, edited by Stephen Elstub and Oliver Escobar, 572–82. Cheltenham Glos: Edward Elgar.

Smith, Graham. 2021. *Can Democracy Safeguard the Future?* Cambridge: Polity Press.

Smith, Trevor. 2017. *Politicizing Digital Space: Theory, the Internet and Renewing Democracy*. London: University of Westminster Press.

Smith, William. 2016. 'The Boundaries of a Deliberative System: The Case of Disruptive Protest'. *Critical Policy Studies* 10 (2): 152–70. https://doi.org/10.1080/19460171.2016.1165128.

Spiegel, Jennifer. 2015. 'Masked Protest in the Age of Austerity: State Violence, Anonymous Bodies, and Resistance "In the Red"'. *Critical Inquiry* 41 (4): 786–810.

Spivak, Gayatri Chakravorty. 1988. 'Subaltern Studies: Deconstructing Historiography'. In *In Other Words: Essays in Cultural Politics*, edited by Gayatri Chakravorty Spivak, 197–221. New York: Routledge.

Stein, Gertrude. 2011. 'Guerrilla Girls and Guerrilla Girls BroadBand: Inside Story'. *Art Journal* 70 (2): 88–101. https://doi.org/10.1080/00043249.2011.10791003.

Steinholt, Yngvar. 2013. 'Kitten Heresy: Lost Contexts of Pussy Riot's Punk Prayer'. *Popular Music and Society* 36 (1): 120–4. https://doi.org/10.1080/03007766.2012.735084.

Stone, Allucquere Rosanne. 1991. 'Will the Real Body Please Stand Up? Boundary Stories about Virtual Cultures'. In *Cyberspace: First Steps*, edited by Michael Benedikt, 81–118. Cambridge: MIT Press.

Suler, John. 2004. 'The Online Disinhibition Effect'. *CyberPsychology & Behavior* 7 (3): 321–26.

Süß, Rahel. 2021. 'Horizontal Experimentalism: Rethinking Democratic Resistance'. *Philosophy and Social Criticism* 48 (8): 1–17. https://doi.org/10.1177/01914537211033016.

Swan, Melanie. 2013. 'The Quantified Self: Fundamental Disruption in Big Data Science and Biological Discovery'. *Big Data* 1 (2): 85–99. https://doi.org/10.1089/big.2012.0002.

Tambakaki, Paulina. 2017. 'Agonism Reloaded: Potentia, Renewal and Radical Democracy'. *Political Studies Review* 15 (4): 577–88. https://doi.org/10.1177/1478929916635882.

Tanasoca, Ana. 2020. *Deliberation Naturalized: Improving Real Existing Deliberative Democracy.* Oxford: Oxford University Press.

Taylor, Keith. 2016. *Political Ideas of the Utopian Socialists.* New York: Routledge.

Thiel, Thorsten. 2017. 'Anonymity and Its Prospects in the Digital World'. 38. PRIF Working Paper. Frankfurt am Main.

Tiqqun. 2008. 'How Is It to Be Done?'. http://cnqzu.com/library/Politics/Invisible-Committee-How-it-be-done.pdf.

Travers, Ann. 2003. 'Parallel Subaltern Feminist Counterpublics in Cyberspace'. *Sociological Perspectives* 46 (2): 223–37. https://doi.org/10.1525/sop.2003.46.2.223.

Turkle, Sherry. 1984. *The Second Self: Computers and the Human Spirit.* London: Granada.

Turkle, Sherry. 1995. *Life on the Screen: Identity in the Age of the Internet.* New York: Simon & Schuster Paperbacks.

Turkle, Sherry. 1996. 'Rethinking Identity through Virtual Community'. In *Clicking In: Hot Links to a Digital Culture*, edited by Lynn Hershman Leeson, 116–22. Seattle: Bay Press.

Turkle, Sherry, ed. 2007. *Evocative Objects: Things We Think With.* Cambridge, MA/London: MIT Press.

Vedel, Thierry. 2006. 'The Idea of Electronic Democracy: Origins, Visions and Questions'. *Parliamentary Affairs* 59 (2): 226–35. https://doi.org/10.1093/pa/gsl005.

Véliz, Carissa. 2018. 'Online Masquerade: Redesigning the Internet for Free Speech through the Use of Pseudonyms'. *Journal of Applied Philosophy*, 1–16. https://doi.org/10.1111/japp.12342.

Vinci, Leonardo da. 2005. *The Da Vinci Notebooks.* London: Profile Books.

VNS_Matrix. 1991. 'Cyberfeminist Manifesto for the 21st Century 1991'. http://www.sterneck.net/cyber/vns-matrix/index.php.

Voß, Jan Peter, Jannik Schritt, and Volkan Sayman. 2021. 'Politics at a Distance: Infrastructuring Knowledge Flows for Democratic Innovation'. *Social Studies of Science* 52 (1): 1–21. https://doi.org/10.1177/03063127211033990.

Wagner Decew, Judith. 2015. 'The Feminist Critique of Privacy: Past Arguments and New Social Understandings'. In *Social Dimensions of Privacy*, edited by Beaate Roessler and Dorota Mokrosinska, 85–103. Cambridge: Cambridge University Press.

Wajcman, Judy. 2004. *TechnoFeminism.* Cambridge: Polity Press.

Walker Rettberg, Jill. 2014. *Seeing Ourselves through Technology: How We Use Selfies, Blogs and Wearable Devices to See and Shape Ourselves.* Houndmills: Palgrave Macmillan.

Wallace, Kathleen. 1999. 'Anonymity'. *Ethics and Information Technology* 1 (1): 23–35.

Ward, Irene. 1997. 'How Democratic Can We Get? The Internet, the Public Sphere, and Public Discourse'. *JAC* 17 (3): 365–79.

Warren, Mark. 1992. 'Democratic Theory and Self-Transformation'. *American Political Science Review* 86 (1): 8–23.

Warren, Mark. 1996. 'What Should We Expect from More Democracy?' *Political Theory* 24 (2): 241–70.

Warren, Samuel, and Louis Brandeis. 1890. 'The Right to Privacy'. *Harvard Law Review* 4 (5): 193–220.

Waskul, Dennis, and Mark Douglass. 1997. 'Cyberself: The Emergence of Self in On-Line Chat'. *The Information Society* 13 (4): 375–97. https://doi.org/10.1080/019722497129070.

'We Are the 99 Percent'. 2011. 2011. http://wearethe99percent.tumblr.com/.

Wenman, Mark. 2013. *Agonistic Democracy: Constituent Power in the Era of Globalization*. Cambridge: Cambridge University Press.

Wesch, Michael. 2012. 'Anonymous, Anonymity, and the End(s) of Identity and Groups Online: Lessons from the "First Internet-Based Superconsciousness"'. In *Human No More: Digital Subjectivities, Unhuman Subjects, and the End of Anthropology*, edited by Neal Whitehead and Michael Wesch, 89–104. Colorado: University Press of Colorado.

Westin, Alan. 1984. 'The Origins of Modern Claims to Privacy'. In *Philosophical Dimensions of Privacy: An Anthology*, edited by Ferdinand Schoeman, 56–74. Cambridge: Cambridge University Press.

Whitson, Jennifer. 2013. 'Gaming the Quantified Self'. *Surveillance & Society* 11 (1/2): 163–76.

Wilde, Oscar. 1996. *The Critic as Artist*: Critical Writings of Oscar Wilde. New York: Random House.

Wingenbach, Ed. 2011. *Institutionalizing Agonistic Democracy: Post-Foundationalism and Political Liberalism*. Surrey: Ashgate.

Wojciechowska, Marta. 2018. 'Towards Intersectional Democratic Innovations'. *Political Studies*. https://doi.org/10.1177/0032321718814165.

Wolin, Sheldon. 1994. 'Fugitive Democracy'. *Constellations* 1 (1): 11–25. https://doi.org/10.1111/j.1467-8675.1994.tb00002.x.

Woo, Jisuk. 2006. 'The Right Not to Be Identified: Privacy and Anonymity in the Interactive Media Environment'. *New Media & Society* 8 (6): 949–67. https://doi.org/10.1177/1461444806069650.

Woodford, Clare. 2018. 'Has Democracy Failed Women'. Broad Agenda Blog. 2018. http://www.broadagenda.com.au/home/has-democracy-failed-women/.

Wright, Erik Olin. 2010. *Envisioning Real Utopias*. London/New York: Verso.

Wright, Erik Olin. 2013. 'Transforming Capitalism through Real Utopias'. *Irish Journal of Sociology* 21 (2): 6–40. https://doi.org/10.1177/0003122412468882.

Young, Iris Marion. 1987. 'Impartiality and the Civic Public: Some Implications of Feminist Critiques of Moral and Political Theory'. In *Feminism as Critique: On the Politics of Gender in Late-Capitalist Societies*, edited by Seyla Benhabib and Drucilla Cornell, 57–76. Cambridge: Polity Press.

Young, Iris Marion. 1989. 'Polity and Group Difference: A Critique of the Ideal of Universal Citizenship'. *Ethics* 99 (2): 250–74.

Young, Iris Marion. 1990. *Justice and the Politics of Difference*. Princeton: Princeton University Press.

Young, Iris Marion. 1992. 'Social Groups in Associative Democracy'. *Politics & Society* 20 (4): 529–34.

Young, Iris Marion. 1994. 'Gender as Seriality: Thinking about Women as a Social Collective'. *Signs* 19 (3): 713–38.

Young, Iris Marion. 1996. 'Communication and the Other: Beyond Deliberative Democracy'. In *Democracy and Difference: Contesting the Boundaries of the Political*, edited by Seyla Benhabib, 120–35. Princeton: Princeton University Press.

Young, Iris Marion. 1997a. 'Deferring Group Representation'. In *Ethnicity and Group Rights*, edited by Ian Shapiro and Will Kymlicka, 349–76. New York: New York University Press.

Young, Iris Marion. 1997b. 'Difference as a Resource for Democratic Communication'. In *Deliberative Democracy: Essays on Reason and Politics*, edited by James Bohman and William Rehg, 383–406. Cambridge: MIT Press.

Young, Iris Marion. 2000. *Inclusion and Democracy*. Oxford: Oxford University Press.

Young, Iris Marion. 2001. 'Activist Challenges to Deliberative Democracy'. *Political Theory* 29 (5): 670–90.

Young, Iris Marion. 2005. *On Female Body Experience: 'Throwing Like a Girl' and Other Essays*. Oxford: Oxford University Press.

Zakaria, Rafia. 2017. *Veil*. New York: Bloomsbury.

Index